The
Conversational
Circle

The Conversational Circle

Rereading the English Novel, 1740-1775

Betty A. Schellenberg

THE UNIVERSITY PRESS OF KENTUCKY

Copyright © 1996 by The University Press of Kentucky

Scholarly publisher for the Commonwealth,
serving Bellarmine College, Berea College, Centre
College of Kentucky, Eastern Kentucky University,
The Filson Club, Georgetown College, Kentucky
Historical Society, Kentucky State University,
Morehead State University, Murray State University,
Northern Kentucky University, Transylvania University,
University of Kentucky, University of Louisville,
and Western Kentucky University.

Editorial and Sales Offices: The University Press of Kentucky
663 South Limestone Street, Lexington, Kentucky 40508-4008

96 97 98 99   00   5 4 3 2 1

Library of Congress Cataloging-in-Publication Data

Schellenberg, Betty A.
    The conversational circle : rereading the English novel,
1740-1775 / Betty A. Schellenberg.
        p.   cm.
    Includes bibliographical references and index.
    ISBN 0-8131-1990-1 (acid-free paper)
    1. English fiction—18th century—History and criticism.
2. Conversation in literature.   3. Literature and society—England—
History—18th century.   4. Domestic fiction, English—History and
criticism.   5. Oral communication in literature.   6. Social
interaction in literature.   7. Friendship in literature.   8. Speech
in literature.   9. Family in literature.   I. Title.
PR858.C66S74   1996
823'.509355—dc20   96-23024

FOR CHRISTIAN

Contents

Acknowledgments

Financial support for the earliest stages of this project was provided by Social Sciences and Humanities Research Council of Canada doctoral fellowships. For intellectual support and professional advice throughout I thank April London, who guided my research through the dissertation process, and Peter Sabor, who first encountered it as thesis examiner. More recently, Mary Ann Gillies, Leith Davis, and June Sturrock of the Department of English at Simon Fraser University read parts of the manuscript, offering advice and timely encouragement; I thank Lois Chaber for doing so as well. The fresh perspectives of Jerry C. Beasley and Elizabeth Kraft were most helpful as the project neared completion. An early version of chapter 3 appeared in *Eighteenth-Century Fiction* 4, 1 (Oct. 1991) as "Enclosing the Immovable: Structuring Social Authority in *Pamela* Part II." Parts of chapter 4 appeared in *Studies on English Literature 1500-1900* 34, 3 (summer 1994), as "Using 'Femalities' to 'Make Fine Men': Richardson's *Sir Charles Grandison* and the Femininization of Narrative." I thank these journals for permission to use these materials. A number of student assistants, in particular John Gray and Suzanne Klerks, lent their skills to the preparation of the manuscript.

Finally, I acknowledge the flexibility of my two sons, Samuel and Luc, who have shared me with this book during their first years of life. And since there would not have been a book without the practical and longsuffering support of my husband, I dedicate it to him.

Introduction:

Narrating Sociability in Mid-Eighteenth-Century England

In 1742, David Hume published an essay entitled "Of Essay Writing," which begins with a pair of apparently self-evident classifications: "The elegant part of mankind, who are not immersed in mere animal life, but employ themselves in the operations of the mind, may be divided into the *learned* and the *conversable*."[1] Hume goes on to describe an exclusive and leisured "world" devoted to conversation:

> The conversable world join to a sociable disposition, and a taste for pleasure, an inclination for the easier and more gentle exercises of the understanding, for obvious reflections on human affairs, and the duties of common life, and for observation of the blemishes or perfections of the particular objects that surround them. Such subjects of thought furnish not sufficient employment in solitude, but require the company and conversation of our fellow-creatures, to render them a proper exercise for the mind; and this brings mankind together in society, where every one displays his thoughts in observations in the best manner he is able, and mutually gives and receives information, as well as pleasure. [568]

While Hume appears to consider this conversable world admirable in its capacity to exchange information and exercise the mind while producing mutual pleasure, it clearly has the potential, in his view, to engage in even more challenging and socially profitable "exercises of the understanding." Indeed, he confidently asserts that "the separation of the learned from the conversable world," which "seems to have been the great defect of the last age," has now been rectified by a newly formed "league" between them (568). This league has rendered the realm of conversation not only more pleasurable but also productive. It is to be the source of a revitalized culture in which the commodities of learning—discursive forms—will be manufactured out of the materials of "common life and conversation" (569) in order to guarantee the cultural ascendancy of "sound understandings and delicate affections" (570). There remains a great deal to be done, however; the league is to be furthered by a literary model—conveniently, the essays he is publishing will provide such a model. In other words, Hume is prescribing a new and self-consciously constructed pattern of sociability while claiming to describe a natural and established one. Such doubleness is fundamental to the essay. Hume acknowledges, for example, "the fair sex" as "the sovereigns of the empire of conversation," whom he approaches "with reverence" (570), but he goes on to censure not only their "false taste" in reading (572), but also, by implication, their superficial taste in men. By the end of the piece, the reader questions whether the new sociability of the leisured orders Hume is purportedly celebrating has any basis other than in the desires of the writer.

This use of a popular literary form to model, in the guise of reflection, a behavioral ideal represents a common feature of the mid-eighteenth-century discourse of sociability in England. Recent students of the period of the 1740s to 1770s have noted a marked concern with the need for building consensus as the basis of a renewed and authoritative social structure—and in that concern the implication that confidence in an absolute and objectively verifiable political, religious, and epistemological order had been irreparably shaken. John Mullan's 1988 *Sentiment and Sociability: The Language of Feeling in the Eighteenth Century,* which begins with Hume, argues that "the work of producing—of modelling or staging—society as a scheme of consensus and unanimity, and of warning against the forces or habits which threaten such a scheme, is an undertaking common to different types of writing" in this period, including the moral philosophy and narrative fiction upon which he focuses.[2]

It is the purpose of this study to examine a number of mid-century fictions that experiment self-consciously with conversational structures as a means of embodying a socially conservative—in other words, an anti-individualistic, anti-conflictual—ideology. Most of the fictions of which I speak have long been dismissed by critics as aesthetic failures because they do not fit the criteria of plot and character generalized as characteristic of the "classical" novel. If the novelistic paradigm is constructed from John Bunyan's Christian turning his back on his family and fleeing toward the Celestial City, or Daniel Defoe's Robinson Crusoe working out his solitary salvation, or Samuel Richardson's Pamela struggling desperately to preserve her virginity, then the domestic Christiana, the patriarchal Crusoe, and the married Pamela can be of little interest. Twentieth-century historians of the early novel, most influentially Ian Watt and Mikhail Bakhtin, have canonized, under defining terms such as "formal realism" and "dialogism," fictions that portray the desirous individual in sustained tension with his or her social environment.[3] Such fictions bring traditional and subversive voices into conflict with one another and privilege a strongly linear, teleological narrative structure. This critical value has clearly been influenced by "progressivist" histories of the eighteenth century as the period of increasing social mobility and individualism, emergent capitalism, and conflict between an aristocracy and a bourgeoisie. It has also reflected a teleological focus on the nineteenth-century novel as the unconscious goal of eighteenth-century fiction. But the resulting history of the early novel increasingly appears restricted and unrepresentative. As just one example, much mid-century fiction, hidden in the shadows of *Clarissa, Roderick Random,* and *Tom Jones,* shows a marked effort to employ the energies of the "new species of writing" in modeling the intimate and exclusive conversational circle as both a paradigm for and a means toward social consensus.

Literary histories of the novel have begun to fill in the gaps of this partial picture. For example, John Bender, in *Imagining the Penitentiary: Fiction and the Architecture of Mind in Eighteenth-Century England,* argues that Bakhtin's uniform ideological coloring of heteroglossia as subversion overlooks the orthodox effect of that heteroglossia's formal containment in the early novel. The genre, in Bender's view, embodies in language a more divided social impulse: "The novel acts out, it represents iconically, the interplay between the unbounded heterogeneity of population in cities (their polyglot assembly of voices) and the bounded unity of their walls, fortified compounds, governmental structures, and systems of communication (their inscription of 'facts,' their insistence on point of view, and their assimilation of authority from approved genres through parody, burlesque, irony)."[4]

Michael McKeon, in his *Origins of the English Novel, 1600-1740,* clearly places such opposing impulses within a model of the genre itself, discussing the emergent English novel as maintaining "a formal tension between what might be called the individual life and the overarching pattern," characterized by an emphasis upon "'horizontal'" historical truth and "'vertical'" transcendent truth, respectively; this framework leads to the incorporation in the novel of both a "progressive ideology," expressed in "the formal posture of naive empiricism," and a "conservative ideology," expressed as "extreme scepticism." McKeon's study is therefore important in that it introduces into the literary history of the novel a model of varied responses to perceived moral, political, and social issues. Although in the broad sweep and teleological structure of his survey he must inevitably generalize, he makes it clear that a helpful redefinition of the novel genre will take into consideration its eighteenth-century manifestations as fictional discourse responding to its environment in a wide range of subversive or reactionary, prescriptive or reflective terms. Such a definition is McKeon's description of the novel as "an early modern cultural instrument designed to confront, on the level of narrative form and content, both intellectual and social crisis simultaneously."[5]

It is not my intent here to propose a new canon of eighteenth-century British fiction. More simply, I wish to examine together a handful of mid-century novels that cuts across the traditional study groupings—novels both sentimental and satiric, novels by both "canonical" and "non-canonical" writers (or, to put it another way, novels by both male and female writers), novels centered on both male and female characters. While I do not pretend to an organizing principle less arbitrary than these traditional ones, such an exercise is always valuable in that a new grouping foregrounds features that have been overlooked, or, more significantly for these novels, that have been dismissed as indicators of the writer's failure to meet novelistic standards of characterization and plot. Indeed, these novels and the circumstances of their production and reception first captured my attention because of shared features that suggest a common project of mid-century writers: the circumscription of socially threatening individualistic desire in a plot structure that models a community of consensus as the ideal unit from which a stable society is constructed. Incorporating elements generally recognized as novelistic—a continuity of past and present rather than a rejection or distancing of the past, a firm anchorage to contemporary physical and social realities rather than an allegorizing or abstracting lack of specificity, a multi-voiced, prosaic register rather than a monologic, elevated tone, and characters individually differentiated rather than typically interchangeable—these works do not employ such elements to the ideological ends identified by theorists like Watt and Bakhtin. Rather, they serve the conservative purposes of affirming traditional authority structures while modifying those structures into more egalitarian modes of morality, social relations, and textual interpretation.

While such tendencies might be identified to varying degrees in numerous mid-eighteenth-century fictions, including *Pamela, Clarissa,* and *Tom Jones,* I have chosen texts whose formal and thematic commitments to the conversational circle are explicit and predominant, and which at the same time represent a range of strategies and ideological ends. It is significant, I believe, that these texts arise out of two generalizable contexts. One group consists of later works—sequels, or works that complete a group of novels—by male authors who, while initially obscure, have moved, largely through their successful use of print, into position as the new authorities of English society. Here I include Samuel Richardson's *Pamela* Part II and *Sir Charles Grandison,* Henry Fielding's *Amelia,* and Tobias Smollett's *Humphry Clinker.* The second group is the work of two of the female writers authorized by these male figures, for whom conformity is the pre-condition of their being encouraged initially, and yet for whom the interface of desire and consensus appears in their mature works to pose problems not raised by their male counterparts. Sarah Fielding's *David Simple,* together with its narrative sequel, *Volume the Last,* and Sarah Scott's *Millenium Hall* will be examined closely here.

Since both of these clusters of writers seek to satisfy the desires of an established audience while fulfilling expectations of social leadership in an age of widespread cultural anxiety, their works tend to reinscribe the isolated protagonist within a stable and intimate social group. Thus these works will be seen to share, as part of their formal engagement with issues of genre, authority, and society, a use of the circle at several levels of structure. The principal structural unit, and even the principal consciousness in some cases, is that of a social circle functioning on the model of the intimate conversational group central to the discourse and ideals of the period. Even at the level of setting and imagery, adventure or courtship is replaced by settled life, motion by fixity, linear temporality by circular repetition, the closet by the tea table. In the most optimistic of these fictions, mid-century ideology of gender provides the basis for the containment of individualistic desire, through a focus on the exemplary female at the center of the circle in the case of male desire, and through a sublimation of the self in the beloved other in the case of female desire.

In the prescriptive rather than descriptive mode, these fictions rework form at every level to embody a model of the self not as a uniquely expressive essence but as a relational and role-defined part of a larger whole. Thus characterization, for example, tends to rely upon techniques of reinforcement—such as the cumulative weight of repetitive description, a series of situations obviously designed to illustrate exemplary behavior, and an admiring chorus—in building a stable and objectified portrait rather than upon techniques emphasizing the conflicts and epistemological uncertainties of self-contradictory desires and multiple perspectives.

As a result conflict, which most commonly supplies the energy of narrative, is replaced by an impulse towards alignment, consensus, and mutual reinforcement, while the normativeness and commonality of human experience are emphasized more than its complexity and uniqueness. The authority of individual experience and interpretation is strongly qualified in these works in favor of more vicarious and communal modes of knowing. Indeed, a tacit recognition of epistemological issues results in a privileging of the language of consensus over witty debate; the communal achievement of harmony is valued more than a conclusive arrival at truth. At the same time, these fictions provide a portrait of social harmony achieved at the price of exclusion, and at the price of begging questions of inequality and dependence. Ultimately, the capacity of the social circle to subsume desire in consensus, upon which its prescriptive and interpretive authority is founded, proves problematic in that no fixed framework for this consensus can be established.[6]

For this reason earlier portrayals of the community of consensus tend to be more optimistic about the applicability of the model to society at large, while later portrayals increasingly seal off the community from its context, rendering it at best an alternative to, at worst the victim of, a chaotic and irredeemable society. However, an undertone of defensive exclusivity can be heard from the first, and the rigid boundedness of the most optimistic models betrays an ultimate retreat from prescription into acknowledged idealism. I will begin with Sarah Fielding's *Adventures of David Simple* (1744) and Richardson's sequel to *Pamela* (1741), in which the ideology and its formal embodiment are at their most explicit and self-conscious. From there I will move to Richardson's and Henry Fielding's final novels, *Sir Charles Grandison* (1753-54) and *Amelia* (1752). While Sarah Fielding and the early Richardson center their circles around exemplary characters who incarnate a purified moral and social tradition and polemically direct its interpretation and application outward, the second pair of fictional circles balances exemplification with a need to circumscribe (female) desire and its narrative manifestations within a narrowly domestic sphere. Scott's *Millenium Hall* (1762) subverts this circumscription by making the feminine sphere the only redeemable one, and Smollett's *Humphry Clinker* (1771) intensifies circumscription to the point of paralyzing the ideal by affirming a lost social order. In both of the latter cases, imitation becomes impossible; thus prescription gives way to description. Sarah Fielding's *Volume the Last* (1753), although published earlier, serves as a fitting concluding statement by this "theorist" of "conservative socialist ideas."[7] Here the author of the early manifesto of conversational community that concludes *David Simple* abandons the prescriptive project altogether, allowing antagonistic desire to invade her domestic circle, fragmenting it into individual units of consciousness and action.[8] Ultimately, the novel of the conversational circle falls victim to the failure of the social model it portrays to provide a widely acceptable authoritative framework that can replace traditional religious, political, and social models. Its ideal is displaced into the future state promised in the resolutions of later novels—either a heavenly paradise where harmony of purpose replaces fragmentation or the earthly paradise created by the newly married pair beyond the pages of the novel.

At this point I must observe that several subgroups of eighteenth-century fiction that have received careful attention in the last few years share some of the concerns and formal qualities of the works I will examine here. Mullan's grouping of literature of sentiment, together with studies such as Janet Todd's *Sensibility: An Introduction,* highlights a mid-century phenomenon that uses feeling as the source of social consensus in reaction to intellectual and economic fragmentation. However, while sentimental fiction rejects the conflict-driven plot, feminizes its protagonists, disrupts linear temporality, and emphasizes the intimate domestic group, its suspicion of language and its rejection, especially in its later manifestations, of active social prescription distinguishes it from my group. Nevertheless, several of the texts I discuss—especially *David Simple, Sir Charles Grandison,* and *Amelia*—are sometimes categorized, albeit cautiously, as sentimental, suggesting the arbitrary nature of all such groupings, my own included. Nancy Armstrong's *Desire and Domestic Fiction: A Political History of the Novel* treats as "domestic fiction" or "feminized discourse" works that create an idealized domestic circle as the ostensibly apolitical locus of true sociability. Armstrong argues that domestic fiction ultimately served the quest of the bourgeois class for social ascendancy; while my works, again, privilege the feminine and the domestic to hegemonic ends, I see these ends as more narrowly reactionary efforts to unwrite or deny a political agenda, rather than as strategic moves in a long-term struggle for cultural dominance.

As a preface to my study two fundamental questions, raised by my brief examination of Hume's double image of the conversable world, must be dealt with. First, what cultural forces might draw both established male writers and marginalized female writers into turning a "progressive" form to "conservative" ends? Second, what meanings do conversational and circular forms bear in eighteenth-century discourse that make them the chosen vehicles for these impulses? In the following chapter, I will examine these contextual questions.

1

Consensus,
the Conversational Circle,
and Mid-Eighteenth-Century Fiction

It is generally accepted that the instability of English political structures in the seventeenth century left eighteenth-century English society a legacy of uncertainty about the unquestioned right of any particular model of political authority. Linked to questions about political authority were debates in the realm of belief—over the nature of the monarchy, the place of revelation in the face of an increasingly empirical and psychological understanding of (human) nature, and the social implications of pietistic Christianity. Furthermore, the development of newly complex and intangible economic structures contributed to a sense of flux and financial vulnerability. Thus, as J.G.A. Pocock has explained in detail, political, religious, and economic changes resulted in an eighteenth-century sense that the ground was shifting under the old foundations of authority.[1]

Recently a somewhat revised version of this view, or at least of its manifestation in relations between societal groupings of the first sixty years of the century, has emerged. While general ideological shifts and the development of new economic interests certainly contributed to a real increase in socioeconomic complexity and to a perceived fragmentation of society into special-interest groups and alienated individuals, the response to these pressures was a vigorous upholding of both traditionally hierarchical and communal values. J.C.D. Clark's 1985 revisionist study, *English Society 1688-1832,* among others, has argued strongly that the first sixty years of the century saw the consolidation of church establishment, state, and aristocratic powers in a reinforcement of political and religious hierarchies as a matter not only of oligarchic imposition but also of general belief across all social strata. E.P. Thompson has reiterated his belief that despite "the growth throughout the century, in numbers, wealth and cultural presence, of the middling orders who came . . . to create and occupy a 'public sphere,'" these orders lacked a collective identity and power primarily because "patrician culture stubbornly resisted any allowance of vitality to the notion of 'middleclass' until the end of the century." As a result, Thompson argues, the gentry and the mob participated in a "paternalism-deference equilibrium" that held English society in a dialectic of interdependence. From the Marxist end of the spectrum, Tom Nairn has argued to enable its post-1688 overseas expansion, England "required, above all, conservative stability at home. It demanded a reliable, respectful hierarchy of social estates, a societal pyramid to act as basis for the operations of the patrician élite." Thus, according to Nairn, the urban middle class, over the course of the eighteenth and early nineteenth centuries, became increasingly allied with, and ultimately merged with, the politically, economically, and socially dominant landowning elite.[2]

CONSTRUCTING THE SOCIABLE SELF IN EIGHTEENTH-CENTURY ENGLAND

An example of this tendency to reinforce and consolidate can be traced in one turn-of-the-century response to the threat of disorder: the attempt to revive, in the ideal of the gentleman, traditional aristocratic theory linking external attributes such as title, family, land, and manners, with innate qualities of benevolence and good taste. The virtues of taste, sympathy, and benevolence used by the third Earl of Shaftesbury to characterize the gentleman were appropriated by writers like Addison and Steele of *The Spectator* as suitable for imitation by a self-conscious and self-justifying urban readership. The currency of the philosophy of sympathy in the early part of the eighteenth century thus attests at once to the ongoing power of the aristocracy to define standards of behavior and to the determination of the urban middling sort to achieve social acceptance by adopting those standards.[3]

As much as it was opposed to earlier notions of aristocratic display, *The Spectator*'s blend of "moral sense" and good taste resisted essentialist thought like that of William Law's influential *Serious Call to a Devout and Holy Life* (1729). This work is striking in its repeated claim that to have "a right knowledge of ourselves" is to see ourselves as beings who are neither irrevocably set within time and social space, nor united in the institutions of church and nation, but "pure spirits," "spiritual and rational in nature."[4] The perceived threat of social disruption from such an internalized ground of moral and political behavior helped to encourage a counter-emphasis upon sympathy as an effective yet relatively communal basis for a new kind of social authority, which would fill the vacuum left by the rejection of traditional paradigms.

Dialogue between the principal characters of *Felicia to Charlotte*, a 1744 narrative by Mary Collyer, illustrates the use of the doctrine of a natural moral "taste" to fill the gap between received notions of authority and individualistic pietism. In the words of the novel's sensible hero-philosopher, Lucius, "The moral sense, Madam, is a taste for what is amiable; that distinguishing faculty of the mind which makes us *feel,*—sensibly and strongly *feel,*—the harmony and discord of actions. It is the *touch,* the *ear* of the soul; while reason is the *eye* to regulate the exertions of this sympathetic faculty. The moral sense feels instantaneously without waiting for the slow deliberation of the rational powers, to know if it ought to do so." This doctrine is received by Felicia as, on the one hand, a replacement for the established church's doctrine of original sin as a tasteless and ineffective means of exerting authority over behavior: "What a delightful representation . . . have you given us of human nature! How very different from those gloomy discourses we daily hear of the wretchedness and deformity of all the race of Adam! Too many of our clergy seem to take a peculiar pleasure in degrading mankind. . . . [Nothing] can be more injurious to the cause of virtue, than such false representations." On the other hand, by making these attractive young lovers the representatives of a rational theology of benevolence, Collyer contrasts such doctrines favorably with the egotistical pietism of the novel's villain, whose exploitation of the notion of Providence allows "her immaculate soul [to triumph] over the crimes of the multitude, and [to] . . . look down upon them with a sacred indignation" while she indulges her own lusts in secrecy.[5]

The *Spectator* papers document such a sentimental and optimistic view of the basis of sociability. At the same time, the exclusivity of the ideal becomes apparent. Richard Steele locates true sociability above all in a distinct social position, located "between" that of the man of public entertainments and that of the man of business. Ideal men, according to Steele, are "such as have not Spirits too Active to be happy and well pleased in a private Condition, nor Complexions too warm to make them neglect the Duties and Relations of Life. Of these sort of Men consist the worthier Part of Mankind; of these are all good Fathers, generous Brothers, sincere Friends, and faithful Subjects. . . . These are the Men formed for Society, and those little Communities which we express by the Word *Neighbourhoods.*"[6] Thus, while it is still naturalized as a matter of the "spirit" or "complexion," admirable sociability is identified with certain social roles. Although the kinds of relationships named are theoretically available to all men, their ideal manifestation is limited to men of the gentry and upper middling sort, neither so exalted in the social hierarchy as to have public political and social responsibilities, nor so humble or entrepreneurial as to be engaged in trade. The result is a self-contradictory notion of manners that in part replaces a rhetoric of artifice with a rhetoric of nature and yet retains for that rhetoric a normative and status-defined manifestation. A later discussion of the ideal companion neatly captures this attempt to combine nature and nurture models of social behavior:

the true Art of being agreeable in Company, (but there can be no such thing as Art in it,) is to appear well pleased with those you are engaged with, and rather to seem well entertained, than to bring Entertainment to others. A Man thus disposed is not indeed what we ordinarily call a good Companion, but essentially is such, and in all the Parts of his Conversation has something friendly in his Behaviour, which conciliates Men's Minds more than the highest Sallies of Wit or Starts of Humour can possibly do. [3:449-50]

To possess "Art," but to avow that it is tainted by "no such thing as Art"; "to appear" and "to seem," but to express what one is "disposed" to or "essentially is" by so appearing—the requisites of good manners are carefully delineated in the same breath as the necessity of their prescription is denied.[7]

Among didactic writers for a primarily urban, socially mobile, yet insecure and even alienated audience, then, the self is being constructed as an essentially social being. While this self affirms the social status quo, its motive for doing so is not conviction of the basis of that status quo in an absolute moral law, but rather, commitment to affective ideals such as those of loyalty, family feeling, and shared experience, as well as fear of the consequences of rejecting such a controlling structure.[8]

The fictional family described in Defoe's 1715 conduct guide, *The Family Instructor,* exemplifies the discursive difficulties encountered in adapting old structures of authority to new views of the sociable self. A previously permissive father is at first presented by Defoe as admirable and justified in his reformed attempt to command obedience: "But I will take care that you shall not help it [being confined on Sundays] while you call me father, for I will not bear the title without the authority." However, his son's report of the comment conveys both a disdain for such outmoded arguments ("he has not spared abundance of threatenings, and other positive testimonies of his patriarchal authority") and a sense of uncertainty about the outcome of this crisis of authority ("a new family government is to be erected, I don't know of what kind"). The son suffers the wages of his sinful rebellion, but his sister is awarded the more cheerful fate, despite estrangement from her father, of a tender husband whose patience and refusal to restrain her ("for I can allow of no submissions and subjections between you and me, but those of love") eventually woo her to repentance.[9] It appears that patriarchal authority is no longer ideally figured by the father's law, but rather by the more ostensibly egalitarian model of conjugal persuasion.

It is appropriate that in the example from *The Family Instructor* the self that comes to an accommodation with established authority is a female one. For the eighteenth-century woman even more than for the *Spectator*'s male reader, the social roles permitted by the patriarchal family and by class set the boundaries within which her self was defined, and beyond the limits of which even sympathy or other "natural" social impulses could not easily extend. Since a woman's identity in the period was constructed in relation to her intimate others, she stood at the ideal median point between public action—increasingly seen as corrupt, self-serving, and dissipated, rather than truly sociable—and self-indulgent withdrawal. This central female figure was not only shared by the upper and middling classes, but also straddled the ideological gap between the hierarchical marriage of a traditional patriarchal system and a more egalitarian model of marriage as a relationship between complementary partners. Moreover, commentators on the period have argued that the new sociable self I have been describing can be understood as a feminized self; that is, in terms of a cluster of qualities gendered as female and generally idealized by the 1740s—private and imaginative, but relationally defined, domestic, and passive.[10]

To speak of a mediating position is not, however, to speak of a theoretically or practically coherent social role, either for women specifically or for the feminized individual they came to epitomize. *The Spectator,* for example, is perfectly capable of at one moment describing marriage as a "Patriarchal Sovereignty" (4:273) and at the next outlining a husband's duty as "a regular and uniform Endeavour to make [him]self valuable, both as a Friend and Lover, to one whom [he has] chosen to be the Companion of [his] Life" (4:371). Indeed, it is because of the high, yet contradictory, expectations attached to family relationships that the domestic circle serves as such a fruitful locus for the period's fictional analyses of social interaction. The individual, in particular the woman, portrayed in this setting becomes the focus of tensions between notions of a self comprehended entirely by its social alignments and a self whose integrity is expressed in a private, affective sphere.

LANGUAGE, COMMERCE, AND CONVERSATION

The refiguring of hierarchies of authority into intimate groups made up of sociable selves was parallelled by a new understanding of language, not as a series of signs in fixed correspondence to absolute meanings, but as a relational system, in which components acquire meaning by association with other components and by the consensus of their users. Words are used as signs, says John Locke, "not by any natural connexion, that there is between particular articulate Sounds and certain *Ideas,* . . . but by a voluntary Imposition, whereby such a Word is made arbitrarily the Mark of such an *Idea.*"[11] Thus the metaphor of commerce becomes ideal for the description of language as an exchange of signs with agreed-upon values. Both naming and accounting are empirical forms of reckoning, Thomas Hobbes explains; "*Subject to names,* is whatsoever can enter into or be considered in an account, and be added one to another to make a sum, or subtracted one from another and leave a remainder."[12] Indeed, "commerce" is for this pre-capitalist culture more than a metaphor taken from trade: it as frequently refers generally to "Intercourse in the affairs of life; [and]

dealings" of any kind, as it does more specifically to an exchange of "the products of nature or art" (*OED*). "Conversation," although distinct from "Business," according to the *Spectator* No. 468 (4:154), shares intimately and almost interchangeably with "commerce" this sense of an exchange of signs invested with a value according to usage.[13] Moreover, the broad application of the word "conversation" in the period in its now obsolete sense of "consorting or having dealings with others; living together; commerce, intercourse, society, intimacy" (*OED*), indicates that even when the term is used narrowly to refer to a verbal exchange, it serves as a metonym for social interaction as a whole.

The notion of words as counters was received in the eighteenth century more as a threat to be resisted for its associations with moral relativism and degeneracy than as a discovery of language's potential for "wider application and greater flexibility," as Bakhtin has hailed it in retrospect.[14] *Spectator* No. 103, for example, quoting from the latitudinarian archbishop Tillotson's 1694 sermon on sincerity, describes complimenting as an inflationary phenomenon, the result of which is that a man from the past would need a dictionary in order "to know the true intrinsick Value of the Phrase in Fashion, and wou'd hardly at first believe at what a low Rate the highest Strains and Expressions of Kindness imaginable do commonly pass in current Payment." This "hollow kind of Conversation" is morally reprehensible even if all participants take into account "the current Value" of the compliments, because men's words as signs at this point are not only as valueless as "meer Cyphers," but also act as "hardly any Signification of their Thoughts"; conversation is therefore but "driving a Trade of Dissimulation" (1:430-31). Commerce which perverts or is detached from truth can be no more healthy for a conversing society than for partners in trade. From the time of Thomas Hobbes's warning of 1651 that "words are wise men's counters, they do but reckon by them; but they are the money of fools, that value them by the authority of an Aristotle, a Cicero, or a Thomas, or any other doctor whatsoever, if but a man," the period is preoccupied with the implication that words as arbitrary signs, dependent for their meaning both upon individual perception and upon consensus, can be employed for the purposes of moral obscurity and personal gain as much as for mutual benefit.[15]

Hence the kind of free play of signifiers glimpsed in Jonathan Swift's *A Tale of a Tub* and celebrated in Laurence Sterne's *Tristram Shandy* and Christopher Smart's *Jubilate Agno* is not the eighteenth-century rule; the primary concern of the developing sciences of textual study, linguistics, lexicography, and grammar is rather with fixing the standards, with limiting the endless possibilities for misinterpretation—and with using "polite" language as an instrument of social coherence. Samuel Johnson's *Plan* for his dictionary of the English language, published in 1747, stipulates a work "by which the pronunciation of our language may be fixed, and its attainment facilitated; by which its purity may be preserved, its use ascertained, and its duration lengthened."

The lexicographer, indeed, describes himself as a Roman soldier about to invade "Britain as a new world. . . . I hope, that though I should not complete the conquest, I shall at least discover the coast, civilize part of the inhabitants, and make it easy for some other adventurer to proceed farther, to reduce them wholly to subjection, and settle them under laws."[16] Henry Fielding's concern with linguistic slippage and its indication of a degeneration of social morality is clear in his "Modern Glossary" of *The Covent-Garden Journal* for January 14, 1752, with its definitions of "Gallantry," for example, as "Fornication and Adultery," and "Modesty" as "Aukwardness, Rusticity."[17] This concern with the problem of fixing value in linguistic exchange is exacerbated by the Grub Street phenomenon—by the growth of a publishing industry that made writers and readers members of a vastly increased and newly anonymous and indeterminate discursive field. Pope's *Dunciad* as well as other Scriblerian texts have made familiar the anxieties aroused in literary circles that formerly enjoyed a privileged status.

Just as the select and carefully enclosed circle of family and friends is the preferred framework for social intercourse in the eighteenth century, its modes of interaction represent an ideal of conversational behavior that manages language to sociable ends. Again, *The Spectator* has grave reservations about the "indecent License" to which an individual with any degree of delicacy may be exposed in the conversation of travelling coaches, assemblies, or other public settings, as well as in the masculine enclaves of the clubs and coffeehouses.[18] In paper No. 68, a disadvantage of even polite public conversation emerges: "Conversation is never so much streightened and confined as in numerous Assemblies. When a Multitude meet together upon any Subject of Discourse, their Debates are taken up chiefly with Forms and general Positions. . . . In Proportion, as Conversation gets into Clubs and Knots of Friends, it descends into Particulars, and grows more free and communicative: But the most open, instructive, and unreserved Discourse, is that which passes between two Persons who are familiar and intimate Friends" (1:289). Simply stated, the size of a group is inversely proportional to the quality of its conversation because a lack of intimacy inhibits. Thus both an inability to control content and an excess of form limiting that content make public and socially mixed conversation undesirable.

Within the intimate conversational circle, the feminization of the ideal self and the new uneasiness over the possibility of gaining universal assent to objective truth mean that the language of debate is replaced by a language of consensus. Since to be agreeable and conciliatory is preferable to "the highest Sallies of Wit or Starts of Humour" (3:450), the ideal role is "the Part of Moderator" (2:275). Thus good conversation is set in opposition to antisocial uses of language, whether self-indulgent or aggressively confrontational. "Of all things," Lord Chesterfield's son is told, "banish the egotism out of your conversation"; to convert a conversation into a monologue is "in some degree a fraud; conversation-stock being a joint and common property."[19]

Although the fundamental metaphor of conversation as commerce—as an exchange of verbal currency based upon a consensus of value—remains a constant throughout the period, a shift of other prominent metaphors reflects this reworking of the model of conversational exchange from a "masculine" one—public, intellectual, witty, and aggressive—to a "feminine" one—private, affective, discreet, and accommodating. Conversation in Edward Young's *Night Thoughts* (1742-45) is figured by a mix of aggressive swordplay and motherly nurture in such passages as:

> What numbers, sheath'd in erudition lie,
> Plung'd to the hilts in venerable tomes,
> And rusted in; who might have borne an edge,
> And play'd a sprightly beam, if born to speech;
> If born blest heirs of half their mother's tongue![20]

Although conflict imagery dominates here, and conversation as heir is decidedly masculine, language itself is a blessing associated with the feminine. Young's aggressive metaphors are, of course, implied in the famous conversational tactics of Chesterfield and Boswell's Johnson.[21] Writing to Samuel Richardson in 1755 about a conversational evening with an elderly couple of low "social station," Mary Collier is conscious of the model being rejected:

> I hardly ever met with more simplicity and good sense than they both have, and it is with some degree of pleasure that I sit in an evening with them, and hear the discourse and gossippings of the day: it makes me smile often, and sometimes rises to a downright laugh; and whatever promotes and causes this, with innocence and good humour, is as eligible (as far as I know, in the way of conversation) and as worthy to be ranked of the sort called delightful and pleasing, as in the routs and hurricanes of the great, or at court, or even in company with my Lord Chesterfield.[22]

Not surprisingly, the gentleman will find his greatest conversational happiness in his own home, in the company of his wife. In the ideal marriage, "The Wife grows Wise by the Discourses of the Husband, and the Husband good-humour'd by the Conversations of the Wife. . . . Their Virtues are blended in their Children, and diffuse through the whole Family a perpetual Spirit of Benevolence, Complacency, and Satisfaction" (*Spectator* 2:11). This model of conversation as an intimate, mutual and informal exchange of satisfactions is valued for a transparent sincerity which can be achieved only within its stable and affective confines. Leland E. Warren has noted that such statements of a conversational ideal "share . . . [a] basis in openness and equality among the participants. But we notice that openness requires closing out all but a very few."[23] The corrupt mind that makes conversational life resemble "that of Daemons" rather than "the Life of Angels," pure in its morals and delicate in its manners, is clearly to be shunned (*Spectator* 1:422).

Of particular interest to this study are formal manifestations of the new conversational model, which appear at this time in the genres of portraiture and the periodical essay.[24] The conversation piece or conversation painting, associated with the rise of the burgher class in northern Europe and apparently introduced into England by Dutch painters in the seventeenth century, was at the height of its popularity in the mid-eighteenth century. The typical English conversation piece is a small-scale painting of a family group in a detailed domestic setting; stylized placement and gestures are used to indicate the nature of the relationships between members of the group.[25] For its patrons, the genre appears to have been attractive in its portrayal of the kind of refined, leisured intimacy idealized in *The Spectator*.[26] For the artist, on the other hand, Ronald Paulson suggests that the form provided an appropriate locus for treatment of the kinds of cultural tensions I have been discussing: between traditional iconography and individual expression, role-playing and intimacy, order and disorder, safe enclosure and imprisonment. Moreover, the genre can be contrasted to contemporary treatments, best known in Hogarth's progresses, of the alienated individual passing through a disordered world, just as the novels to be examined here oppose the plot of an individual's journey through the world with the story of a domestic circle.[27]

The concept of the conversation painting is transferred to contemporary discourse in the form of prose sketches of intimate social circles and the codes of values, tastes, and behaviors that bind them together. In *Spectator* No. 424, for example, a letter on behalf of readers retiring to the country asks for "a Lesson of Good-humour, a Family-Piece" to help overcome the discord which inevitably arises "when our Conversation is confin'd"; the letter then offers its own "family-" or conversation-piece, describing a house party of intimate friends whose fear of "a certain Satiety" in each other's company has led to the establishment of an infirmary for the ill-humored in their residence (3:591). A later *Spectator* again uses the limited rural "Circle of Neighbours" as its reason for proposing a club of hunters and drinkers, a "green Conversation-Piece" based upon a shared value for broken bones, whose members, "for their own private . . . as also the publick Emolument, should exclude, and be excluded all other Society" (4:177-79).

My argument to this point has assumed the influence of the social doctrines of the early eighteenth-century periodical essay on the ideology of the conversational circle. More significant to novelistic structure than the authorizing of certain forms of social interaction, perhaps, is these periodicals' modeling of those interactions; as Michael G. Ketcham argues, the *Spectator* phenomenon is that of "a social structure being created out of a literary structure."[28] From the fiction of a club as source of the essays, to the encouragement of reader participation because "it is an impertinent and unreasonable Fault in Conversation, for one Man to take up all the Discourse" (4:4), to the treatment of topics such as gossip, a conversational group is demonstrated to be the most authentic source of subject matter, the most authoritative voice in which to convey it, and the fullest illustration of its complex truth. If this mediation of social ideals through the conversational circle is the principal influence of the periodical essay on the novels of my study, other more discrete, but related traces of the earlier genre include an inclusivity of forms and subject matters that contributes to the subsuming of plot, a tendency to move between dramatic representation and narrative commentary that similarly renders plot more diffuse, and an experimentation with the use of multiple characters to illustrate a range of situations and points of view.

CIRCULAR FORMS AND THE FICTIONS OF CONSENSUS

In the discourse of eighteenth-century England, conflicting views of history and of human experience are made concrete in terms of competing spatio-temporal paradigms.[29] Satire portrays temporal process as regressive, as the fourth book of Pope's *Dunciad* illustrates, while works portraying spiritual or intellectual growth, such as Bunyan's *Grace Abounding* and *The Pilgrim's Progress,* employ time as the medium of progressive change. A third type of text, one which like satire criticizes perceived cultural change while idealistically modeling a self and a society mutually reforming and reformed, links the achievement of social harmony with temporal fixity and spatial stability in a kind of secularized echo of the medieval Christian paradigm. When writers of this period choose centripetal and static narrative structures rather than linear, teleologically-oriented, asymmetrical patterns, their choices bear ideological weight.

A circular image of time suggests stability as well as continuity in the form of recurrence. A circular image of space allows for the self-perpetuating activities of inclusion and exclusion. A circular model of the social group implies that it is held together by an equilibrium between the gravitational pull of its central figure and the balanced forces of the individuals who make up its circumference. Thus the intimate circle begs the problematic issue of authority by substituting for a hierarchical social model an ostensibly more egalitarian relation between self and other, while retaining the traditional value of group before self.

A few brief examples from eighteenth-century writing other than prose fiction will serve to illustrate these uses of the circle image in support of conservative ideologies. At the turn of the century, Swift portrays the self-satisfied individual with his famous image of the spider, "which by a lazy Contemplation of four Inches round; by an over-weening Pride, which feeding and engendering on it self, turns all into Excrement and Venom, producing nothing at last, but Fly-bane and a Cobweb."[30] Nevertheless, a life of security and contentment, given a social rather than an intellectual coloring, becomes for many of Swift's genteel contemporaries an ideal; according to a correspondent of Mr. Spectator, "the very Enquiry after Happiness has something restless in it, which a Man who lives in a Series of temperate Meals, friendly Conversations, and easy Slumbers, gives himself no Trouble about" (2:268-69). The first *Spectator* paper immediately attaches a positive value to enclosure and fixity in its description of the family estate, "bounded by the same Hedges and Ditches in *William* the Conqueror's Time that it is at present, and . . . delivered down from Father to Son whole and entire, . . . during the Space of six hundred Years" (1:1-2). Like nature's "unchangeable constancy" as it "moves on through the varied tenor of perpetual decay, fall, renovation, and progression," the ideal society, Edmund Burke argues in his 1790 *Reflections on the Revolution in France,* recognizes time as a cyclical perpetuity of domestic forms, a natural repetition with variations.[31] At its most open and optimistic, the circle is portrayed as part of an interlocking system of spheres that makes up society as a whole. Thus, for Pope, a "circle mark'd by Heav'n," whether "a bubble" or "a world," delineates the proper sphere of each creature, but these spheres are themselves links in the Chain of Being. Alternatively, the self is but a small pebble at the center of "one close system of Benevolence" made up of concentric circles representing all social categories, from "Friend" to "all human race" to "ev'ry creature . . . of ev'ry kind."[32]

Henry Fielding shows himself shrewdly self-conscious of the constructed and ideological nature of such imagery in the 1752 *Covent-Garden Journal* No. 37. Describing the "People of Fashion," the urban elite of England, he speaks of "the Use which these People [of Fashion] have always made of the Word Circle, and the Pretence to be enclosed in a certain Circle, like so many Conjurers, and by such Means to keep the Vulgar at a Distance from them"; examples of such popular usages are "a polite Circle, the Circle of one's Acquaintance, People that live within a certain Circle." Fielding goes on to describe the efforts made by the fashionable to "guard against any Intrusion of those whom they are pleased to call the Vulgar; who are on the other Hand as vigilant to watch, and as active to improve every Opportunity of invading this Circle, and breaking into it"; he traces the flight of "the Circle of the People of Fascination" before "the Enemy" through a series of neighborhoods until they are "stopped by the Walls of Hyde-Park."[33] Writing after the publication of *Amelia,* Fielding here captures the fate of the circle figure as it is used in the novels of this study: increasingly unable to claim prescriptive power, it becomes a mere fiction of social uniformity, meaningful and coherent only insofar as it can exclude that which is unlike itself.

These static, consensual, and exclusive colorings of the circle accord well with at least one eighteenth-century theory of fiction. Samuel Johnson's *Rambler* No. 4 begins with a characterization of contemporary fictions that assumes a static, rather than an historically particular, view of time and of human experience in time. The popular fictions in question, he says, "exhibit life in its true state, diversified only by accidents that daily happen in the world." Whereas the fantastic events of heroic romance are the product of idiosyncratic isolation, in which a writer need merely "retire to his closet, let loose his invention, and heat his mind with incredibilities," the new writing, if it is to be authoritative, demands a basis not only in "that learning which is to be gained from books," but also in "that experience which can never be attained by solitary diligence, but must arise from general converse, and accurate observation of the living world." This basis can therefore be subjected to the test of consensus, since "every one knows the original, and can detect any deviation from exactness of resemblance." Further, the writer's purpose is not self-expression or public acclaim, but the fulfilment of a social role; for "the young, the ignorant, and the idle," fiction provides "lectures of conduct, and introductions into life." Yet, like the intimate social group as opposed to the world at large, fiction's "chief advantage . . . over real life" is its capacity to include and exclude, for its "authors are at liberty, tho' not to invent, yet to select objects, and to cull from the mass of mankind, those individuals upon which the attention ought most to be employ'd."[34] Such socially conservative and anti-individualistic principles find expression in the circular forms employed by mid-century fictions.

Some novels, then, are best read as responding to a cultural need for fictions that represent individual experience as contributing to, rather than as in inevitable conflict with, a shared and received wisdom. In the view of one correspondent of Mr. Spectator, the writer who, "instead of the necessary vexations which are generally insisted upon in the Writings of the Witty," portrays "the Way of Life which plain Men may pursue, to fill up the Spaces of Time with Satisfaction," will perform "a very good Office to Society." That way of life includes "the Relations and Affinities among Men, which render their Conversation with each other so grateful, that the highest Talents give but an impotent Pleasure in Comparison with them," as well as "Good-nature," an "endless Source of Pleasures," and "domestick Life, filled with its natural Gratifications" (2:269). That the writers of mid-century fictions would see themselves as needing to perform good offices for society is not surprising given the general sensitivity of the period to the new conditions of authorship created by the shift towards professionalism and a broader audience range. This sensitivity could only be reinforced by the need to establish an authoritative voice on a work-by-work basis in a genre which was still significantly indeterminate.

What roles might one expect the initially somewhat marginalized authors in this study—a learned and financially dependent gentlewoman, a socially insecure master printer, the lawyer offspring of a younger branch of the nobility, an escapee from an unhappy marriage who founded a pious community of women, and a Scottish surgeon-turned-author—to play in modeling and reinforcing authoritative patterns of sociability? One need only think of *David Simple's* first chapter, of *Pamela* and *Clarissa*, of *Jonathan Wild* and *Joseph Andrews*, of *The History of Cornelia*, and of *Roderick Random* to recognize that the earliest fictions of Sarah Fielding, Samuel Richardson, Henry Fielding, Sarah Scott, and Tobias Smollett include a sharp critique of corruption in the clerical, professional, political, and aristocratic spheres of society. True to generalizations about the "rise of the novel," that critique takes the form of an isolated and relatively innocent individual's victimization by representatives of these classes. Built into the critique, however, is always the offer of purifying, and hence reinvigorating, existing social institutions through a redemptive absorption of the individual into the offending structure. This fundamental allegiance to "the system" on the part of the principal mid-century novelists suggests that they saw their social role as one of guiding the individual's social integration. Their condemnation is applied to both abusers of power and resisters of authority, but does not attack instituted authority itself. In the later fictions of these writers, who are then speaking from a relatively more authoritative position, the balance shifts even more firmly from detailing the need for resistance to modeling a submission of individualistic desire to the demands of the group.

More specifically, what social offices are performed by the conversational circles constructed in the texts I will be discussing? Although I have answered this question in a general way in my introduction, the model of the intimate conversational group examined in this chapter does tend to be represented in a number of quite specific forms. When the plot structured upon the dualistic framework of a self-society conflict is replaced by a plot of consensus, the diminished drive towards resolution is felt in a greater focus on individual units of structure—not actions contributing to a chain of causes and effects, but rather, conversational exchanges, which may be related to one another logically and topically rather than temporally, and which are governed by a movement toward mutual sympathy and a reaffirmation of social authority.[35] The conversational unit thus provides the means both of characterizing the individual as a social being and of drawing lines of authority; like the conversation painting, these units often give the impression of semi-ritualized tableaux or ceremonies. Action is important primarily as the gesture that accompanies speech. Indeed, the conversational novel's primary counters are spoken words, which, though threatened by inflation and fraud in the broad context of the world, are successfully anchored by the intimate group to some mutually acceptable foundation for authority. Thus, successful closure is represented, not by marriage, but by the achievement of full stability and a self-perpetuating rhythm of life. This achievement is often reified in a detachable text: a blueprint for the duplication of this ending in the reader's world, an allegory encapsulating one's experience, an announcement in a newspaper, a referral to the New Testament.[36]

The reader projected by these fictions is not encouraged to identify with an isolated and misunderstood protagonist in defiance of society; instead, she or he is invited into the novel's intimate circle, responding according to the ideal established by that circle to its central authority figure or figures. To facilitate such a response these novels always create a contemporary and familiar setting. More exclusively even than does the novel of the period in general, they focus on the domestic interior and, in that interior, on the drawing room and breakfast room, the dining table and tea table, rather than the closet or library. The notion of language as a fixed and shared currency is of course reflected in the style of these works as well. Characters mirror one another's language, with repetition rather than expansion used to establish clusters of key terms so that their meaning becomes unmistakable and inescapable within the enclosed circle. Together with correct speech, correct reading and correct interpretation are carefully modeled for the reader.

Although he puts it much more facetiously than would Sarah Fielding or Samuel Richardson, Sterne's words in *Tristram Shandy* can, with a twist, be applied to the novel of the conversational circle, with its dedication to a project that carries beyond its covers into the reader's social world: "Writing, when properly managed, (as you may be sure I think mine is) is but a different name for conversation: As no one, who knows what he is about in good company, would venture to talk all;—so no author, who understands the just boundaries of decorum and good breeding, would presume to think all: The truest respect which you can pay to the reader's understanding, is to halve this matter amicably, and leave him something to imagine, in his turn, as well as yourself."[37] It is into the conversational circles constructed by the feminized hero David Simple and rendered authoritative by the married Pamela that I now invite the reader.

2

Constructing the Circle in
Sarah Fielding's *David Simple*

Although little is known about the life of Sarah Fielding, the extra-literary traces that have remained, particularly in correspondence by, to, and about her, indicate the precarious dependency of the unmarried gentlewoman of very limited means, exacerbated by the suspicion with which the mid-eighteenth-century female of intellectual tastes and aspirations was viewed. The principal feature of human life as it is portrayed in the fictions of Sarah Fielding might be said to be the mutability of circumstances and relationships; perhaps from knowledge of that fundamental uncertainty of earthly existence comes an obsession with finding rest in an intimate and accepting community. That the ideal of the conversational circle is a deeply felt one for Fielding is suggested in a 1755 letter to Samuel Richardson about his household, where she had on occasion been a guest:

> To live in a family where there is but one heart, and as many good strong heads as persons, and to have a place in that enlarged single heart, is such a state of happiness as I cannot hear of without feeling the utmost pleasure. Methinks, in such a house, each word that is uttered must sink into the hearer's mind, as the kindly falling showers in April sink into the teeming earth, and enlarge and ripen every idea, as those friendly drops do the new-sown grain, or the water-wanting plant. There is nothing in all the works of nature or of art too trifling to give pleasure, where there is such a capacity to enjoy it, as must be found in such an union.[1]

Sarah Fielding went well beyond inarticulate desire, however; she has recently been accurately described as an important "theorist" of community.[2] Thus her early *Adventures of David Simple* (1744) and its 1753 narrative sequel provide a useful frame for my study in their explicit construction and then abandonment of the conversational circle as both a social and a narrative ideal. The impulse to defeat isolation and change through community is the structural basis of Fielding's debut novel. Change is ostensibly ordered through the familiar narrative form of the quest, as the subtitle "Containing an Account of His Travels through the Cities of London and Westminster in the Search of a Real Friend" indicates. However, the first portion of the novel in effect denies the power of linear form to lend any sort of progressive meaning to the social fragmentation of London society that has resulted from an apparently universal abuse of social and economic power to gratify individualistic desires. The protagonist's frustrated quest for friendship evolves rather into the purposeful construction of an intimate community as a stable alternative to that fragmentation. Thus *David Simple* traces in narrative form the cultural shifts I have identified in the previous chapter, providing a sort of blueprint for the transformation of an archetypally linear and individualistic plot into a fictional model of the conversational circle. The self-serving hero is exposed, while the passive and collaborative protagonist becomes the ideal; the impulse to journey towards a goal of fulfilled desire is proven a chimera and replaced by the stasis of the conversational group; hierarchical and authoritarian conflict is followed by egalitarian consensus on the model of an intimate family network of brother and sister, husband and wife; abuses of language are portrayed in detail before giving way to transparent conversation.

The novel culminates in a manifesto that insists upon the real possibility of such a social formation, concluding, "And, as strong a Picture as this is of real Happiness, it is in the power of every Community to attain it, if every Member of it would perform the Part allotted him by *Nature,* or his *Station in Life,* with a sincere Regard to the Interest and Pleasure of the whole."[3] Nevertheless, as the conclusion of this chapter will suggest, visible just beneath the optimism of this narrative structure and its final summation are the stress fractures created by the necessity of excluding conflict, of acknowledging the ultimate individuality of consciousness, and of reintegrating the egalitarian circle within existing social structures. These fissures can be seen as symptoms of the inevitable strain experienced by Fielding as a social outsider and an unauthorized (because female) author needing to obtain the support of powerful mentor figures such as Richardson and her brother Henry Fielding. It is not in the novel's triumphant conclusion, however, but only in its 1753 sequel, *Volume the Last,* that Fielding assumes for herself the authority to deconstruct the conversational circle as a failure, a passing dream. For this reason, *Volume the Last* will be discussed in chapter 8, the final chapter of this book.

UNWRITING THE QUEST FOR FRIENDSHIP

In the meantime, the novel begins with twin heroes—brothers, in fact—David and Daniel Simple, who appear to represent our ideal from the start. As schoolboys, "[the] strict Friendship they kept up was remarked by the whole

School; whoever affronted the one, made an Enemy of the other; and while there was any Money in either of their Pockets, the other was sure never to want it: the Notion of whose Property it was, being the last thing that ever entered into their Heads" (9-10). It is soon revealed, however, that while David is indeed perfectly sociable in his disposition, Daniel is an imposter who, "notwithstanding the Appearance of Friendship he had all along kept up with his Brother, was in reality one of those Wretches, whose only Happiness centers in themselves; and that his Conversation with his Companions had never any other View, but in some shape or other to promote his own Interest" (11). Daniel forges their father's will to exclude David; as the first in a long series of egotists, he thereby proves that to the individual bent on attaining the object of his own "will," friendship is merely instrumental to self-fulfillment.

This maxim next proves true in the case of heterosexual love, when David's betrothed abandons him for an "old and ugly" man who is "immensely rich" (34), and continues infallible in the behavior of characters at all social levels, from landladies and shopkeepers to whist-players and bluestockings. While among the high, "in Conversation, the real Thoughts are often disguised," in the more adversarial exchanges of the gaming table, "the Mask is thrown off, and Nature appears as she is" (78). That nature, it appears, is one in which all play the role of "Competitors," in one moment the joyful "Conquerors" and in another the despairing "Vanquished." Sociability is only a veneer, leading "an *unexperienced* Man" to believe mistakenly that pleasure lies "in serving each other"; the reality of card-playing provides rather the "Proof of the selfish and mercenary Tempers of Mankind" (79).

In contrast, David emerges from the initial crisis "wishing he could meet with a human Creature capable of Friendship" in order to create "a little Community, as it were of two, to the Happiness of which all the Actions of both should tend with an absolute disregard of any selfish or separate Interest." This ideal leads him to take "the oddest, most unaccountable Resolution that ever was heard of, *viz.* To travel through the whole World, rather than not meet with a real Friend" (26-27). David's continual disappointments, however, soon transform the quest into a seemingly endless oscillation of hope and hopelessness with an ever-diminishing possibility of success. After his discovery of his beloved Nanny's mercenary passions, for example, he is left "in the same Condition as when he discovered his Brother's Treachery. The World [is] to begin again with him; for he [can] find no Pleasure in it, unless he [can] meet with a Companion who deserve[s] his Esteem" (45). What hope David does retain rests not in an educative process that will ultimately enable him to express his social impulses successfully, but rather in a fixed and essentially sociable nature that is utterly other than the nature of those he meets. It is David's "own Mind [which is] a Proof to him, that Generosity, Good-nature, and a Capacity for real Friendship, [are] to be found in the World" (46).

In the first portion of the novel, then, Fielding rejects the hero-on-a-quest pattern for fiction both on the moral ground that it is inherently antisocial and on the representational ground that it falsely claims the individual can be improved through knowledge of the world. Since London society in *David Simple* is a chaotic mass of egos held together by structures of self-interest, where "all the Women [are] tearing one another to pieces from Envy, and the Men sacrificing each other for every trifling Interest" (46), the broad social experience represented by a journey through the world can only offer an arbitrary sequence of deception followed by disillusionment. In other words, meaningful progress towards a goal devolves into the aimlessness and arbitrariness characteristic of the picaresque.

The danger of deception is particularly pronounced in David's world because of rampant abuses of language. His first traveling encounter is with a man who uses the epithets "good" and "wise" to describe a dishonest but wealthy stock-trader, in a manner reminiscent of the society satirized in Fielding's "Modern Glossary." In fact, most of the characters David meets share the card-players' hypocritically sociable use of language. They are ultimately exposed through the truth-revealing devices of an overheard conversation or a new character on the scene who knows the "history" of the previous speaker. In this way, truth about a character is constantly deflected away from the direct source to another, who is in turn dishonest about his own motives. Again, David's method of inquiry, in which he is relying upon the verbal transparency of a number of guide-figures, proves inadequate; indeed, the very possibility of language as a means of establishing objective truth and grounding human ties comes into question as one "truth" replaces another in a horizontal slide.

CONSTRUCTING THE CONVERSATIONAL CIRCLE

David's encounter with Cynthia therefore signals the decisive shift in his fortunes and a correlative shift in narrative form. The "something . . . good-natured in [Cynthia's] countenance" (100) which attracts David initially proves perfectly congruent with her actual behavior, and her conversational integrity is indicated by the fact that she entrusts David with the history of her whole life. In other words, what earlier characters have hidden for David's accidental and indirect discovery is here brought to the surface with a transparency that for Fielding is in itself a sign of truth. The telling of a character's life story, which in the first part of the novel is used to show the true depths hidden beneath the attractive surface of a new acquaintance, and thereby to illustrate that no one's story can be accepted at face value, gives way to a use of narration as vicarious experience, which is less in direct opposition to lived experience than a broadening of its scope.[4] Through conversation, the privileged and untraveled male auditor can learn what it is to be a dependent female toadeater, or a beautiful gentlewoman disguised as a hunchbacked beggar, or a French marquis who has murdered his best friend.

As David listens to Cynthia's lengthy story, it is evident that the moral and functional definition of the hero is being modified further. Already evolved from older brother and heir into wandering sentimental picaro,[5] David now relinquishes his own story as he becomes the auditor of the stories of others. While he continues to play the traditional male roles of protector, suitor, and benefactor, the extent of his sympathetic identification arguably transforms him at times almost into injured female virtue itself. Thus, curiosity to hear Cynthia's story draws him to her place of residence on numerous successive days and he implicates himself by finding her a means of escape from the abusive Lady _____; later, Camilla's story makes him "afraid every time [she] open[s] her Mouth, what he [shall] hear next; for he [finds] himself so strongly interested in every thing which concern[s] her, that he [feels] in his own Mind all the Misery she [has] gone through" (168). Parallel to this feminization of the hero is the accompanying elevation of female narrative as a series of admirable women—Cynthia, Camilla, and Isabelle—tell their stories.[6] The overall effect, however, is one less of feminocentricity than of the replacement of the single male traveler by a protagonist group. Although David's point of view remains interesting, it becomes only one of a range of perspectives, whether in response to a story or experience, or in a round of sharing one's thoughts during a coach ride, or in the narration of the emotional fluctuations of the four lovers.

David has already shown himself an altruist who has "no Ambition, nor any Delight in Grandeur" and whose "only Use . . . for Money, [is] to serve his Friends" (26), in contrast to Daniel, "hugg[ing] himself in his Ingenuity" at cheating David of his fortune (15), and to a later miser and spendthrift who share a common "Selfishness, which makes every thing center wholly in themselves" (60). At this point in the novel he becomes the sole financial support of Cynthia, followed soon after by Valentine and Camilla. David's lack of any sense of "mine" and "yours" illustrates the same expansiveness of the ideal social self beyond its own circumference that is revealed in his sympathetic listening. While dispensing money is also a conspicuous activity of Richardson's sociable heroes, Mr. B. and Sir Charles Grandison, their generosity generally functions to reward or encourage the performance of specific duties within well-defined structures of dependency.[7] *David Simple* treats property in its undispensed form as belonging equally to all members of the circle, suggesting a radical dismantling of the power which generally accrues to wealth in a direct rejection of the abusive economic dependency which the group members have variously suffered.

Although Cynthia leaves for the country soon after telling her story, leaving David "to begin the World again" (125), the fact of his having found a friend who confirms his ideals of virtue implies that the random thread of David's wanderings is soon to be drawn into a domestic circle. The protagonist's immediately subsequent encounter with Camilla and Valentine fixes his own quest, and ultimately that of Cynthia, who is the long-separated lover of Valentine. When Cynthia's restless travels return her to London, "like People in a burning Fever, who, from finding themselves continually uneasy, are in hopes by every Change of Place to find Relief" (175), David seeks her out to complete the foursome. In a deliberate resolution of the *Paradise Lost* motif, we read that "they sat [*sic*] out together, to find all which either of them valued in this World" (186).

With the end of the solitary, peripatetic portion of the novel signalled thus, the narrative form shifts to a static, socially connected model. Writing with particular reference to Henry Fielding's *Tom Jones* and Tobias Smollett's *Peregrine Pickle*, Ronald Paulson has noted that "in England, picaresque structures of satiric exposition, as they grew increasingly more complex, tended to become intense knots of . . . chance relationships," particularly through the use of the family as a locus for "replacing coincidence of recurrence with causality."[8] In *David Simple*, the reader sees this transformation from narrative line into conversational circle occurring as individuals encountered by chance form a network of related characters bringing past and present into congruence and enabling the foundation of an ideally familial community. Thus, the atheist who sours Cynthia's stagecoach journey is discovered to be David's treacherous brother, who disappeared soon after the novel's opening, and whose death definitively removes him from further interference either as villain or as dependent family member; Camilla is revealed to be the companion of Cynthia's youth and Valentine the young gentleman she has secretly loved since then; the brother and sister's estranged father arrives repentant at the door; and Cynthia's clergyman-suitor becomes a catalyst for the construction of this network, reappearing first to give an identity and history to the atheist and later to perform the double marriage that creates the extended family of the novel's conclusion. In *David Simple*, the family-as-causality of which Paulson speaks provides the context that grounds and vindicates relationships established through conversation. Thus, David's esteem for Camilla, aroused by his intimate acquaintance with her behavior and story, is confirmed by the revelation that "she [is] the person whom *Cynthia* had mentioned in so advantageous a Light" (172), while the clergyman's moralized account of "*the Life of an Atheist*" (285) becomes a means of portraying to his friends David's history of goodness and sensibility.

Indeed, once David, Cynthia, Camilla, and Valentine have become an established foursome, any traveling they do takes the form of short coach and barge excursions providing stimuli to the conversational reflections of "Minds, so philosophical as their's" (252). Stories and travels become interchangeable

according to the weather as the group's interest in one another's sentiments replaces the search for friends. Narrative attention is focused therefore upon the
stories of other social groups and the modulations of character within them—
the tragic story of Isabelle's self-destructive circle, the absurdity of Camilla's
father and his friend, the two young ladies at Paris and their various suitors. In
its pleasure in one another's company the group represents the exemplary social
circle. As ideal moderator, who combines intelligence and knowledge of the
world with submission to the will of the group, Cynthia proposes subjects
which draw out all members in turn, or tells stories herself to provide entertainment for the others. David plays the part of encouraging tutor to the
self-doubting Camilla, whose willingness to doubt the validity of her sentiments is the guarantee that her individualistic interpretations will be inter-
cepted by the group before they can lead her into error.

In fact, the interpretive activities of this group are treated with a certain
amount of irony. When Camilla imagines the houses they pass as full of
"*Mothers-in-Law,* working underhand with their Husbands, to make them
turn their Children out of Doors to *Beggary* and *Misery*" (190), she is clearly
reading all she sees as a variation upon her own experience. Similar to Camilla's
attribution of her own family history to strangers are the quartet's conjectures
about Isabelle's mysterious circumstances:

> *Camilla* could not forbear enquiring of *Cynthia,* if this *young Lady*
> *had not a Father alive,* and *whether it was not probable his marrying*
> *a second Wife might be the cause of her Misfortunes:* But before there
> was time for an Answer, *David* said, '*I think, Madam, you men-*
> *tioned her Brother; he possibly may have treated her in such a manner,*
> *as to make her hate her own Country, and endeavour to change*
> *the Scene, in hopes to abate her Misery.*' In short, every one guessed
> at some Reason or other, for a Woman of *Isabelle*'s Quality lead-
> ing a Life so unsuitable to the Station Fortune had placed her in.
> [194-95]

However, these instances of blindness, as well as those caused by the partiality or anxieties of love, are narrated with a lightness that suggests their
relative safety within a setting of transparent and virtuous conversation. More
important than an absolute abstracted truth as the goal of the group's conversation is the integrity of self-representation between its members. Thus
exchanges between David and his earlier guide-narrators, in which strictly ve-
racious accounts of others are nevertheless the product of hidden and evil
motives, are replaced by a kind of self-revelation conducive to spiritual intimacy. In addition, the parallel between these cases of subjectivity and that of
the earlier character, Mr. Spatter, who "look[s] through the Magnifying-Glass

at all their Defects [i.e. those of every person discussed], and thro' the other end of the Perspective on every thing commendable in them" (93), underscores the necessity for multiple viewpoints as an epistemological corrective.

In its distinguishing features of transparency, consensus, and stasis, this conversational group is, as I have said, virtually a model for the intimate circles portrayed in the contemporary fictions to be discussed in this study. In several respects, however, Fielding's version of the circle can be said to set a standard that the subsequent texts do not approach. One of these is the prominence of the David-Cynthia axis of the circle. As the first two of its members to be introduced, as well as the most fully characterized, David and Cynthia establish a heterosexual friendship of mutual benefit and satisfaction which at times makes the addition of Camilla and Valentine as their respective lovers appear merely a device for legitimizing the friendship through a kinship tie.[9] Secondly, Cynthia's worldly wisdom and intellect make her the leader of this mixed group, while David's naive sympathy and his possession of a small fortune assign him the role of mentor and benefactor. By distributing conversational roles between Cynthia as intellectual leader and David as chief sympathizer, as well as by reversing the usual gendering of such roles, Fielding establishes a more equitable distribution of power than do the Richardson and Henry Fielding social circles, centered as they are upon an exemplary figure who is either an authoritative male or authorized by one.[10]

The Adventures of David Simple ends emphatically, in terms both of its resolution of the four characters' stories and its certainty that, in an imitation of the "Scheme of Life . . . followed by this whole Company" (303), a perfectly harmonious social stability can be achieved by any intimate group. "*David*'s Travels," we read, "were now at an end"; Camilla's "Happiness was compleat"; "*Valentine* and *Cynthia* had not a Wish beyond what they enjoyed" (303). Through what April London has called a "virtual catalogue of eighteenth-century metaphors of order"[11]—the roles which combine to produce a theatrical performance, the parts which constitute a machine and "regulate its Motions" (304), the shrubs and trees which compose a beautiful prospect (with a couplet from Pope's *Windsor-Forest*)—the text insists that social happiness "is in the power of every Community" where natural and ordained places are maintained and where the sociable talents are shared for the common enjoyment of all:

> If every Man, who is possessed of a greater Share of *Wit* than is common, instead of insulting and satirizing others, would make use of his Talents for the Advantage and Pleasure of the Society to which he happens more particularly to belong; and they, instead of hating him for his *superior Parts,* would, in return for the Entertainment he affords them, exert all the Abilities Nature has given

them, for his Use, in common with themselves; what Happiness would Mankind enjoy, and who could complain of being miserable? (305)

Retrospectively, then, it is not David Simple's desires that initiate his quest, but a society which has been so corrupted by envy and self-interest that it has degenerated into a mere mass of individuals, each vying for the privilege "*of playing the Top-part*" (304). In consequence, David as the inherently sociable self has necessarily been excluded from the larger society and remains detached until he finds a "little Society" (304) of equally sociable selves. The journey therefore takes on meaning in hindsight as a state of transition en route to a heaven on earth, where the exercise of differing gifts in the common interest will override apparent differences of interest. Having arrived at the ideal narrative form with which to construct this social ideal, Fielding replaces the conventional dichotomy of self in opposition to society, established at the novel's opening, with a dichotomy of the actual fragmentation of society as a whole in opposition to the potential coherence of intimate communities for the ultimate "Happiness of Mankind."

A Fool's Paradise?

The thoroughness of this modification may enable the reader to forget the sense of overwhelming corruption and social degeneracy with which the first part of the novel is imbued. Nevertheless, further examination reveals a degree of disjunction between an apparent rejection of all social structures because of egotistical individuals who abuse their positions of power—whether as parents, husbands, employers, patrons, financial advisers, or hosts—and a concluding reintegration of David and Cynthia's egalitarian circle into the larger social framework, a reintegration that implies the rightness of hierarchical structure. Just as the final manifesto draws on the "metaphors of order" that, in mid-eighteenth-century society, at any rate, are used to justify differences of station (for example, "The lowly Hedge, and humble Shrub, contribute to the varying and consequently beautifying the Prospect, as well as the stately Oak and lofty Pine," 304), so an ostensible restructuring of the intimate group is counterbalanced by a conservative gesture towards traditional patterns of authority.[12]

David and Cynthia are orphans, the former's uncle dies at the beginning of the novel, and Valentine and Camilla's father and stepmother have driven them from their home. All of the worldly-wise guides in whom David places his confidence at the start of the novel, like Cynthia's cruel patroness and Valentine and Camilla's relations who have accused them of incest, have failed in their social responsibility. It appears that they must, however, be replaced by a parental figure of some kind, who will symbolically reconcile the group to the society that has forcibly ejected them. Although a temporary structural vacuum has freed the group to establish the relationships of lovers and friends, an impasse has developed at the point where love and dependency are to be formalized through marriage ties and structures of support. Thus the death-bed confession of the stepmother, the transformation of the nobleman who admires Camilla from seducer to advocate, the redeployment of the clergyman from unwelcome suitor to performer of weddings, and above all the metamor-phosis of Valentine and Camilla's estranged father into fond parent function to legitimize the foursome as a new kinship structure.[14] Not surprisingly, how-ever, legitimization can also be read as appropriation, mutual dependence as a reforging of the Chain of Being.

If this final denial of a radical disjunction between the anti-individualistic social circle and a hierarchically ordered society subtly undermines the ideal, the viability of the ideal itself is also questioned indirectly at several points in the novel. The emphatic early description of David's goal of a "little Commu-nity" as a "Fantom," an "Idol," which the protagonist worships as an "Enthu-siast" (26-27), points uncertainly in two directions, either to the false cynicism of the larger social world, or to the naiveté of chasing after a chimera. The re-peated power of selfish plotters over the innocent in the early experiences of David and Camilla and Valentine, which appears overcome by the strategy of group interpretation, can again be read alternately as an unconquerable naiveté and incapacity for independent judgment on the part of a character such as David. Similarly, the potential malice of the envious outsider towards members of the exclusive intimate circle is illustrated by the jealousy of Cynthia's mother and sisters at her friendship with Camilla, where the outsider's suspicion of the power of friendship is captured in Cynthia's comment about her mother: "I verily believe, she thought we should draw *Circles,* and turn *Conjurers*" (107).

More extensively, the history of the mysterious French gentlewoman, Isabelle, becomes a kind of tragic translation of the group's own comic experi-ence, as its members' "inward Exultings of their Minds, at the Thought that they [have] met with the same Happiness in each other" (219) indicate during the early stages of her narration. This story, with its evident parallels to the situation of the protagonist group, in one sense deflects the dangers of plot from that group's own experience, as do most of these mid-century novels. At the same time, it functions as well to illustrate the vulnerability of the sympa-thetic circle to conflict that arises from within in the form of a revived desire for self-gratification on the part of any one member. The group's sociable optimism is defeated in the face of Isabelle's experience; they can only agree with her that she is "in the right, in her Resolutions of retiring from a World, in which it [is] impossible for her to meet with any thing worth her Regard, after what she [has] lost" (250). More fundamentally, the final claim that "it is in the power of every Community to attain [real Happiness]" (304) is thrown into question; ironically, the fatal catastrophe for Isabelle's circle is triggered by the attempt of her brother to render perfect the group's intimacy by the marriage of his sister to his best friend.

In the face of this demonstration of vulnerability, the notion that perfect sympathy is equivalent to perfect happiness, first stated in David's insistence that "if he ever did attain to what he was in pursuit of, he should be the *happiest Creature* in the World" (76), is an invalid assumption. Indeed, Camilla discovers the opposite when her brother's life-threatening illness exacerbates her own despair and forces her to take desperate risks. The principle of conversational transparency nourished by complete sympathy can also succumb in reality to well-meant affectation on the one side and a resulting state of self-deception on the other. As a result, David's long-sought happiness is described, even at the moment of its apparent fulfillment as the product of a fanciful mind:

> *Valentine* and *Camilla* often sighed at the Remembrance of their Father's Usage; but they cautiously hid from their *generous Benefactor,* that any uneasy Thoughts ever intruded on their Minds: He fancied them entirely happy, and that their Happiness was owing to him. None but Minds like *David*'s can imagine the Pleasure this Consideration gave him. *Cynthia* saw through *Valentine*'s Behaviour; and yet sometimes she could not help fearing that his Thoughtfulness might arise from some other Cause than what she would have it; and her great Anxiety concerning it, naturally produced Suspicion. [277]

While David lives in a fool's paradise, in other words, his intimate companions are disguising from him various states of uneasiness, fear, anxiety, and suspicion. Although deluded happiness becomes real through the marriages that replace desire and uncertainty with fulfillment, the capacity for worldly or practical concerns to disturb the peace of the community here hints at the ultimate impossibility of all desires being fulfilled, even within the confines of the safely isolated group.

Seen in this light, the reduction of conflict for the protagonist, which has been the general tendency of the plot structure since the beginning, appears to be not merely a matter of resolution within the group itself but also a dangerous indulgence of David's desire to escape conflict rather than confront it. David's initial quarrel with his diametrical opposite, his brother, becomes the overheard disagreement between Nanny Johnson and the friend who takes David's part, and from there is even more distanced through the intermediary guide-narrators, who tell the stories that reveal his acquaintances' failings. The protagonist's pattern of response is to "[run] down stairs, [get] as far out of their hearing as he [can], and [leave] the House that very Night" (48). Thus Fielding's exemplary social circle is again typical, in that the confident promise of an egalitarian, transparent, unindividualistic, non-conflictual, and self-sufficient means of attaining social stability is nevertheless fulfilled in terms of traditional hierarchy, polite deception, a denial of desire, an exclusion of sources of conflict, and a dependence on the material supports of leisured sensibility.

CREATING AUTHORIAL SPACE

I wish to return now to the starting point of this chapter: Sarah Fielding's own precarious social position and apparent attraction to community. While it is not certain that she knew, or was known to, Richardson at the time of *David Simple's* publication, she would undoubtedly, as an educated and avid reader, have been aware of *Pamela* and her brother's parody, *Shamela;* she is further believed to have contributed Leonora's letter to Horatio in *Joseph Andrews.* At any rate, Richardson was an admirer of her *Familiar Letters between the Principal Characters of David Simple* (1747). In 1756 he wrote to her: "I have just gone through your two vols. of Letters. Have re-perused them with great pleasure, and found many new beauties in them. What a knowledge of the human heart! Well might a critical judge of writing say, as he did to me, that your late brother's knowledge of it was not (fine writer as he was) comparable to your's. His was but the knowledge of the outside of a clock-work machine, while your's was that of all the finer springs and movements of the inside." (*Correspondence* 132). Fielding's attitude towards Richardson was, in turn, one of intense admiration, both of his work and, as we have seen, of the circle over which he presided at Parson's Green. Henry Fielding, similarly, took an active, if somewhat patronizing, interest in his sister's writing. Thus, in his preface to the second edition of *David Simple* (also 1744), he apologizes for "some Grammatical and other Errors in Style in the first Impression, which my Absence from Town prevented my correcting," insisting, however, that these are "small Errors, which Want of Habit in Writing chiefly occasioned, and which no Man of Learning would think worth his Censure in a Romance; not any Gentleman, in the Writings of a young Woman."[14] Like Richardson, he sees the "Merit" of the novel in its "vast Penetration into human Nature, a deep and profound Discernment of all the Mazes, Windings and Labyrinths, which perplex the Heart of Man." Indeed, this penetration is "the greatest, noblest, and rarest of all the Talents which constitute a Genius" (5).

Jane Spencer has suggested that, positioned between the rival mentors of her brother and Richardson, Fielding would have experienced a combination of serious encouragement and carefully delimited expectations of female writing.[15] Janet Todd makes the plausible argument that "the humility and gratitude of the stance" created by Henry Fielding for his sister in his preface may well have received her endorsement as appropriate for her as a female writer;[16] one is reminded of the fictional Pamela, whose behavior as social actor and didactic writer models such a stance. Fielding's own statements to Richardson indicate not merely self-conscious strategy but the attitude of a literary disciple and a woman needing the reassurance of having something to say— she begins one letter to Richardson with the words "[you] cannot imagine the pleasure Miss Collier and I enjoyed at the receipt of your kind epistles. We were at dinner with a *hic, haec, hoc* man, who said, well, I do wonder Mr. Richardson will be troubled with such *silly women;* on which we thought to ourselves (though we did not care to say it) if Mr. Richardson will bear us . . . we don't care in how many languages you fancy you despise us" (*Correspondence* 123).

The community created by *David Simple* is one in which a man and a woman gradually take on a shared authority, but only when the hero whose story this ostensibly is willingly takes on the role of audience, allowing the woman to tell her story to him.[17] This authority is shared, moreover, only within an intimate circle that provides a retreat from, or at least a safe zone within, the larger social structure. Moving outwards to the textual apparatus which mediates between author and audience, we find that a timid and anonymous writer submits herself to her readers in the "Advertisement" to the first edition, giving them free rein to approach the work as a "Moral Romance (or whatever Title the Reader shall please to give it)," apologizing for it as "the Work of a Woman, and her first Essay."[19] The tone of *David Simple*'s narrator is complex and uncertain. Moments of self-conscious formality ("Upon which ensued the following Dialogue; which I shall set down word for word; every body's own Words giving the most lively Representations of their Meaning," 35) alternate with apology ("And I believe my Reader, as well as myself, is heartily glad to quit a Subject so extremely barren of Matter, as that of Gaming; and into which I would not have entered at all, but that it would have been . . . ," 81) and self-deprecation ("to describe this Scene . . . requires a *Shakespear*'s Pen; therefore I am willing to close it as soon as possible, being quite unequal to the Task," 294). The overall impression is one of a narrator who is the naive alter-ego of the protagonist, trusting him to speak her message just as the members of his circle initially need him to authorize their self-narrations; she in fact informs us early that "this History is all taken from his own Mouth" (10). Further, as I have noted, from the novel's second edition onwards, its preface was supplied by Fielding's famous brother. Authorization thus begins with a series of male voices supporting a rather tentative narrator, and concludes, as my discussion of the novel has emphasized, with a confident assertion of social possibility that nevertheless relies upon conventional metaphors of order. Like David Simple, the female writer of the social circle must first create the space within which she may be heard and then reinsert that space into an existing social structure.

In Richardson's sequel to *Pamela,* the next work to be discussed in this study, the intimate circle becomes a raised and outwardly radiating exemplar, bringing the larger social world into orbit around its female center. Whereas *David Simple* creates for a few women a safe retreat whose structure can only be miscommunicated to the world in terms of traditional metaphors that do not in fact fit, Richardson uses a mirrorlike resonance between Pamela's husband and his admiring social set, on the one side, and a submissive heroine on the other, to create the tightly enclosed structure that nevertheless exalts and lends authority to Pamela's broad social and discursive powers. The editor of *Pamela* Part II, I will argue, possesses the optimism to narrate the story of Pamela successfully effecting social change. The hard-won narrative voice of *David Simple,* as this chapter has shown, promises change through the multiplication of intimate groups; when it comes to portraying the interaction of the intimate group and the larger social world in *Volume the Last,* it is perhaps inevitable that the ideal community falls victim to attacks of egotism from without and its own virtues from within.

3

Social Authority and the Domestic Circle in Samuel Richardson's *Pamela* Part II

Critics have generally found Richardson's 1741 sequel to *Pamela; or, Virtue Rewarded* easy to dismiss. For T.C. Duncan Eaves and Ben D. Kimpel, "the great fault of the continuation of *Pamela* is that there was nothing which could happen in it, and the best excuse that can be offered for it is that Richardson was evidently forced to write it, without any urge from inside." Even Margaret Anne Doody's relatively sympathetic reading of the sequel is entitled "*Pamela* Continued: Or, The Sequel that Failed."[1] Summarizing these and other evaluations in her recent discussion of *Pamela* Part II, Terry Castle concludes with "What then to say . . . about a work for which little may be said? Where to go with a text that seems to go nowhere?" Castle finds that even among the problematic class of literary sequels, "the novel is more than a disappointment. At times it seems almost to insult us, to affront our expectations, including our very desire for repetition."[2]

Castle's comments usefully identify two expectations frustrated by this sequel—the expectation of a plot which provides linear thrust and the expectation that a reading experience will repeat itself. Castle's solution to this problem is to recuperate the novel's masquerade sequence as a "capsule of narrative delight in a narrative of few delights," a happy accident resulting from the coincidence of Richardson's and his readers' repressed desires for a repetition of Part I's subversive, disorderly plot. Reading Part I as a narrative of carnivalesque desire fulfilled, and Part II as imaginatively successful only inasmuch as it repeats Part I's "sheer transgressive energy," Castle applies to this novel the Bakhtinian assumption that the essence of the genre is found in the individual's radical subversion of the dominant social codes. From this perspective, the masquerade becomes "an indispensable plot-catalyst" allowing it to fit her identification of the eighteenth-century novel as the genre which "registered most symptomatically the paradoxical carnivalization of eighteenth-century society."[3]

Castle's attractively transgressive "misreading," like the earlier dismissals she cites, skirts the possibility that the author sets out deliberately to "insult" and "affront," to frustrate reader desire. I believe in fact that Richardson is doing just that: while he cannot be said to oppose anachronistically a critical tradition which will privilege the novel of teleological and conflictual structure over one whose narrative is more static and consensual, he is clearly reinforcing a conservative reading of *Pamela* Part I by contextualizing his heroine and thereby setting boundaries to the interpretation of her life story.[4] Carol Kay has suggested that Richardson's work in general reflects his hope of "social reconciliation and unification . . . invested in the authority of moral discourse," an authority whose "rules . . . seem to emanate from everywhere and nowhere" and which is upheld by the self-regulation of exemplary characters who "subject themselves to the limitations of convention." More specifically, *Pamela* Part II illustrates what Kay has noted as a tendency for the authority conferred upon an author through literary recognition to be represented in "the rise in status and authority of central characters from first novel to second novel."[5] Richardson was credited by one party of *Pamela's* first readers with writing a book that "will do more good than many volumes of sermons"; by another party, he was accused of encouraging lasciviousness in youth, impertinence in servants, and interference in dependents by means of "this poison."[6] Thus Part II of *Pamela* can be read as a text which formally and explicitly confronts, and posits resolutions to, issues raised by the reception of its precursor through the increasing authority of its heroine. Terry Eagleton has reminded critics that a lack of sympathy for the ideological values served by Richardson's forms does not in itself justify a dismissal of those forms on aesthetic grounds;[7] to this I would add that a search for one kind of form should not blind the reader to another.

Enclosing Pamela in Part II involves for Richardson a defense of two aspects of Part I: its courtship story and its claims of Pamela's fitness for her raised status. Further, rewriting within the bounds of an exemplary marriage (by eighteenth-century standards) calls for a narrative structure that does not depend on the development of an interiorized self in conflict with its context. Whereas in Part I Richardson's female center of consciousness, who defends her honor and the value of her soul as equal to those of a gentleman, inevitably appears to oppose a social structure which does not reflect that equality, the heroine of Part II, as a wife, becomes the center of moral authority and interpretation within the social structure. The original's correspondingly reactive, breathless structure of counter-intrigue and breach-stopping gives way to a text radiating outwards in methodical alignment around a center of disciplined self-regulation. In other words, this supposedly plotless, directionless work carefully centralizes authority in the exemplary figure of Pamela, while presenting her as the ideally submissive manifestation of the conventions of the social circle she has penetrated. Potentially disruptive desires and their stylistic manifestations are either brought into line with the terms of Pamela's discourse or deflected and excluded from her circle.[8]

Richardson's concern, then, is to work within social realities as natural, to deflect conflict between the encroaching and the defending sexes into channels less threatening to domestic happiness, and to both establish and contain the discursive authority of the virtuous female; *Pamela* Part II can be roughly divided into three movements reflecting these emphases in turn. In the first portion of the text, Pamela's fitness for her newly powerful social role is demonstrated and affirmed through a minutely detailed portrayal of her performance as Mrs. B. Subsequently, the public world of London poses a challenge to the stable domestic circle by exerting a counter-pull on Mr. B.'s attentions. Finally, Pamela leaves "this undelightful town"[9] for private life, in which her now-firmly established authority is paradoxically exerted throughout ever-wider social and literary spheres. In other words, Pamela's destiny as wife is figured not in terms of progress towards a defined if unattainable happiness, but in terms of an ever-increasing atemporality and abstraction as the centre of a stabilized circle, the still point gradually aligning a spinning social world around its morally fixed self.

Before this, however, Richardson's correspondence and the sequel's preface raise the issues with which he is faced and point to the strategies to be employed in dealing with them. The regulation of desire by a naturalized social structure is suggested by the claims that Part II, like its predecessor, is "equally written to NATURE," yet presents rules "equally *new* and *practicable*," that it is "not unworthy of the *First* Part; nor disproportioned to the more exalted condition in which PAMELA was destined to shine" (v). In keeping with this careful contextualization of the sequel and the heroine is the preface's emphasis upon boundaries and circumferences; the novel of marriage and social relations must voluntarily subscribe to the same kinds of limits as must its female protagonist. Like the proper domestic woman, whose "watchful eye" enforces the "rules and directions" prescribed in her husband's household (393), the Editor has "labour'd hard to rein in [his] Invention, and made it a Rule with [him] to avoid unnecessary Digressions, & Foreign Episodes."[10] Indeed, he has sought "to bring [a multitude of important subjects] within the compass which he was determined not to exceed" (v).[11] "To perfect the Design" of *Pamela* is Richardson's goal, and as a result, "there cannot, *naturally*, be the room for Plots, Stratagem and Intrigue in the present Volumes as in the first" (*Letters*, 51, 53). Commenting upon one of these letters, Eagleton suggests that for this author "the indecent liberties of 'invention' must be suppressed in the cause of instruction, ideological closure achieved by a *calculated* sacrifice of *jouissance*."[12]

PERFORMING IN A BOUNDED SPHERE: BEDFORDSHIRE

Thus, defending the bulwarks of besieged virtue in the social limbo of Part I becomes, in the first part of the sequel in particular, a detailed drawing of the boundaries circumscribing female roles and behavior under more common-place conditions. Richardson uses a dual strategy to construct a female authority which functions in support of the status quo: he defines personal integrity as ideal role-playing, and he has Pamela insist upon limiting her activities to the domestic sphere. Personal integrity in all of Richardson's fiction is achieved through correct placement of the self within a coherent matrix of social and moral values. For example, his retrospective statement that *Pamela* is the story of a "Libertine . . . perfectly reclaimed," first by his mother's instruction, then by his love of Pamela, and finally by "her amiable Example, and unwearied Patience" as his wife, suggests that a deviant situation has been corrected by realignment with fundamental social and moral values.[13] Pamela's achievement in Part I is therefore the recognition of Providence's ordained role for her. In Part II, her exemplary response to her marriage, the hope that she will thereby be made "an humble instrument in the hand of Providence to communicate great good to others" (63), establishes the keynote for her acts of reclamation and modeling that will set her context in order around her center. Most importantly, it is Providence that directs a passive Pamela into her position of power within the existing hierarchy, so that she can be portrayed as the upholder of social forces without incurring the responsibility, dangerous in an upstart, for their existence and perpetuity.

As Pamela establishes herself as mistress of B.'s Bedfordshire house, she is encircled by an audience of her betters by birth, who assume the providential prerogative of assigning roles for her to perform. In elaborate and ceremonial exchanges B. and others plead with Pamela to determine such issues as the awarding of titles and church livings, overruling her demure disclaimers and then responding to her pronouncements with grateful tears or ecstatic praise, later reinforced by the accolades of correspondents. Furthermore, the increasingly broad social authority exercised by this woman and former inferior is carefully channeled through her husband, who on one occasion proclaims, "Whenever I put power into your hands for the future, act but as you have now done, and it will be impossible that I should have any choice or will but yours" (154). This statement illustrates what Kay has called the B.'s's "Humean realization of mutual satisfaction in limiting the full play of power," but more especially, the limitations within which the power of a subordinate finally operates. At any rate, Pamela's role-playing is not a mystification of her true identity, as Castle would have it, but proof of her essential fitness for her ordained part, in the manner of a concept of character that Elizabeth Deeds Ermarth associates with spiritual autobiography.[14] Desireless, yet perfectly consistent with her essential self, Pamela's role-playing provides an exemplary contrast to that of the upcoming masquerade, where she is proven mistaken in her assumption "that all that was tolerable in a masquerade, was the acting up to the character each person assumed" (259).

As Pamela's roles change with her marriage, the virtues of humility, honor, duty, and pride alter their manifestation in her. The harassed servant-girl who calls her master's behavior "poor and mean" in Part I (1:12) does not contradict herself in Part II when she carefully describes herself as "withstand[ing] the greatest of trials and temptations, from a gentleman more worthy to be beloved, both for person and mind, than any man in England" (129), because she is now a proper bride for whom virtue includes seeing virtue in her husband. In other words, this text's generalized bounding of self-expression by socially (and providentially) defined roles is more specifically, for Pamela, a matter of mastering the role of wife. Prudentia, the heroine of one of Pamela's nursery fables, cultivates those "domestic virtues, which shall one day make her the crown of some worthy gentleman's earthly happiness: and which, *of course,* . . . will secure and heighten her own" (470-71). Although Pamela's friend Polly Darnford is at one point moved to exclaim, "What a public blessing would such a mind as [Mrs. B.'s] be, could it be vested with the robes of royalty, and adorn the sovereign dignity!" (250), Pamela's exemplary influence is made possible precisely because, like Prudentia, she "shines, to her last hour, in all the duties of domestic life, as an excellent wife, mother, mistress, friend, and Christian; and so confirms all the expectations of which her maiden life had given such strong and such edifying presages" (471).

Pamela's ideal performance is paradoxically strengthened by a feminist subtext which is developed in Part II not as a subversive but rather as an adaptive strategy. The often-noted commentary Pamela intersperses with her account of B.'s curtain-lecture upon her behavior as a wife in Part I is now expanded into a running exchange between women, of whom the principals are Pamela, Lady Davers, and Polly Darnford. This exchange claims for itself such privileges as the discussion of strategies for circumventing B.'s "haughty way of speaking of our sex" (42) and the sharing of specifically female experiences and fears "on an occasion upon which our sex may write to one another; but . . . gentlemen should not desire to see" (217), as well as the freedom for generalized commiserations over that "constant parching drought" during which "all [a lady's] attributed excellencies [are] swallowed up in the quicksands of matrimony" (178). Nevertheless, because these discussions uphold humility and extreme delicacy as the only modes of expressing resistance, they serve in themselves to reinforce the notion of female power as necessarily circumscribed. By encouraging one another in acquiescence as a reality of marriage, these women defuse what might presumably manifest itself in undesirable forms of rebellion. Pamela's educational writings and conversations similarly co-opt feminist critique for the purposes of a naturalized hierarchy of gender. Thus the frequent superiority of intelligence over their husbands which she observes in wives she uses to argue that women should receive a better education in order to "make better daughters, better wives, better mothers, and better mistresses" (416-17). More strikingly, she counsels her ward, "in your *maiden state,* think yourself *above* the gentlemen, and they'll think you so too, and address you with reverence and respect. . . . In your *married state,* which is a kind of state of humiliation for a lady, you must think yourself subordinate to your husband; for so it has pleased God to make the wife" (467).[15] It is only within the bounds of an established matrimonial hierarchy, then, that Pamela may exercise her moral and social authority, and it is by these boundaries as well that Richardson will delimit his plot of consensus.

Although still ostensibly writing letters, Pamela frequently modifies her form in the sequel to that of a series of "conversation-pieces" recording household routine. The term is used self-consciously by Pamela and her correspondents (58, 97, 119), suggesting that Richardson deliberately selects this form as a structuring device suitable to contextualizing the solitary and besieged individual of Part I. The heroine describes these pieces as informal in structure and content, apologizing for "dispens[ing] with some forms," for "hav[ing] no regard, when it would fetter or break in upon my freedom of narration, to inscription or subscription," and for "blots and blurs" (89-90). Nevertheless, this ostensibly informal and expressive mode is ultimately monologic in its reflexivity; the informal and the intimate thus give way to the more formal and generally applicable and, by implication, the more imitable.

This monologic effect comes in part from the fact that, despite an increased range of tones and styles in the sequel, Pamela adapts to and manages each as a demonstration of her suitability to her station. Indeed, the irascible Sir Simon Darnford recognizes his own structural role as a necessary "foil . . . to set off some more edifying example, where variety of characters make up a feast in conversation" (78). Pamela's admonishment to Sir Simon in a decorous version of his own jocular style, juxtaposed with her letter to Mrs. Jewkes, beginning "You give me, Mrs. Jewkes, very great pleasure, to find, that, at length, God Almighty has touched your heart, and let you see, while health and strength lasted, the error of your ways" (63-64), proves her mastery of what Bakhtin calls not true heteroglossia but "a forensic and polemical discourse,"[16] positing the existence of an absolute and definable standard of social action applicable to all experience.

Typical of Part II's monologic conversation is the fact that when B. tells his version of the courtship story, Pamela's definition of honor, so contested in Part I, is revealed to have been his own all along: "Yet my love was a traitor, that was more faithful to *her* than to *me;* it had more honour in it at bottom than I had designed," he explains (116). B.'s marriage to Pamela is now described by her as a resignation on his part of the prerogative of naming: "When he could not have me upon his own terms," she declares, "God turned his evil purposes to good ones; and he resolved to submit to mine" (49). In other words, the requirement of linguistic consensus, shared by all of these mid-century texts, is in this case achieved through the affirmation of Pamela's language as the only right one. Lady Davers, in particular, shifts from the epithet of "beggarly brat" in Part I (1:355) to calling the heroine "my charming Pamela; my *more than sister*" (130), and announces, "Beloved, deservedly beloved of the kindest of husbands, what a blessing art thou to this family!" (142-43). Her verbal conformity shows that she has resolved to be guided by the moral example of Pamela, her inferior in age and in birth; a similar significance lies in the gestures of such characters as the formerly hardened Mrs. Jewkes, who places Pamela's letter, like a sacred talisman, next to her heart, and Jackey, the illiterate dandy, who "vows he'll set pen to paper and turn letter-writer himself" (34). To borrow Aaron Hill's description of Richardson's novels, "verbosity becomes a virtue" and "redundance but conveys resemblance."[17]

The conformity of Pamela's social circle to her discursive practice produces two related effects: the transformation of Pamela's past into an artifact of shared social memory and the exclusion of criticism of her from her social circle. As Pamela's past is circulated in the form of a bundle of papers or even the single word "story" in order to draw others into moral alignment with her, the most problematic memories of Part I are recontextualized or replayed in altered form.[18] B. and Lady Davers both explain their apparently dishonorable actions in ways which allow for the aptness of Pamela's original responses while salvaging their own claims to nobility of character. As Kinkead-Weekes has noted, Sir Jacob Swynford reenacts an ignorant and boorish version of Lady Davers's initial rejection of Pamela, only to be thoroughly and humiliatingly convinced of his error.[19] In general, the party of her admirers steadily absorbs its opposition to form an increasingly symmetrical chorus: Mrs. Jewkes joins Mrs. Jervis, Sir Jacob Swynford follows Lady Davers, and Mr. Peters joins Mr. Williams. Thus, Pamela is hemmed in by a circle of the like-minded, who reinforce and universalize her values.

In fact, Pamela's audience within the text constantly reflects back to the heroine, and to her reader, the success of her performance, reinforcing the pattern of exemplary behavior authorized through the consensus of its context. In one sequence, Pamela records first praise of herself for "an understanding which comprehend[s] every thing, and an eye that penetrate[s] into the very bottom of matters in a moment," and then the response to this audience response as a kind of infinite replication of mirror images:

> Judge how pleasing this was to my best beloved, who found, in their kind approbation, such a justification of his own conduct as could not fail of being pleasing to him, especially as Lady Davers was one of the kind praisers. Lord Davers was so highly delighted, that he rose once, begging his brother's excuse, to salute me, and stood over my chair, with a pleasure in his looks that cannot be ex-

pressed, now-and-then lifting up his hands, and his good-natured eye glistening with joy, which a pier-glass gave me the opportunity of seeing, as sometimes I stole a bashful glance towards it, not knowing how or which way to look. [134]

The correspondents to whom these accounts are directed, as Carol Kay points out, "are addressed as representative social authorities, [who] have a right to pronounce judgment on the behavior of the letter writer and join in the interpretation of other characters."[20] The reader as most peripheral correspondent is situated both at the circumference of this circle, her scrutiny focused inward on its center, and at its center, in the person of Pamela regulating her own behavior for an ever-present audience. This tightly reflexive structure embodies Kay's above-noted description of social rules in Richardson as at once originating "from everywhere and nowhere" and self-generated by a subject who has perfectly internalized the conventions.

By the conclusion of the Bedfordshire section, therefore, Pamela's very range of speaking and role-playing powers serves, paradoxically, to reinforce the emphasis upon her unchanging virtue. B. tells us he was first brought to think honorably of the servant-girl Pamela by "a virtue [he] had never before encountered, so uniform and immovable" (116); in the second part of the sequel, her assertion of her wifely prerogatives through the supposed trial of her own conduct will confirm this conclusion; B. will tell Pamela that he has "weighed well [her] conduct" and "[finds] an uniformity in it, that is surprizingly just" (318).

RESISTING THE PLOT OF CONFLICT: LONDON

A number of these strategies for establishing Pamela's bounded authority in the first portion of the sequel clearly minimize the structural and thematic significance of conflict. The absorption of Pamela into the hierarchical status quo through the revelation that her courtship was in fact less conflictually structured than her papers had presented it to be, through her ostentatiously passive embodiment of authority invested in her by others, and through her use of a potentially subversive language to conservative ends, have all been seen to dissolve apparent oppositions into consensus. Most importantly, as the ideal wife of the autocratic husband, Pamela is one of those "infatuating creatures" who, "instead of *scornful* looks darted in return for *angry* ones, words of *defiance* for words of *peevishness,* persisting to defend *one* error by *another,* and returning *vehement wrath* for *slight indignation; . . .* can thus hide their dear faces in our bosoms, and wish but to *know* their faults, to *amend* them!" (74). As this oppositional description of the wife Pamela is *not* indicates, the B.s' marriage can never be threatened from within because Pamela's perfect role-playing will never allow her to treat B. as her equal and adversary.

Nevertheless, while the first portion of the sequel minimizes conflict in this way, it profits from the momentum supplied by a number of mock conflicts. B. pretends anger with Pamela on several occasions, only to approve and enlarge upon her course of action. Such incidents heighten suspense, while providing roundabout approaches to further praise of the heroine. Perhaps most significantly, they develop the category of imagined evil, which both reinforces the new explanations that have been provided for some of Pamela's sufferings before her marriage and introduces the only adversarial form Richardson can safely allow into the marriage plot: the conflict of misunderstanding, heightened by the sensible female imagination. Thus, Pamela is on several occasions almost overpowered by fear of B.'s anger, exhibiting her exemplary desire to please her husband above all things but also, the text makes clear, her heightened emotional susceptibility as a pregnant woman.[21]

Into this non-conflictual idyll is inserted the visit to London with its masquerade episode, constituting a test both of the sequel's conjugal ideal and of Pamela's ability to deal with conflict in a context within which the old binary patterns of opposition are inappropriate and potentially fatal to happiness. That the London sojourn brings a test of this marriage is not unexpected, given the contrast between Pamela's carefully delineated domestic circle and the disorderly, "overgrown capital" with its "vast circumference" and "public diversions" (224). The reader has been prepared to read this test as B.'s straying out of the orbit of Pamela's center through explicit projections such as her "if I can but find him not deviate, when we go to London, I shall greatly hope that nothing will affect his morals again" (119). Terry Castle has noted that the London of *Pamela* Part II is a place of confusion and multiformity, and that the masquerade Pamela attends reluctantly is the very emblem of the city's social disorder. However, as the pregnant Quaker wife at the assembly, Pamela represents not "the visual embodiment of carnival confusion," as Castle would have it, but rather realized domestic order standing in contrast to the "gaudy prospects" (314) of unregulated desire which attract B. in the person of the flirtatious nun. Indeed, Pamela is portrayed as a motionless center at once attracting the attention of, and standing apart from, all the masqueraders; she is not Castle's "queen of misrule" (131), but the speaker of "a general satire on the assemblée" (*Pamela* 2:261).[22]

When Pamela believes her husband to be embarking upon an extramarital affair with the Countess Dowager of _____, which amounts in her view to polygamy, she sees herself under divine obligation to refuse any part in the arrangement.[23] Her authoritative management of the mock-trial scene is therefore allowable both in terms of her social role—"the character I ought to assume as his wife"—and her moral duty—"that one hope I had, to be an humble means of saving the man I love and honour, from errors that might be fatal to his soul" (306). She thus manages to appear "uniform" to B., and to the reader, despite the "boldness" (306) of her staged trial scene, on the strength of her proven fitness for her position. Castle argues rightly that the affair resurrects the suggestion that a highborn wife would in fact have been a more suitable one for B., and that it is this suggestion which the heroine emphasizes as the primary charge against herself.[24] The real effect of this return to the old issue, however, is to display once and for all exactly why Pamela is the ideal spouse for B. Thus her defense masterfully turns an acknowledgment of her inferior origins into an argument that she is nevertheless superior to the countess in her moral qualifications—those qualifications which B. himself has equated repeatedly with his social ones—because her love for him extends beyond his physical and social attractions to his mind and soul.

As after the crisis of Part I, Pamela is later able to look back upon "how happily God's providence has now, at last, turned that affair," through the resultant conversion of B. into "a *religious* man" (420). Because Richardson is working with the non-conflictual mode of marriage, however, this happy turn can only be fully realized through a universally satisfactory solution, as Pamela explains to Lady Davers: "I . . . hope my next will be a joyful letter; and that I shall inform you in it, that the affair . . . is absolutely concluded to my satisfaction, to Mr. B's and the Countess's; for if it be so to all three, my happiness, I doubt not, will be founded on a permanent basis" (332). True happiness, in other words, is built not upon the defeat of an outside rival for one's husband, but upon achieving a shared satisfaction. Thus, B. and the countess each tell Pamela their versions of the story, versions whose apparent contradictions with Pamela's view of the affair are managed by an appeal once more to the heightened imagination of Pamela, this time as a new mother. Richardson does not go so far, however, as to question Pamela's rightness and timeliness in taking action; her concern throughout represents the response of virtuous love, if not of worldly-wise strategy. As she insists later, "The dear man *was* to be on the brink of relapsing: it was proper, that I should be so very uneasy, as to assume a conduct not natural to my temper" (422). Confirming the moral authority of Pamela's position, the repentant countess hopes to become "as solid, as grave, as circumspect, though not so wise, as Mrs. B" (370), and B. relinquishes reliance upon his own strength of character altogether, in favor of Pamela's moral guidance. Scriptural allusions, by means of which Pamela links herself with the prophet Nathan before King David, Queen Esther before King Xerxes, and St. Paul before the governor Felix—all relatively powerless figures in terms of earthly hierarchies but fighting for the victorious spiritual cause—further assert that moral authority throughout the episode. Pamela herself rejoices in the new surety of a husband "in all probability, mine upon better and surer terms than ever" (315). When social and moral frameworks are once again temporarily divided, as they were during B.'s initial pursuit of Pamela, the heroine and the moral structure she represents remain the immovable center against which deviation is measured.[25]

TRANSCENDING THE DOMESTIC CIRCLE:
ON THE ROAD AND IN THE NURSERY

As this center, Pamela emerges from the trial fully exemplified as "virtue itself" and as B.'s "tutelary angel" (314). Thus the latter portion of the sequel focuses upon an abstracted Pamela as virtue itself, reminding the reader again that Part II is telling the story of "Virtue Rewarded." In keeping with the consistent emphasis of the sequel upon the individual as role-player, however, the virtue preserved and rewarded here is not Pamela's sexual purity, but rather what is proper to B.'s wife. Despite her immediate sensation, therefore, of "a thankfulness so exalted, that it left me all light and pleasant, as if I had shook off body, and trod in air" (315), Pamela's victory is marked, not by a Clarissa-like transcendence that places her above the limitations of social convention, but by an apotheosis of the wife at the center of the household. That household, as Richardson's ideal social structure, is modeled on the perfect harmony and stasis of heaven.

The third portion of the sequel begins with the B. family withdrawing from London to Pamela's parents' farm in Kent, where Pamela can preside over a regrouped and expanding circle of "all [she] delight[s] in, upon one happy spot together" (320). Renewed congruence is marked by a heightened rhetoric of stability and cyclical motion that reaches its peak with the religious conversion of B. as an outgrowth of his London failure.[26] At this point, all potential for tension, to which the marriage remained vulnerable for as long as B.'s values were divided between those of his social world and those of his wife, is removed. The B.s's marriage has indeed become a heaven on earth: "Methinks I am already, dear Sir," cries Pamela to her husband, "ceasing to be mortal, and beginning to taste the perfections of those joys, which this thrice welcome declaration gives me hope of hereafter!" (424). This spiritualized world of pure and matched desires is again embodied in a reflexive language; thus Pamela describes her marriage as an equilibrium obliterating distinctions of dominance and submission, present and future, in which "this *heavenly* prospect . . . [is] added to all my *earthly* blessings! . . . that [Mr. B.] is, and will be mine, and I his, through the mercies of God, when this transitory life is past and gone, to all eternity" (423).

In the light of eternity, particularities of time and space, of daily activities and changes of location, lose their significance. "In a family so uniform and methodical as ours," Pamela apologizes, there is no news, only repetition, "the same things, . . . with little variation, occurring this year, as to our conversations, visits, friends, employments, and amusements, that fell out the last"

(419). Although B. and Pamela travel more and more widely and even for years at a time, her writings do not describe their travel experiences, but rather limit themselves increasingly to the private concerns of family life and the education of her children. The momentarily linear plot of the exemplary marriage under siege becomes a static focus on the family circle as a viable alternative to the dissipations of London and Continental society. Thus, domesticity is not a last-ditch retreat from a corrupt public world but rather an optimistically and extensively developed alternative to it.[27]

From this condition of stasis the sequel takes the final step of resolving into tableaux and maxims that convert the narrative past tense into a transcendental present. "Imagine you see me seated, surrounded with the joy and the hope of my future prospects, as well as my present comforts," she writes (462), as she embarks on a transcription of one of her nursery tales. Pamela as authoritative educator of the young distills experience into its moral essence; "naughty" and "good," so problematic as epithets for Mr. B. in Part I, for example, have now hardened into moral categories which determine inclusion within, or exclusion from, the circle of the virtuous and the blessed. According to this system, "good Masters seldom fail to make good gentlemen; and good Misses, good ladies; and God blesses them with as good children as they were to *their* parents; and so the blessing goes round!" (463), while a corollary "sad" law states that "every one that is naughty, first or last, must be *certainly* unhappy" (470). In the case of the "naughty" sons and daughter of one of Pamela's nursery tales, their initially precarious status as the children of "a poor, poor widow woman" (463) is transformed into definitive expulsion from the social structure by divine punishments in the form of seafaring and resultant drowning, thieving and resultant hanging, unemployment and resultant exile, and sloth and resultant fatal illness.

The universality of this law in Pamela's world is indicated by her justification of the use of rewards for children with the argument, "for is it not by this method that the whole world is influenced and governed? Does not God himself, by rewards and punishments, make it our *interest,* as well as our *duty,* to obey him?" (377). Nor does Pamela's experience falsify the providential plot: she herself is the "happy, and the happy-making" Prudentia of the nursery tale with which the sequel concludes, as Miss Goodwin recognizes. Characters who, like Lord and Lady Davers, are given the grace to align themselves about Pamela's ideal figure find themselves greatly improved in "conversation" and "temper" (428). As instructor of young ladies, Pamela presides over a teatable to which even "the pulpit . . . may be beholden" (451). Indeed, Pamela's fame spreads across the world, according to the former Sally Godfrey, who credits her with the power to ensure "the good of thousands" (357). By maintaining nevertheless a tension between Pamela's normative example and its abnormal excellence, Richardson shields her social rise from would-be imitators, channeling desire into moral emulation on the part of all who come within the heroine's gravitational field.[28] By contrast, most of the "naughty" remain almost out of sight in this narrative, at best cautionary flashes whose egocentric courses carry them momentarily through Pamela's stable universe. The fallen Sally Godfrey, for instance, whose story negatively mirrors Pamela's, writes from "an awful distance" (355) that geographically illustrates her exclusion from the exemplary inner circle, if not from the penitent outer one. Other such characters are rakes and coxcombs, as representatives of all that Pamela's reformed sociability condemns. Lord Davers's nephew Jackey, as one whose "delights are centred in himself," and who "will not wish to get out of that exceeding narrow circle" (350), is doomed to suffer, not directly at the hands of the passively virtuous Pamela, but simply by breaking the rules of this fictional universe. The decisive point in Jackey's original downfall is his decision to leave the family and go to London alone; he thereby excludes himself from the B. circle through his deliberate defiance. After being made a public laughingstock through his "abominable folly" (433), Jackey is readmitted to the circle when he "[throws] himself upon the protection of Mr. B" and marries a prudent and virtuous woman "of Lady Davers's recommendation" (473).

Although the text of course excludes from representation its own acts of exclusion, they are nonetheless suggested through brief summaries and stylistic negations. The drama of reform in Pamela's own household is never recorded, implying that the process has been uniform and unresisted. We are merely told after the fact that "the good have been confirmed, the remiss have been reformed, the passionate have been tamed," so that "there is not a family in the kingdom . . . more uniform, more regular, and freer from evil, and more regardful of what they say and do, than [Mr. B.'s]" (391). The ideal tutor who will further such family values is described in terms so resonant with "avoid," "shall not," and "nor" as to lead Pamela herself to admit that he has been "negatively described" (387-88). When Pamela's waiting maid, Polly Barlow, allows herself to be drawn by Jackey into an indiscretion, it becomes necessary to remove her from Pamela's person and from the household circle—appropriately, through an unsuitable marriage whose uncertain future will be the just reward of her scheming desires.

As the above examples of Pamela's educational activities suggest, the heroine's achievement of moral stasis for herself and her world is matched by the establishment of her authority over those genres to which, in Richardson's view, the domestic woman can extend her literary practice. Criticizing public forms such as the theatre (for its lack of "proper regulations" [252], its whirlwinds of passionate love, and its players, who prostitute themselves to play any character), the opera (for its "mere temporary delight" [256]), and the masquerade (for its lack of "a standard . . . by which one could determine readily what *is*, and what is *not* wit" [261]), Pamela indicates that the role of cultural critic is appropriately feminized. Her extensive comments on Locke's educational theories make it clear that the education of children is particularly her province, as "watchful mamma . . . employed like a skilful gardener, in assisting and encouraging the charming flower through its several hopeful stages to perfection" (376). Beyond educational theory, Pamela engages in the practice of producing curricular materials, developing her conversation pieces and character sketches into "characters of persons . . . whose conduct may serve for imitation or warning" to young ladies and children (461). Pamela's texts, like her example, are gradually detached from her person and circulated in increasingly anonymous forms to an ever-wider circle of beneficiaries. Thus B.'s description of Pamela as "virtue itself" is paralleled in the discursive sphere by the claim "that *virtue* itself [speaks]" when she does (453).

Indeed, the sequel would seem to end at the moment in which abstraction overwhelms narrative—in which the individual Pamela has been completely subsumed in the typological Prudentia, and in which Pamela's story has fragmented itself into an anthology of exemplary narratives with lives of their own. In a sense, such a view supports the critical claim that a narrative without a unified plot and without a protagonist who embodies individualistic desire is unviable and unreadable. Richardson's text, however, has gone to literally great lengths to arrive at this unreadability, this complete frustration of the desire for a tension-driven plot. Privileging the social over the individual, Part II of *Pamela* is constructed according to the image of a family clockwork, in which Pamela is "the master-wheel, in some beautiful pieces of mechanism, whose dignified grave motions is to set a-going all the under-wheels, with a velocity suitable to their respective parts" (25). Uniform virtue has rescued the text, as well as B., from the moment-to-moment tensions and reversals arising from "the guilty tumults that used formerly to agitate [his] unequal mind" (2). Pamela's charitable impulses have been regularized into a "*benevolent weekly round*" (185), while spiritual and social energies are so perfectly congruent in her "heaven of a house" that "wound up . . . constantly once a week [by Sunday prayers], at least, like a good eight-day clock, no piece of machinery that ever was made is so regular and uniform as this family is" (250).[29]

In achieving this stability, the author has taken the domestic and conversational circle with a woman at its center and granted it a broad moral, social, and aesthetic authority of interpretation, evaluation, and prescription. Although Pamela's authority must be firmly established through, and properly aligned with, existing social structures, she exercises an ordering power within those bounds that is affirmed by both Providence and the watching world. The structural, social, and linguistic circle into which *Pamela* Part II draws itself is, among the collection of texts I am discussing, the most tightly controlled and least penetrable model of the consensual ideal. It seems to me, then, that this sequel leaves the modern reader not so much with the sense that desire has been repressed as with a sense that an anxiety about the social and moral dangers of the new prose fiction has been controlled by delimiting the "compass" which the individual's text must not "exceed."

In *Sir Charles Grandison,* Richardson appears, on the other hand, at the height of his optimism and sense of social responsibility. By dividing plotting and narrating functions in the novel along the lines of gender, placing a well-born and wealthy hero at the center of a circle of narrating female admirers, he enables himself both to address explicitly the issue of individualistic desire and to portray an intimate circle with the power to expand its authority across the spectrum of polite society. At the same time, true to the paradox of these novels in general, *Grandison* successfully circumscribes desire in the interests of a more rigidly patriarchal structure of authority than that of *Pamela* Part II. In *Amelia,* Henry Fielding similarly genders exemplary and narrative functions; in contrast to Richardson, however, he places an ideally silent and passive heroine at the center of her familial circle, allowing the story of her ultimate success in securing her wandering husband within her orbit to be given meaning by an authoritative male spokesman. As a result, again, the authority of Amelia's virtue is proven more powerful than that of Pamela in the egotistical excesses from which she manages to reform her husband, while she is not allowed any desire which deviates from that her society has prescribed for the domestic female. Thus, the next pair of texts to be examined represents the height of both optimism and conservatism for the novel of the conversational circle.

4

Socializing Desire and Radiating the Exemplary in Samuel Richardson's *Sir Charles Grandison*

Although Samuel Richardson tells his readers, in the guise of Editor of *Sir Charles Grandison*, that with this novel he has "completed the Plan, that was the Object of his Wishes . . . to accomplish," the notion of completion has become considerably more complex than it was in the case of the sequel to *Pamela*.[1] On one level, this "public View [of] the Character and Actions of a Man of TRUE HONOUR" is a companion piece to *Clarissa* as an intimate anatomy of the "Heart, always excellent, refined and exalted" of the "truly *Christian Heroine*"; the active, public, masculine self is offered as a necessary balance to the suffering, private, feminine self. In another sense, both of the earlier novels are represented as stages in the project of painting an ideally sociable self, not just a "Libertine . . . reclaimed," and certainly not the "Destroyer . . . buoyed up with Self-conceit and vain Presumption" who remains "unreclaimed," but rather, the man who is "happy in himself, and a Blessing to others." Finally, Richardson asserts that this novel has at once "enabled [him] to obey . . . his Friends, and to complete his first design," portraying the work as the realization both of audience desire and of an authorial plan (1:3-4).

Thus, in the very rhetoric of completion and closure Richardson appears to open the bounds of his text to a heteroglossia of fictional and societal voices. The attempt at interpretive control that is embodied in the tightly centralized authority of *Pamela* Part II's exemplary heroine gives way to a model of the text as stimulus for conversation. Although Richardson's notion of the novelistic text and the extra-textual correspondence it generates has been a porous one since as early as the first proofs of *Clarissa*,[2] this strain becomes the dominant motif in the early epistolary references to *Grandison*, probably begun in 1750. At this juncture in the process of literary production, the reading circle is invited into the text, well beyond mere stylistic correction or moral pointing, to its very heart: the nature of the protagonist as the "TRULY GOOD MAN" (3:462).[3]

Most striking among Richardson's repeated invitations to his female readers to supply attributes and actions for the prospective hero is his half-assertion–half-complaint that "it is more in the power of young ladies than they seem to imagine, to make fine men" (*Letters,* 164). The phrasing here suggests first that women, by virtue of their sex, have a unique creative or formative power over men—in other words, Richardson conceives of the imagination in gendered terms. At the same time, he clearly views the female imagination with a deep ambivalence; because it is associated with sexual desire, it at once supplies a generative impulse and poses an antisocial threat, whether through moral apathy that allows the imagination to remain inactive altogether, or through a preference for less-than-"fine" constructions, such as Lovelace, as its objects.[4] By further implication, Richardson sees his authorial self in a double role, dependent upon that feminine source of creative energy in producing his own narrative, yet needing to activate, authorize, and censor that energy.[5]

Richardson is far from relinquishing his belief in textual authority, in fact. Just as the novel is at once generated by audience desire and controlled by its author, so Sir Charles Grandison the character is both the creation of his admiring social circle (John Mullan describes Sir Charles as "an effect of feminine awe"[6]) and the authorizer of that circle's narrative of himself. In contrast to Pamela's circle, characterized above all by a hard-won linguistic and social stasis constructed through redefinition, reflexivity, and exclusion, this novel's dynamic circle socializes individualistic desire by centering it upon Sir Charles as the instrument of social good, and enlarges the circumference of its influence by expanding one private sphere to take in a much broader sweep of society. To understand the model of the social circle's authority erected in *Grandison,* then, one must examine the interaction of hero and circle. This chapter will begin with the text's portrayal of the problem of female desire and its narrative manifestations, then proceed to the focusing of that desire on narration of the exemplary hero. Once the hero has taken his place at the center of the domestic circle, his roles, first, in ordering and expanding the exemplary circle, and second, in circumscribing the feminine discursive impulse, will be examined. Finally, it will become clear that Richardson's attempt to encode mid-eighteenth-century ideology of gender in fiction's structure and style reveals the logical inconsistencies inherent in those assumptions.[7] The text appears even to highlight inconsistencies in its exploration of the impossible situations in which society's expectations place the female self and in its hints at an androgynous discursive ideal. Nevertheless, the model of the conversational circle in *Sir Charles Grandison* is at once the most fully developed and the most optimistic of those I will discuss.

THE PROBLEM OF FEMALE DESIRE AND
ITS NARRATIVE MANIFESTATIONS

Sir Charles at one point claims, "I am not an absolute stranger to the language of women" (2:84); defining and moralizing such a language is a central focus of this novel. There can be no doubt that Richardson's narrative structure is shaped by contemporary doctrines of gender and their naturalization. At the symbolic culmination of the novel, on the morning after the marriage which consummates the love of the ideal Sir Charles and his principal narrator, Harriet Byron, the author inserts a debate intended to prove "a natural inferiority in the faculties of the one Sex" and a "natural superiority in those of the other" (3:246). In this debate, the primary male qualities, enumerated by the virtually infallible Sir Charles and accepted as empirically verifiable by his audience, are "strength, firmness, . . . a capacity to bear labour and fatigue; and courage to protect the other [sex]," while the female attributes, again defined by Sir Charles with the assistance of Harriet, are "delicacy, softness, grace," "meek[ness]," "beneficen[ce]," and "pusilanim[ity]" (3:247-48). As always in the discourse of sociability I am examining, the argument uses nature to reinforce social necessity: "were it not so, their offices would be confounded, and women would not perhaps so readily submit to those domestic ones in which it is their province to shine," waiting patiently for their men to "at last, lay all our trophies, all our acquirements, at your feet" (3:248).

Harriet's early experience confirms for her the ideal locus of female existence: "frighted by the vile plot upon me at a masquerade, I was thrown out of that course of diversion [the public one], and indeed into more affecting, more interesting engagements; into the knowledge of a family that had no need to look out of itself for entertainments" (2:406-7). Nevertheless, Sir Charles's sister Charlotte's descriptions of herself as her husband's "chattels, a piece of furniture only" (2:501) and as a bird in a cage chosen for her, who "has nothing to do, but sit and sing in it" (2:504) suggest that the boundedness and domesticity which reflect woman's very essence are paradoxically what her wandering instinct most resists. Elsewhere in the text, the authoritative Harriet and Sir Charles join in associating women with wayward desire, referring to "womens eyes" as "sad giddy things" that "will run away with their sense, with their understandings" (1:182), and as "wanderers" that "too often bring home guests that are very troublesome to them" (2:8).

Female softness and grace conspire with waywardness to produce an instinctive preference for the curve, for affectation. In fact, the text elaborates a specialized vocabulary to describe this characteristic. Using Harriet's Uncle Selby, in particular, Richardson introduces the term *Femalities* and its synonym *scrupulosities* to describe the "little forms and affectation" of feminine delicacy (3:253; 3:77-79; 3:95-98); Selby cannot simply be dismissed as a humorist since the outspoken Charlotte admits that his term is apt, "tho' I do not love that men should be so impudent, as either to find us out, or abuse us" (3:114; also 3:237). Another term of Selby's coinage, "the whole *circumroundabouts* of female nonsense" (3:97), is not only retrospectively approved by Charlotte (3:112), but is anticipated by frequent references to conversational "*circumambages*," "roundabouts" and "turns" as peculiarly female techniques for avoiding open dealing (1:274-75; 1:442; 2:103; 2:303).

Fearful, passive, and domestic, women in their waywardness are nevertheless insatiably curious about the affairs of others and about the outside world. Charlotte, again, admits to "an immoderate quantity of curiosity" (2:413), and when Sir Charles's ward Emily begs to attend the wedding of the guardian she is secretly in love with, Charlotte comments, "The first vice of the first woman was curiosity, and it runs through all her daughters" (3:202). One manifestation of this desire for forbidden knowledge is excessive flights of the imagination, exacerbated by weak judgment; again, Sir Charles states the principle: since "Women's minds have generally a lighter turn than those of men," "a boundary [must be] set to [their] imaginations" (2:8).

As my examples have indicated, these five qualities—weakness and passivity, domesticity, waywardness, curiosity, and imagination—are consistently belittled in the novel as discursive foibles which betray more serious moral failings. A cluster of diminishing terms are clearly used by women to describe their own writing—Harriet, Charlotte, and Emily, for example, repeatedly speak of their "impertinent remarks" (1:22), "little chit-chat" (2:71), "pertness" (1:210), "silly prate" (2:420), and "*pen-prattle*" (2:550). On the part of the novel's male speakers, as Charlotte wryly observes, "The epithets *pretty,* and *young,* and *little,* are great qualifiers of harsh words" (2:85); they cannot obscure the critique embodied in "pretty trifler" (2:85), "pretty playfulness, on serious subjects" (2:99), or "Charming copiers [of affectation]" (2:97). When Sir Charles speaks of the language of women, he is rebuking Charlotte; when Lord L., Sir Charles's brother-in-law, refers to women's preference for "tak[ing] a compass before they explain themselves" (1:442), he does so in the context of apologizing for their dishonesty. Charlotte's dangerous tendency to indulge the "levity" and "wantonness" of her wit beyond the bounds of "justice" and "decorum" (3:29; 2:662) draws repeated censure from the more self-disciplined Harriet. Harriet's dreams, which expand the narrative through terrifying alternatives to the happy ending, are "imbecillities of tender minds" against which Sir Charles warns his "dear Ladies" to "Guard," and which "give a superiority to" the male sex (3:242).

These dangerous characteristics nevertheless form the basis for Richardson's elaboration of an ideal narrative style, sensible yet playful, capable of endless elaboration as it circles delicately and exhaustively around its subjects, focused on the inward and private yet generating speculations and cautionary tales regarding the male world beyond its boundaries. It is not difficult to see how this feminized narrative style serves Richardson's purposes in spinning a very lengthy novel out of the rather meager plot of virtue in distress rescued by a "modern Anglican knight of sensibility,"[8] obstructed by the knight's prior love entanglement, and then rewarded by marriage to the rescuer.[9] It is precisely "in these points [of love]," that Lord L. notes the tendency of "ladies" to "take a compass before they explain themselves." As one of the principal narrators,

Charlotte prides herself on possessing "a talent to make subjects out of *nothing*" (3:261), and she insists, "why should not we women, after all, contrive to make hurry-skurries . . . and make the world think our affairs a great part of the business of it, and that nothing can be done without us?" (3:202). Several readers have commented upon a sense of life lived in the subjunctive mode in *Grandison;* this narrative mode is clearly suited to the circumscribed existence of the domestic woman of the eighteenth century. Indeed, John Sitter has described the novel as "a map approaching the size of the territory it depicts," and therefore "not an interpretation of experience but its replacement."[10]

NARRATING THE FINE MAN, SOCIALIZING DESIRE

Despite elaborate cautions about the dangers of feminine discursive qualities, the novel begins by establishing positive versions of these qualities in Harriet, thereby authorizing her as primary narrator. She is described as the most admirable woman in England, possessed of "all the feminine graces" (3:248). As ideally vigilant keeper of the house of her own body, Harriet has "been careful ever to shut the door of [her] heart against the blind deity, the moment [she] could imagine him setting his incroaching foot on the *threshold*" (1:67), and is no less wary of the dissembling wooer, a "male hyaena" who "will come to us, even into our very houses, fawning, cringing, weeping, licking our hands" (1:24). Her early London letters illustrate the delicate sensibility that makes her a precise judge of those she meets and renders her highly susceptible to offense and terror at Sir Hargrave Pollexfen's unwanted attentions; the value she places on domestic life leads her to write affectingly of her "adopted" father and brother, Sir Rowland Meredith and Mr. Fowler, while her delicate turns of phrase allow her to reject their suits without wounding them; her imagination is used to invent portraits of herself as a range of characters at an assembly might describe her. From the beginning, Harriet's narration is presented in explicitly gendered terms. She calls herself, quoting her family, "*a fanciful girl*" (1:68), and her lengthy accounts reflect her uncle's view that "Two girls talking over a new set of company . . . are not apt to break off very abruptly" (1:44).

Meanwhile, the need of this admirable woman for adequate male protection is emphasized by the plot. The novel's opening structural paradigm is a linear one of Harriet's flight before the pursuit of unwelcome suitors, culminating in her abduction by Sir Hargrave. Having left her wise and supportive relations behind in the country, Harriet laments on several occasions the inadequacy of her London host as a protector from unwelcome advances, especially those of the wealthy Sir Hargrave. Harriet cannot "be allowed the same free agency that [she is] ready to allow to others," Sir Hargrave himself tells her bluntly, simply because "Every man who [sees her] must wish [her] to be his; and endeavour to obtain his wishes" (1:95). As Gerard A. Barker has noted,

Harriet's growing recognition of the social unworkability of female freedom, sharpened by the inadequacy and even perfidy of her succession of suitors and protectors, combines with the reader's anticipation of the appearance of the title character in a deliberate effect of desire heightened by delay.[11] Writing to the impatient Lady Bradsheigh, Richardson explains: "He [the good man] must not appear till, as at a royal cavalcade, the drums, trumpets, fifes and tabrets, and many a fine fellow, have preceded him, and set the spectators agog, as I may call it. Then shall he be seen to enter with an eclat; while the mob shall be ready to cry out huzza, boys!" (*Letters,* 179). Harriet's "huzza" is in fact a relinquishing of her self to Sir Charles; when he asks, "Will you, madam, put yourself into my protection?" she replies, "O yes, yes, yes, with my whole heart—Dear good Sir, protect me!" (1:140).

Sir Charles's speech, at his introduction into the novel as Harriet's rescuer, seems intended to signal potent action in its succinct and paratactic contrast to her highly sensible narrative of her sufferings: "I ordered my coachman to break the way. I don't love to stand upon trifles. My horses were fresh: I had not come far" (1:139). Indeed, Sir Charles's "active, . . . restless goodness . . . absolutely dazles" the virtuous Harriet (2:38). She uses a gravity metaphor to describe her love of Sir Charles as inevitable, as a natural desire for virtue: "It is virtue, it is goodness, it is generosity, it is true politeness, that I am captivated by; all centred in this one *good man*" (1:389). Harriet's own plot, with its threatened repetition of Clarissa's tragedy, is now at an end, and she enters the privileged inner circle of the Grandison family as its admiring and dedicated scribe. Although this circle displaces itself frequently between city and country houses, Harriet's sudden fixity of attention results in a curious sense of narrative arrival. "I can write nothing now but of Miss Grandison and her brother," she says (1:195), and despite her relations' repeated suggestion that she escape the growing attraction of Sir Charles, she lingers on, continually excusing, and thereby emphasizing, her mesmerized state.

Harriet's new center of attention, Sir Charles, inspires in her the "*sublime stile*" and "overflowings" of a "*grateful* enthusiasm" (1:178). Indeed, all of the novel's predominantly female speakers and writers find in him both the inspiration of narrative and its shaping theme. "My heart always dilates, when I enter into the agreeable subject, and I know not where to stop" (1:279), Charlotte says; later, "Forgive me, that I bring *him* in, whenever any good person, or thing, or action, is spoken of. Every-body, I believe, who is strongly possessed of a subject, makes every-thing seen, heard, or read of, that bears the least resemblance, turn into and illustrate that subject" (1:136). It is Harriet, however, who elaborates such "turns" into an excursiveness that "has carried me out of my path" (1:186), that has "seized, and [run] away with, my pen" (1:195), and into "a better subject" that compensates for the pain of her apparently unrequited love (1:349).

Harriet is the ideal narrator of Sir Charles's story because her love for him, according to Richardson's psychology of female love, enhances the useful qualities already inherent in her narrative style. As Sir Charles generalizes, "The most *sensible,* I will not say *subtle,* creature on earth, is certainly a woman in Love. What can escape her penetration? What can bound her curiosity?" (2:650). In an admirably modest woman, heightened sensibility and curiosity are accompanied by humility; Harriet observes, "Is it not the nature of the passion we are so foolishly apt to call *noble,* to exalt the object, and to lower, if not to debase, one's self?" (2:78). Indeed, the closer Harriet approaches to her union with Sir Charles, the more her sense of the distance between them increases, and she writes: "Ah, my partial friends! you studied your Harriet in the dark; but here comes the sun darting into all the crooked and obscure corners of my heart; and I shrink from his dazling eye; and, compared to Him . . . appear to myself such a Nothing—" (3:132). Thus, a woman's self-doubting admiration of her lover provides Richardson with a technique for the portrayal of his hero that serves the requirements of an exemplary and engaging narrative while avoiding the awkward effects, felt in *Pamela* of a heroine's self-narration.

Making a fine man, in other words, is not an *ex nihilo* act that celebrates the potency of the male deity or writer, but the creation of an environment of female modesty and admiration that encourages male essence to reveal itself fully. In Harriet as lover-narrator, *Grandison* provides its readers with the model of a narrator who has marginalized herself in her own story in order to structure her narrative upon the movements of her new center; "Your Harriet was not a mute," she writes on one occasion, "but you know, that my point is, to let you into the character and sentiments of Sir Charles Grandison: And whenever I can do them tolerable justice, I shall keep to that point" (1.430). The anonymous author of the 1754 *Critical Remarks on Sir Charles Grandison,* written before the novel's publication in full, captures this paradoxical position: "Harriet appears to be everything, and yet may be nothing, except a ready scribe, a verbose letter-writer."[12] Harriet herself hints at the psychological cost of love as narrative impulse when she responds to the discovery of the existence of her Italian rival, Clementina: "But now my ambition has overthrown me: Aiming, wishing to be every-thing, I am nothing. If I am asked about him, or his sisters, I shall seek to evade the subject; and yet, what other subject can I talk of?" (2:181).

THE HERO AND THE EXPANSIVE DOMESTIC CIRCLE

Unlike Pamela, who must limit her own authoritative influence with elaborate metaphors of herself as reflecting moon to B.'s sun, Harriet can freely ascribe to Sir Charles a self-generated radiance. The "moment" he enters a room, "sunshine [breaks] out in the countenance of every one" (2:69); petulance is dispelled "the instant he [shines] upon [the Selby circle]" (3:132). In Charlotte's words, "Light is hardly more active than my brother, nor lightning more quick, when he has any-thing to execute that must or ought to be done" (3:114). This active heroism takes on an almost messianic character: "The fame of [Sir Charles's] goodness is gone out to distant countries. . . . All opposition must fly before him" (2:317-18).[13] Unlike selfish uncles, scheming stepmothers, and rakes, those "narrow-hearted creatures [who] centre all their delight in themselves" (1:342), Sir Charles's "enlarged heart can rejoice in the happiness of his friends" (2:608). The grounds of Grandison Hall, we read, are "as boundless as the mind of the owner, and as free and open as his countenance" (3:272).[14] If Sir Charles is immanent in his expansiveness—as "The Soul of us all!" (3:410) and "the life of every company, and of every individual" (3:361)— he is also transcendent. The sense of profound moral distance between Sir Charles as perfect center and his admiring circle results in "a kind of reverence for him" (1:444) that keeps both his internal audience, and presumably the reader, focused on him in an effect similar to that of the *Pamela* sequel.

With a man of impeccable credentials at its center, the social circle of *Grandison* can parallel this double movement of expansion and elevation, making it both more socially inclusive and more morally exclusive than the circle of Pamela as Mrs. B. Whereas Pamela's own hybrid status makes it imperative that she avoid such potentially misconstrued gestures as helping distant relations, Sir Charles can associate with Everard Grandison's City wife, secure in the knowledge that his own status is untouchable. At the same time, while it would have been presumptuous for Pamela to condemn the masquerade countess or Lord Jackey, Sir Charles can with impunity correct women for breaches of decorum and eject upstart captains from his premises.

Nevertheless, while Sir Charles's sphere is clearly a broad, active, and public one, in contrast to the more restricted, verbal, and familial worlds of Harriet and the Grandison sisters, his activities and ambitions are in fact explicitly limited to an intermediate range between the public and the retired, a range most accurately called the domestic. His benevolence is repeatedly exemplified but almost without exception concerns family transactions, in which he ensures that the passages of travel and homecoming, dowering and marriage, death and inheritance are carried out in an orderly and financially generous manner.[15] Sir Charles's favorite charity is "that of giving little fortunes to young maidens in marriage with honest men of their own degree" (2:11). Refusing marriage into a titled family, he proves that he has "conquered . . . ambition" (2:649) and fixed as his "chief glory" the aim "to behave commendably in the *private* life" (3:99). According to the mid-eighteenth-century maxim "that families are little communities; that there are but few solid friendships out of them; and that they help to make up worthily, and to secure, the

great community, of which they are so many miniatures" (1:25), the novel portrays Sir Charles and his family circle as a model of moral excellence applicable
to society as a whole.[16]

As a demonstration of the model's usefulness, this hero's domestic
domain is expanded by a redefinition of "family" not as a blood kinship but as
a fraternity of sentiment and sensibility. Sir Charles as chief proponent of the
model "cannot, ought not to be engrossed by one family" (2:260). On the one
hand, conferring a kinship relation is thus a means of freeing the social model
of the domestic circle to break down barriers between sexes, generations,
nationalities, and faiths. The hero's acts of mediation between generations, for
example, invariably involve correcting the elder's blighting influence upon dutiful and worthy members of the younger, reforming the hierarchical family
into a relatively egalitarian structure. At the same time, a primary function of
the family model in the text is to erect barriers to dangerous desire. Her own
aptitude in this technique proven by her redefinition of Sir Rowland Meredith
and his lovesick nephew as sentimental father and brother, Harriet quickly sus-
pects that Sir Charles "has been *used* to this dialect, and to check the passions
of us forward girls" when he applies it to both herself and Clementina (2:157).
Later, Sir Charles in his turn feels "the *exclusive* force" of Clementina's calling
him brother (2:615).[17]

With the use of letters in *Grandison* primarily to record and comment
on social exchange, the encounters of the intimate group become the fundamental units of narrative. The adversarial nature of earlier exchanges, such as
Harriet's lengthy debate with Mr. Walden on the subject of learning and her
verbal duels with the amorous Sir Hargrave, form a notable contrast to the
serene and ceremonial harmony of the Grandison circle. Like *The Spectator's*
ideal family gentleman, Sir Charles acts as moderator, belonging equally to
everyone, and introducing topics of conversation that allow every member of
the circle to shine in turn. The seriousness with which he treats women in conversation, in contrast to the supercilious Mr. Walden, realizes an ideal of
conversation in which women are given the opportunity for improvement in
matters which are otherwise inaccessible to them (3:244) and in which the
conversation of women serves to "improve a man of sense, sweeten his manners, and render him a much more sociable, a much more amiable creature,
and, of consequence, greatly more happy in himself, than otherwise he would
be from books and solitude" (3:250). As "master of every subject" (3:138), the
hero is able to introduce improvement and edification into every setting, so
that when he meets with Sir Hargrave and his rakish friends, Lord L. is of the
opinion "that his brother's noble behaviour, and the conversation that passed
at table, . . . [will] make more than one convert among them" (1:289).

Given the moral and ideological associations of conversation, it is not
surprising that the conversational units of the novel are more thematic than

dramatic in function; in fact, speakers' subject matter is often summarized rather than recorded in dialogue form.[18] When portrayed more fully, a conversation may be organized so as to show a spectrum of character-revealing and illustrative responses to an issue, such as the appropriate wording of a letter to one's unnatural mother.[19] At such points, dramatic momentum is reduced to a bare minimum, making of the text a collection of sentiments connected by a logic of theme rather than action, and lessening again the sense of conflict. Even where an encounter is presented dramatically, as in the case of Sir Charles's visit to his challenger Sir Hargrave's house, tension is deliberately reduced through Harriet's (and the reader's) prior knowledge of the outcome.[20]

Sir Walter Scott's anecdote of the "venerable old lady" who preferred hearing *Grandison* read to "any other work, 'because, . . . should I drop asleep in course of the reading, I am sure when I awake, I shall have lost none of the story, but shall find the party, where I left them, *conversing in the cedar-parlour'*" is perhaps the wittiest comment upon the generally consensual, timeless effect of this conversational structure.[21] The elaborately formalized circle of Sir Charles often takes on the quality of a stylized conversation-painting or an elaborate dance, with placement symbolizing relationships, and openings and closings representing inclusion and exclusion from the social circle.[22] Seated trios are particularly prominent, portraying various structures of power and protection. When Harriet is accosted by the Grandison sisters regarding her love for Sir Charles, they sit on either side of her, each taking her hand in a gesture of simultaneous encouragement and imprisonment. Sir Charles's settlement of money upon each of his sisters is accompanied by his raising them from their knees to the same seating arrangement, with himself at the center in the role of generous benefactor. In the most gestural sequence, during Harriet's first visit to the Grandison's London house, Harriet is drawn away from the company by the eldest Grandison sister, immediately joined by Charlotte. Sir Charles next comes to them, commenting on their grouping as proof that "goodness to goodness is a natural attraction" and adding, "We men, however, will not be excluded." The sober Dr. Bartlett is then ceremonially drawn into this off-center circle of virtue, which is rapidly becoming the gravitational center of attraction. The arrival of a rakish cousin, Everard Grandison, saying, "What! Is there not another hand for me?" is greeted typically as an "interruption" and by Sir Charles's exclamation, "How the World . . . will push itself in!" At this Everard complains, "But if you exclude me such company, how shall I ever be what you and the Doctor would have me to be?" And so on, concluding with the formation of one large circle at Charlotte's words, "Is there more than one heart among us?" (1:234-35).

Feminine activity, on the other hand, remains peripheral and contingent because of its restriction to discursive functions. Clearly the novel's narrators participate vicariously in Sir Charles's activities outside of the narrow domestic setting. More positively, if not actively, "enlargement of heart" in Harriet is generous response to the stories of others, evidenced by her messages of forgiveness to her abductor and his henchman. In her selfless wish for her rival Clementina's happiness, Harriet resists the temptation to make love "a narrower of the heart" (2:131), modeling rather an ideally sociable use of narrative power. The closest she can come to active generosity is in contributing herself and her property, in the form of a marriage settlement, to an increase of Sir Charles's powers.[23] In fact, even here Harriet is restricted to the passive sphere of imagination. Rather than allowing Harriet a large fortune with which to expand her hero's capacity for doing good, Richardson limits her to fantasies about having power and consigning it to Sir Charles. Thus, soon after meeting him, she wishes "that the best woman in the world were queen of a great nation; and that it was in my power, for the sake of enlarging Sir Charles's to do good, to make him her royal consort. Then I am morally sure, that I should be the humble means of making a whole people happy!" (1:193). In one instance of the novel's socializing project, the realization of female desire in Sir Charles here paradoxically circumscribes its potential: Harriet's destiny is to become neither a creator of fictions nor a queen choosing her instrument of doing good, but rather the objectified and financially inadequate "reward" of Sir Charles's goodness (2:339). As Terry Eagleton has described it, feminized discourse is hereby "recuperated by patriarchy and centred on a man."[24]

So strong is the socialization of individual desire in *Grandison,* moreover, that the narrative can no more conclude with a marriage as private point of arrival and closure than Harriet can be allowed sole possession of Sir Charles. Unlike the apotheosis which allows Pamela to attain stasis and exemplified abstraction in the midst of her domestic circle, stability of the social circle in *Grandison* is fully detached from the individual's experience. Thus her arrival at Grandison Hall as Lady Grandison reduces Harriet from the chosen bride of its proprietor to one of a long line of Lady Grandisons, represented by the "unbroken series" of pictures in the gallery; with her marriage the focus of her desire shifts from the hero to the possibility of being one day "allowed a place among [those portraits]," thereby achieving the permanence of a family ancestor (3:278).

THE HERO AS CIRCUMSCRIBER OF THE FEMININE

Much earlier, once the hero has established his identity as physical protector, the role of "patron . . . to women"[25] is expanded to include the task of saving women from themselves as their own worst enemies. "Ladies," says Sir Charles, "where Love and their own happiness interfere, are the most incompetent judges of all others for themselves" (1:414-15), and as a result, "independent women" even if they "escape the machinations of men, . . . will frequently be hurried by their own imaginations . . . into inconveniencies" (2:368-69). The truly delicate woman is thus invited to give her very will up to this hero, confident that he will act for her as she has not the strength to act for herself. In the most extreme instances, Clementina seeks from Sir Charles himself the power to implement her decision not to marry him, and Harriet in the reverse position is assured by Charlotte that her acceptance of Sir Charles's marriage proposal is a matter that "may all be left to him" who "knows so well what becomes the character of the woman whom he hopes to call his wife" (3:65). From his appearance in response to female desire, then, the hero moves into place as its guardian and implementer, but also as circumscriber of its excesses.

A woman's instinctive discursive affectation, or "femality," poses a double threat—to her own happiness, because it impedes or misdirects male action on her behalf, and to the social circle, because it disguises individualistic forces which may run contrary to the good of the group. Thus this "natural" femality must also be labelled unnatural; according to Sir Charles, an artful woman is "a departure from honest nature," whose "curvings" of eyes and countenance, matched by excessive apologies or reserves, expose her faulty mind to the observer (presumed male) "who himself disdains artifice" (2:53). Sir Charles's greatest challenge in socializing the female narrative impulse is Charlotte, whose wit is employed, not in the establishment of conversational clarity, but in upholding what Sir Charles labels "female pride, which distinguishes not either time, company, or occasion" (2:94). Although Charlotte's "kittenish disposition" reveals "not so much the love of power . . . , as the love of playfulness," she indulges herself egotistically, "let who will suffer by it" (2:330). Whether in the disguise of her own secrets or in the searching out of others', then, Charlotte's "circumambages" (2:94, 2:103) and "excursiveness" (2:663) are symptomatic of a lack of self-knowledge, of poor judgment about whom to confide in, and of an abdication of her social responsibility—exactly those propensities that render female desire dependent upon virtuous male guidance.

The novel's extensive discussions of Sir Charles's reserve towards his sisters make explicit a moral distinction between the principles governing male and female secrecy. Charlotte's and her brother's mutual reserves, which Harriet initially places on the same footing, are soon found to be governed by the gendered dichotomies of strength and weakness, independence and dependence, sociable responsibility and irresponsibility. Sir Charles's reserve derives from his consciousness of the protector role. As a man he must "keep all his troubles to himself, because he would not afflict anybody, and yet study to lighten and remove the troubles of every-body else" (2:109), while "women should unlock [their] bosoms, when . . . called upon" (1:19). Thus, Sir Charles's extraction of the secrets of women, even by flirtatious raillery, as in the case of Lady Beauchamp, is both natural and morally justified: "Surely, Lady Beauchamp, a man of common penetration may see to the bottom of a woman's heart. A cunning woman cannot hide it. A good woman will not" (2:280). Female secrecy is unnatural, therefore affected and deserving of exposure; male secrecy is natural, therefore noble and deserving of respect.

As Charlotte feels to her cost, Sir Charles's power of granting or withholding approval is his most effective socializing force. Whereas Clarissa uses withdrawal from a social group to express independence and a need to retreat from social pressures, Sir Charles uses it as a means of controlling Charlotte's undesirable behavior. Whether pretending he neither recognizes nor hears Charlotte, or actually leaving the room, the hero ostensibly punishes himself by removal from the group, with the effect of heightening the contrast between his own perfection and Charlotte's waywardness. Only her brother's absence in Italy allows Charlotte to persist in insubordination to her husband for as long as she does, for Sir Charles has warned that if she depreciates Lord G., he himself will be "apt to forget that [he has] more than *one* sister: For, in cases of right and wrong, we ought not to know either relation or friend" (2:114). The force of the hero's social attractiveness, which creates a desire to emulate and be approved by him, renders all the more devastating his exclusive moral rigor.[26]

THE SELF-CONTRADICTIONS OF THE GENDERED CIRCLE

I have already suggested that much of the delight of Richardson's narrative is paradoxically supplied by the supposed faults of a female style; Harriet admits more than once that everyone loves Charlotte for her "very faults" of "over-liveliness" (2:409). More to the point here, Charlotte's "*roundabouts,* and . . . *suppose's*" (1:274) are used to disburden other women of their hidden love secrets, and to allow the text to focus obsessively upon them while maintaining decorum. In other words, such elicitations and indirections create acceptable conditions for the communication of female desire, and thus serve a necessary function in a society which prohibits a woman's admission of love where the loved object has not first declared an acceptable passion for her. Even Harriet, frequently praised for her frankness, is shown to exercise a selective reserve in her relations with men. She refuses adamantly to answer Sir Hargrave's questions about the state of her heart because she is not accountable to him, although she will answer the same questions put by the Countess of D. at their first acquaintance. In general, her open admission to all and sundry of her love for Sir Charles while she maintains a cover of neutral composure to her beloved himself does not appear to taint her reputation for frankness. Sir Charles himself claims on the one hand that "It is not in woman to be unreserved in some points" and on the other that "(to be impartial) perhaps they should not"

(2:18).[27] Richardson portrays a polite female discursive style as a necessary evil, a mode of self-defense by which a woman can preserve a semblance of dignity and discretion in the face of a censorious world.

Clarissa's experience with Lovelace of course shows how the requisite female style can work against that woman when she is not matched by a penetrating yet delicate masculine opponent.[28] For this reason the virtuous hero must be master of this form of penetration. A lover, according to Sir Charles, needs the help ("Don't be affrighted, Ladies!" he inserts) of a little disguise "to develop the plaits and folds of the female heart" (1:429); the circuitous approach also serves Sir Charles well with his sister. She complains, "he winds one about, and about, yet seems not to have more curiosity than one would wish him to have," until, "Led on by his smiling benignity, and fond of his attention to my prattle, I have caught myself in the midst of a tale of which I intended not to tell him one syllable" (1:184). Sir Charles may not be called "a little Satan," as is Charlotte when she tempts Harriet to read a wrongfully gained letter (2:6), but since Richardson uses Charlotte's "windings" around other characters to further their relationships in much the same way that Charles uses his serpentine techniques, figuring the sister as a temptress highlights the double standard built into the gendering of social behavior.

Although Richardson presumably trusts the reader to imagine Sir Charles as a good serpent, other awkward uses of the myth of the Fall to censor female discursive qualities reveal further contradictions inherent in at once naturalizing and moralizing gendered behavior. Sir Charles, in attributing affectation to all women, quotes Milton's portrayal of Eve's first meeting with Adam in *Paradise Lost* (2:97). Expressions of curiosity throughout the novel are accompanied by references to Eve; Emily's curiosity has been seen above to reflect the "first vice of the first woman." Even when the object of curiosity is innocuous, the trait is feminized and condemned by this link; Harriet, desirous of seeing Sir Charles's long letter from another woman, writes to Charlotte, "I was very *Eve-ish,* my dear" (3:131). At the same time, curiosity is the ideal response Richardson models for his readers in the requests of the text's internal audience that Harriet "write me every-thing how and about [her courtship]; and write to the moment" (3:40). In effect, he appropriates the feminine for his novel while maintaining a moralistic rhetoric that will keep its expression dependent upon male permissiveness and approval.

Associating a female narrative style with the Fall further implies that prelapsarian narrative and social structure would rise above "natural" gender differences. In an often-cited passage Harriet speculates that if Sir Charles had been Adam, he would have resigned his sinful Eve to her punishment rather than accompany her in the Fall. While the suggestion does little to endear the hero to today's reader, critics have tended to ignore the parallel comparisons of Harriet to an unfallen Eve.[29] Offered a sight of the stolen letter referred to above, Harriet resists the "Little Satan" Charlotte with the cry "Tempter! . . . how can you wish me to imitate our first pattern!" (2:2). She is described by Sir Charles as "an exception" to the affectation which all women show in imitation of their "common grandmother" (2:97). Harriet is exceptional, then, in being something more than female, the perfect balance of female excursive energy and its circumscription: "She is mild, tho' sparkling: She is humble, yet has dignity: She is reserved, yet is frank and open-hearted: Nobody can impute to her either dissimulation or licence of behaviour" (2:647).[30] In another transcending equation, the hero's feminized delicacy and the heroine's rigorous honesty can be seen as complementing one another to achieve a kind of narrative androgyny which avoids the extremes of indelicate male penetration and devious female circularity. Thus it is Harriet's "generous pain" and "noble frankness" that call forth an "equal frankness" on the hero's part (2:113). Sir Charles's and Harriet's exemplary status thus suggests that in an ideal world, the gender dichotomies which structure narrative and the social circle would be rendered unnecessary. Indeed, between Harriet and Sir Charles there appears to be little need for conversation at all; the hero's sister remarks that her brother's and Harriet's notions are "exactly alike, on every subject" (2:91), and Sir Charles very early in the novel—before Harriet can explain herself—presumes "to explain her sentiments in giving mine" (2:85).

In this "real" world, however, the ideal that privileges consensus over conflict, in conjunction with this belief in the sublimating qualities of virtuous love, allows for the use of sympathy as a means of incapacitating the loved object as a source of tension. Thus, when Sir Charles finds his feelings for both Clementina and Harriet beginning to take on the aspect of "a competition," he solves the problem "by Miss Byron's assistance" (3:54)—in other words, by making her a party to his courtship of Clementina through her predictable sympathy for Clementina.[31] Charlotte's recalcitrant insistence on oppositional patterns of relationship to her family and husband clearly does not allow her to play such an accommodating role. She tells Harriet, "Your happiness, child, is in the still life. I love not a dead calm: Now a tempest, now a refreshing breeze, I shall know how to enjoy the difference" (2:329). Charlotte's love of confrontation for its own sake makes her "an enemy . . . of her own happiness" when she enters marriage armed with an inadequate military metaphor for her relationship with Lord G. She is ultimately forced to replace her conflictual metaphors with domestic ones, abandoning "the road of perverseness" in order to "get home as fast as I can" (2:519).[32]

The troubling story of Charlotte's education in submission to a man who is her acknowledged intellectual inferior makes clear that, for Richardson at least, a feminization of social reality does not lead to inevitable congruence between a woman's desires and her social role. Unlike the Pamela of Part II, whose essence is most fully expressed in her wifely role, the relation between the social and the essential selves in *Grandison* is more problematic. As frequent scenes depicting the invasion of a character's closet suggest, the assigned parts of friend, sister, and wife are a necessary burden on the private self, the tangible manifestation of one's duty to submit to a Providence which determines the roles one is to play.[33] Cheerful supporter of another woman's claims to her beloved, Harriet fulfills the assigned role with resignation, not as "an hypocrite," but in recognition that "this case is one of those few in which a woman *can* shew a bravery of spirit" (2:259). To be ideally sociable, in other words, is to understand clearly, and respond sacrificially to, a conflict between self-fulfillment and the happiness of others.

For the hero, with his powers of self-definition, a right balance between sociability and the essential self can be struck; refusing Sir Hargrave's challenge, Sir Charles explains, "I live not to the world: I live to myself; to the monitor within me" (1:206). Almost immediately after this, however, Charlotte is faulted in comparison with the hero's other sister because "by her livelier manner, [she] is not so well understood . . . as she ought to be; and, satisfied with the worthiness of her own heart, is above giving herself concern about what the world thinks of it" (1:210). Charlotte's perilous journey towards a reconciliation between her lively self and the role of wife suggests that just as in the case of female language, this is at once a woman's failure—a result of her particular moral susceptibility—and a consequence of the elaborately delineated social patterns within which she is trapped.

Woman's dependence upon a mysterious and arbitrary male potency, her unattainable and self-destructive desire to submerge the self in the perfection of the "other," and her contribution to her own moral and social circumscription sound a note of sadness in this social comedy.[34] The more ideally feminine the woman, the more her delicacy and imagination will tend to psychic dissolution. When Harriet intends to refuse all other suitors after the loss of Sir Charles, she is warned against "tyrannous over-refinements" and "a maze of bewildering fancy" (2:546). Clementina's "glorious perverseness" in adoring Sir Charles may be "the very soul and essence" of her heroism (3:406), but it is also the origin of her madness. Despite his role as knight-errant in the moral, social, and financial rescues of so many women, Sir Charles can only be allowed to carry one of them in his arms into his own coach. A good portion of the novel's final section is spent commiserating over the love-wounds of Clementina and Emily; the extensive casuistry as to the impossibility of another Pamela in Richardson's earlier sequel is nothing to the anguish of these women, and presumably of the readers, who feel imprinted upon their hearts the impossibility of there being another such hero. Because there is only one Sir Charles, he is "nobody's" (3:232)—not even his bride's on her wedding day—and she must live with the knowledge that despite the attainment of her desires, she is his second choice. Although transcribed into a major key, the feminized narrative voice in *Grandison,* as in *Clarissa,* is ideally suited to express the general truth "that the human Soul is not to be fully satisfied by worldly enjoyments; and that therefore the completion of its happiness must be in another, a more perfect state" (3:19).

THE READER IN THE EXPANSIVE CIRCLE

Like Richardson's preliminary discussions of the hero with his readers, the correspondence generated during and after the composition of *Grandison* appears to invite discussion rather than invoke authoritative closure.[35] Richardson offers his readers the space provided by the relative openness of the novel's ending as an area for imaginative play, repeatedly teasing them with possible continuations of the story,[36] and calling upon "every one of [his] Correspondents, at his or her own Choice, [to] assume one of the surviving Characters in the Story, and write in it" (*Letters,* 306). One of his last statements to Lady Bradsheigh about *Grandison,* in response to her repeated attempts to solve the question of Sir Charles's feelings for Clementina, goes so far as to resign authorial privilege in an apparently un-Richardsonian gesture: "If your Ladyship will have it so, so let it be. The Book is now before you. That must determine us both. I don't desire to be better acquainted with his Mind, than any of his Readers" (*Letters,* 300-1).

If Richardson resigns control, however, it is only to pass it over to his hero, and therefore he immediately adds, "Only let them not suppose things contrary to what appears in his Letters; nor question the Veracity of a Man they think good." Thus, in the very act of relinquishing the text to his readers, Richardson bequeaths to them a model for circumscribing their imaginations: meaning can be found in the novel's center, its hero, but that meaning can only be determined through a prior act of submission to the narrative's central premise, that Sir Charles is a good man. And in that act of submission is the agreement to read as a good woman, a woman who desires a good man. In other words, the consequence of making a fine man is submission to the authority of the finished product.

Sir Charles Grandison, then, is Richardson's final statement about the feminization of discourse and its socializing function as they are realized in narrative. The novel is on one level a celebration of "femality," allowing extensive play to the desires, imaginations, and private concerns of women, and on another a rigid subjection of that femality to the gender hierarchy of the day. Richardson's ultimate model of female sociability is not a Pamela endlessly reflecting upon the self reflected in her social roles, nor a Clarissa scrutinizing the private self stripped of its social context, but a Harriet whose self is defined in the process of creating a narrative center outside of herself in the active virtue of a hero who is also the man she loves. It is his social function, as the ideal subject of the female narrative roundabout, that gives her own self and its discursive modes function and meaning.

At the same time, Harriet's desire, which can never be at rest through absolute possession of its center, assures the endless deferral of self-satisfaction in a dynamic equilibrium between self and other. This dynamic equilibrium will prove to be the highest achievement of the novel of the conversational circle. With Fielding's *Amelia,* the heroine's attractive power at the center of her social circle is both non-narrative and passive, resulting in a circle which can hold its own by offering a stable alternative to a chaotic public world, but which has almost no persuasive or expansive force and is therefore reduced from an authoritative ideal to a private option.[37]

5

Silencing the Center in
Henry Fielding's *Amelia*

For Samuel Richardson, increasing literary authority is accompanied by a growing confidence in the power of his model of the conversational circle to socialize individualistic desire. Henry Fielding would appear to share this expansive confidence in his early "Essay on the Knowledge of the Characters of Men," in which he renders in prose Pope's image of the circle expanding from self-love to social responsibility:

> If a Man hath more Love than what centers in himself, it will certainly light on his Children, his Relations, Friends, and nearest Acquaintance. If he extends it farther, what is it less than general Philanthropy, or Love to Mankind? . . . [No] man can have this general Philanthropy who hath not private Affection, any more than he who hath not Strength sufficient to lift ten Pounds, can at the same Time be able to throw a hundred Weight over his Head. Therefore the bad Son, Husband, Father, Brother, Friend; in a Word, the bad Man in private can never be a sincere Patriot.[1]

The conclusion of *Joseph Andrews* seems also to suggest that the benevolence of a man such as Squire Booby can spread through his household to a larger community of relations and worthy dependents. The search for such an order, however, involves several wholesale changes of location, from city to country, and then from Lady Booby's to Squire Booby's seats. Ideal sociability in *Tom Jones* is even more elusive, existing only in imperfect, promised form: in Tom's unrealized potential for responsible behavior, in the squirearchy of Allworthy, which blunders its way to a state of justice, or in the headship of Tom, inspired by Sophia, over the family projected beyond the novel. In these novels, self-love is not the first step towards sociability, but is rather the force, in the form of individualistic desire, that opposes it.

Amelia, Fielding's final novel, appears to express a new optimism by shifting from the pursuit of an elusive ideal to its incarnation in a stable domestic circle. With an exemplary, silent, and self-effacing heroine at its center, such a circle provides a context within which male potential for social virtue can be most fully realized. At the same time, Fielding juxtaposes that circle to its perverse anti-type, an all-consuming vortex of self-love, which structures public life. This social backdrop is so entirely hostile to the domestic circle that the outward expansion from private sociability to true patriotism, described in the "Essay on the Knowledge of the Characters of Men" and more fully illustrated in *Sir Charles Grandison,* becomes almost impossible. Openness of the domestic circle to the larger social world is as natural for Fielding as the outward expansion of circles in water; there is even less possibility in *Amelia* of the bowling-ball self-sufficiency of the Stoic than there was in *Tom Jones.* Indeed, the urban setting promises neither harmless retreat nor refuge from the fact of interdependence.[2] In this novel, however, the relation between private and public worlds has become disjunct, and the sociable individual is caught between the two. That individual is William Booth, Amelia's husband. As choice-maker placed between the public world, promising influence and security through intrigue and corruption, and the private world, offering the stable harmony of life with Amelia, Booth is attracted because of his own pride and egotism to the false circle, while continually pulled by love and virtue back to the true.[3]

By gendering self-love and sociability in this way, Fielding produces a social model that is, in itself, as tightly structured as the circle of female desire centered on Sir Charles Grandison;[4] because it is centered on a silent and passive female, however, it can only be a fortress under attack, rather than an outwardly expanding influence. The all-consuming center of the public vortex, moreover, is a passionately self-absorbed woman; she and the false notions of honor and duty that govern male social behavior in this society are presented as forces irresistible to all but a very few individuals. Thus, although stability is made permanent for one domestic group when Booth's choice of Amelia becomes definitive, evil has not been excluded from the discursive landscape at the novel's conclusion and the potential for wrong choice remains located in the individual.

This emphasis upon individual moral responsibility is made explicit in the text by Dr. Harrison, the most authoritative character of Fielding's fictional canon. Between the doctor and Amelia, more particularly, Fielding divides the functions of narration and exemplification in much the same way that Richardson does between narrating women and Sir Charles Grandison. The gender reversal is crucial, however: whereas *Grandison* unites, in the hero, authority and the exemplary as the circle's center which attracts and orders female narrative power, the authoritative word, in the person of Dr. Harrison, is located at the periphery of Amelia's circle. Dr. Harrison models an ideal outward expansion from the private into the public realm, but his location, like that of Booth, at the edge of the domestic circle reduces his example to a mere alternative, an idiosyncracy, rather than a demonstrably effective guide to other characters.

At the time of writing *Amelia* Fielding appears to have seen his literary authority as itself contested in a sphere broader than that of Richardson's carefully cultivated audience of correspondents. As when Richardson was writing *Grandison,* Fielding was at the height of his literary reputation and his sensitivity to audience expectations when writing *Amelia;* Fielding's novel was introduced, however, not into an intimate conversational circle, but into a public sphere governed by the figure of the court of law. Just as Richardson fostered his readerly circle, Fielding the magistrate created this context to a large extent through his self-appointed role of censor of politics, manners, and literature in his journalistic writings.[5] Fielding's first discussion of *Amelia* in the *Covent-Garden Journal* takes the form of a trial in the "Court of Censorial Enquiry," in which he acts as advocate for the novel, "this poor Girl the Prisoner at the Bar," before the hostile critics.[6] Within the fictional world of *Amelia,* while Fielding adopts the ideal of the domestic circle centered on an exemplary heroine, his portrayal of ideal femininity as one that refuses to assume narrative authority leaves him with a social model that can establish its own authority only through dramatized contrasts and their effects on the outcome of events: a sort of trial by experience.

In this chapter I will examine the contrasts established between the destructive qualities of the public anti-circle and the virtues of the domestic circle centered on Amelia, the threat posed by the anti-circle to Amelia's circle, and the positions of Booth and Dr. Harrison as representative choice-makers between the two types. In comparing the two circles, I will focus in particular upon the role played in Amelia's circle by conversation, which offers vicarious experience and sympathetic communion as a sociable defense against self-narration and individualistic interpretation. My discussion will make it clear that in *Amelia* the feminocentric social circle, embattled by widespread corruption and able at best to achieve self-enclosure, offers a model ultimately more cautionary than prescriptive. In other words, although the conversational circle achieves a limited kind of victory at the novel's close, the restrictions Fielding places upon its modes of authority suggest problems in the realization of the ideal that will lead to its increasing social isolation and, ultimately, to its reduction to an unrealizable, merely textual vision in the later novels of this study.[7]

THE CIRCLE AND THE VORTEX

For early readers of *Pamela* Part II and *Amelia,* the portrayal of married life appeared as a departure from expectations which were already being formulated for the novel genre; thus the early reviewer John Cleland finds *Amelia,* "from the choice of [Fielding's] subject, . . . the boldest stroke that has yet been at-tempted in this species of writing."[8] In fact, Cleland's admiring description of Amelia echoes closely Richardson's descriptions of Pamela as ideal player in a bounded sphere: "[Amelia] is painted, in fine, as the model of female perfec-tion, formed to give the greatest and justest idea of domestic happiness. She fills every character, in every scene, in every situation, where the tender, agree-able wife, the prudent fond mother, and the constant friend can have leave to shine."[9] Richardson's social ideal in the *Pamela* sequel, however, is constructed in general upon the almost unspoken exclusion of individualistic behavior from Pamela's familial circle and upon that circle's unproblematic separation from the public world of London for the latter portion of the novel. By rather immersing his heroine in a city which aggressively attacks her domestic circle, Fielding heightens both the exemplary achievement of Amelia in holding the domestic circle together and the sense of the domestic circle as a bounded and besieged fortress.

Amelia begins with the announcement that its subject is "the various Ac-cidents which befel a very worthy Couple, after their uniting in the State of Matrimony."[10] The style and structure of this opening, with its placement of the anonymous "worthy Couple"'s unity in a position of temporal anteriority and final emphasis, while beginning with reference to the accidents befalling them, serves as a kind of paradigm for the moral and narrative structures of the novel. Accidents will appear to besiege the Booths but will finally be with-stood by their domestic unit; the contingent and temporary will be given a threatening prominence, but ultimately will serve only to prove the durability of an ideal marriage. Accordingly, the first three books of the novel are devoted to Booth's arbitrary arrest and imprisonment, to his Newgate picaresque, and finally to the meeting and exchange of stories that spark his illicit affair with Miss Mathews, a former rival with Amelia for his affections.[11] In this process the present, in which Booth makes a wrong choice of Miss Mathews over Amelia, is juxtaposed with the story of a younger Booth choosing rightly between them; the accidental moment of individual choice is set in a context of temporal and social connections which insists upon its essential relatedness.

Miss Mathews and Amelia function in numerous ways as polar opposites around which contrasting values cluster and to which Booth is variously at-tracted. Miss Mathews's youthful attraction to Booth was merely an expression of egotistical jealousy over another woman's threatened precedence at a ball, whereas Amelia's love for Booth was a highly refined form of self-love, respond-ing gradually to his sympathy at her disfiguring accident. Miss Mathews's attempts to portray herself as an equally loving alternative to Amelia cannot blind Booth to the fact that her attractions are entirely physical, which can for him only be "the Object of Liking," while Amelia's appeal for him illustrates the sole power of "Love to be the Object of Love" (226). Thus the courtship story of Amelia and Booth illustrates Fielding's earlier statement that ideal self-love radiates outward to encompass first immediate relations and friends and ultimately all of mankind. Love in Miss Mathews, on the other hand, is a jealous and destructive passion: when her vanity allows her to be seduced by a flattering imposter, she attempts to murder him, and when the guilt she feels in having disappointed her father makes her feel uncomfortable, she contrives a hatred of him over a past trifling incident in order "to ease [her]self" (57).

The novel's initial sequence, spiraling Booth inward and downward to Newgate prison with the doubly locked chamber of Mrs. Mathews at its center, creates an image of the public social structure that is confirmed by later descriptions of assemblies at Ranelagh and Vauxhall and of representatives of judicial and political institutions, such as Bondum the Bailiff and the powerful nobleman of Dr. Harrison's acquaintance.[12] Presiding over the mouth of the Newgate vortex is the corrupt Justice Thrasher, who understands perfectly "the Duty of Self-love," and has learned "to consider himself as the Centre of Gravity, and to attract all things thither" (21). Newgate itself is a perverted underworld wherein the apparently virtuous are revealed to be utterly indecent and character is rendered increasingly unreadable through a series of protean shifts. Worse, the unquestionably innocent, such as a frail girl imprisoned for causing bodily harm and an acquitted soldier recommitted for his jail fees, are simply sucked into this maelstrom and destroyed.

Throughout *Amelia* individuals set in positions of authority—from Justice Thrasher and "the Governor of the enchanted Castle" of Newgate (152) to the "little great Man" who swallows Booth's bribe "as a Pike receives a poor Gudgeon into his Maw" (476)—clearly contribute through their voracious self-interest to the corrupt condition of the public sphere. That structure's malfunctioning, in other words, is the inevitable consequence of an agglomeration of faulty parts. Whereas the ideal state, like Pamela's household, should circumvent "the ill Execution" of its laws because "good Laws should execute themselves" as does a well-constituted clock (19), this state's operations are described as "the Wheels in the Great State Lottery of Preferment. A Lottery indeed which hath this to recommend it, that many poor Wretches feed their Imaginations with the Prospect of a Prize during their whole Lives, and never discover they have drawn a Blank" (499).[13] The narrator's lengthy explanation of how Dr. Harrison is brought to employ the crooked lawyer Murphy illustrates the ease with which individual corruption can go undetected by even the most clear-eyed moral authority in the anonymous and compartmentalized city, where the doctor can "remain as ignorant of [Murphy's] Life and Character, as a Man generally is of the Character of the Hackney Coachman who drives him" (515).[14] The result is not the social fragmentation of David Simple's London, however, but a perverted structural logic built upon self-interest. Thus, although to Booth the workings of accident upon him remain essentially arbitrary and inexplicable for the greater part of the novel, Bondum the Bailiff in fact bleeds his victims according to the well-established principles of "the Way of Business" (513), with "no more Malice against the Bodies in his Custody, than a Butcher hath to those in his" (312). That three separate villains employ the same man in their final attack on Booth is no accident because even the "Business of the pimping Vocation" has been institutionalized; "this subaltern Pimp" acts on the commands of "his Superior *Trent*" (495) in a parody of military efficiency.

From the moment when Amelia makes her delayed appearance in the novel through an uncharacteristic voyage into the Newgate vortex to reclaim her husband, she is a center of stability opposed to the perverted structures outside of her home. This function of the heroine is indicated by a rhetoric of balanced contrasts, when upon Booth's experience of "one of the greatest Afflictions which, I think, can befal a Man, namely, the Unkindness of a Friend," the narrator continues, "but he had luckily at the same time the greatest Blessing in his Possession, the Kindness of a faithful and beloved Wife" (186). On an earlier occasion, Amelia herself offers Booth the comfort that, "however other Friends may prove false and fickle to him, he hath one Friend, whom no Inconstancy of her own, nor any Change of his Fortune, nor Time, nor Age, nor Sickness, nor any Accident can ever alter" (175). Amelia's essentially fixed and virtuous nature thus resembles Pamela's in its uniformity through every vicissitude of life.

Amelia's constancy and its stabilizing role in the marriage are more than an abstraction: she is physically fixed in her lodgings in a near-absolute separation from the chaos of public London. After her rescue of Booth, her only excursions are initiated by others, and she resists all public pleasures but those of the masquerade, proposed by the noble lord who has promised to prefer Booth, and a visit to Vauxhall Gardens, proposed by Dr. Harrison. The most striking example of Amelia's active choice of home is her avoidance of the second masquerade, which Mrs. Atkinson attends in her place.[15] "My Inclinations," she assures her husband, "would, I am afraid, be too unreasonable a Confinement to you; for they would always lead me to be with you and your Children, with at most a single Friend or two, now and then" (362). In fact, it is the domestic confinement of Amelia's love, to which Booth can voluntarily commit himself, that offers the only true refuge in this world, in opposition to Booth's forced imprisonments in Newgate and the bailiff's house. When, early in the novel, Booth remains home to avoid arrest, the reader is told not only that Amelia knows "no Happiness out of his Company, nor scarce any Misery in it," but also that Booth gives her "at all times so much of his Company when in his Power, that she [has] no occasion to assign any particular Reason for his staying with her" (192-93). An externally imposed confinement is thus transformed into a celebration of married love, and the kind of miserly love which

Amelia and Booth hold for one another—to use their own image for it (382)—
offers a social stability which London promiscuity cannot provide. It is not
until her husband learns to choose this domestic refuge at all times, however—
we read at the conclusion of the novel that since his move to Amelia's estate he
"hath never since been thirty Miles from home" (532)—that the family's stability is permanent.

If "A Match of real Love is, indeed, truly Paradise" (285),[16] then this
paradise is a precisely located and particularized one. The domestic detail of
delayed dinners, child-care arrangements, and newly redeemed gowns that accompanies the novel's dénouement, for example, is directly opposed to the
rarefied abstraction of the conversational circle in Richardson. Most frequently,
domestic tableaux in *Amelia* are centered upon a table, at which either the
Booths enjoy a simple meal together or Amelia waits alone while her wrongly
choosing husband sits at a gaming table, a tavern table, or the supper table of
Miss Mathews. Amelia has the gift of creating *"Happiness in a Cottage"* (86),
of embracing and transforming the ordinary in the face of poverty and a hostile outside world. Thus we find that she is able to perform "the Office of a
Cook, with as much Pleasure as a fine Lady generally enjoys in dressing herself
out for a Ball" (236), and that "it [is not] possible to view this fine Creature in
a more amiable Light, than while she [is] dressing her Husband's Supper with
her little Children playing round her" (488). For Miss Mathews, on the other
hand, poverty is only a romantic cliché, so that "A Cottage with the Man one
loves is a Palace" (86), and generosity stems merely from the fact that to her
"Money [is] as Dirt, (indeed she may be thought not to [know] the Value of
it)" (158).

This idealization of domestic detail becomes almost sacramental in the
novel's focus on the shared meal as the center of an expansively hospitable conversational circle. Again, the ideal is first portrayed by its antithesis. Conversation round the table of "the Governor of these (not improperly called
infernal) Regions," that is, Newgate, at which are seated such "Persons of
Honour" as Miss Mathews, a gambler, and a corrupt lawyer, predictably degen-
erates from its initial veneer of elaborate courtesy to oaths, open insults, and
recommendations of the efficacy of bribery and perjury "to save the Life of any
Christian whatever, much more of so pretty a Lady" as Miss Mathews (60-64).
Similarly, the refreshment table at Vauxhall is by virtue of its public situation
vulnerable to the intrusion of the two rakes, who are able to destroy "totally . . .
the Mirth of this little innocent Company [of Dr. Harrison and friends], who
were before enjoying complete Satisfaction" (398). By contrast, the table
Amelia presides over is given a dignity that crosses the boundaries of social
station; in Fielding's description, the heroine "bestir[s] herself as nimbly to provide [her husband] a Repast, as the most industrious Hostess in the Kingdom
doth, when some unexpected Guest of extraordinary Quality arrives at her

House" (213). Furthermore, Amelia's table offers a hospitality that represents a just and egalitarian recognition of merit rather than the hierarchical snobbery of the larger world. Dr. Harrison commends Amelia for a friendship with Sergeant Atkinson, "in Opposition to the Custom of the World; which instead of being formed on the Precepts of our Religion to consider each other as Brethren, teaches us to regard those who are a Degree below us, either in Rank or Fortune, as a Species of Beings of an inferior Order in the Creation" (377). Indeed, Amelia's social circle becomes the most truly inclusive of the circles I have examined to this point; the last scene of the novel depicts a dinner table in Amelia's newly inherited house, "at which perhaps were assembled some of the best and happiest People then in the World," including "*Amelia*'s old Nurse, . . . by *Amelia*'s absolute Command, seated next to herself at the Table" (531).[17] The basis of this circle in merit and affection rather than social status or blood relationship suggests that the exemplary is accessible to all. Such accessibility is absent in Pamela's tales opposing the good and wealthy to the naughty and poor, and in Harriet's symbolic induction into the hall of the Grandison ancestors. From the noble lord to Betty the maidservant, those who exclude themselves from this group do so not with the tacit encouragement of its center, but by their own deliberate choice of aggressive and isolating evil.[18]

THE THREAT TO THE DOMESTIC CIRCLE

Seeing all "through the Medium of Love and Confidence" (178), Amelia cannot at the same time be equipped for the public world with the cynicism of a Miss Mathews, in whom such a spirit is part of the "something so outrageously suspicious in the Nature of all Vice" (161). Domestic harmony therefore consists in a precarious and constantly threatened balance. As ideal center of the domestic circle, Amelia's fixity is accompanied by an attractive power which draws not only her husband, but also other men, to her. Thus the narrator compares her, as Harriet does Sir Charles Grandison, to the sun, in that it is as impossible "to withdraw Admiration from [her] exquisite Beauty" as it is not to feel the warmth of the sun. In the reversed gender configuration, however, admiration of Sir Charles by women leads only to their own destruction, whereas admiration of Amelia by men leads to acts of aggression, and therefore cannot remain innocent: "Desire is sure to succeed" admiration, followed by "Wishes, Hopes, Designs, with a long Train of Mischiefs" close behind (232). Amelia's satisfaction with her domestic sphere is therefore matched by an extreme vulnerability when she does venture into the public eye: at her first excursion to the oratorio, she is marked as a target by the disguised noble lord, and thereafter she is constantly accosted, either by him or by unnamed rakes. On the one occasion when she does wish to go to the masquerade, lulled by her belief in the noble lord's disinterested generosity, her confidence is utterly betrayed; her later discovery of Colonel James's deceitful motives for helping her husband indicates that nothing but the utmost circumspection on her part can prevent the success of stratagems against her and against the stability of her marriage.

Amelia is endangered not only by excursions into the public world, but also by malicious invasion of the domestic circle on the part of predatory self-interest, which invariably takes a sexual form. Men who desire Amelia attack Booth by refusing to stand him bail quickly, by offering him a post overseas, by inciting him to gambling, and by challenging his honor. In their exploitation of Booth's financial and personal weaknesses, such actions represent more than a conflict between the predatory male and the virtuous female: they become an attempt to destroy a social unit whose integrity individualism refuses to respect. When Colonel James invades the domestic circle seated around a supper table first at the Booths's lodgings and then at the Atkinsons's, he brings, on the first occasion, the outsider's gaze, which leads to his passion for Amelia, and later, the discordant influence of the partially known deceiver, whose double meaning incites misunderstanding between husband and wife. This abuse of hospitality reveals the fundamental opposition between the laws by which the two worlds govern themselves. When Dr. Harrison argues for the interdependence of private and public social structures in his letter on adultery ("Domestic Happiness is the End of almost all our Pursuits. . . . When Men find themselves for ever barred from this delightful Fruition, they are lost to all Industry, and grow careless of all their worldly Affairs. Thus they become bad Subjects, bad Relations, bad Friends and bad Men," 414-15), the derision of the masquerade bucks emblematizes a society determinedly severing all links with its fundamental unit.[19]

Amelia's only defense in her vulnerable state, therefore, is what characters such as Miss Mathews and Mrs. Atkinson call her prudery, the kind of prudery which, while it refuses to suspect the virtue of "abundance of Women, who indulge themselves in much greater Freedoms than [she] should take," insists that she has no desire other than for her husband (190).[20] Amelia's avoidance of the second masquerade highlights the boundedness of the feminine in this novel in contrast to *Pamela* Part II. Whereas Pamela herself stands at the masquerade as a moral center condemning its social and referential chaos, what Amelia stands for must be spoken at this assembly, in her absence, by the letter from Dr. Harrison on adultery. Miss Mathews's reentry into Booth's life by means of the masquerade emphasizes her affinity with deceit and irresponsibility, in contrast to the essential transparency and modesty which preclude even Amelia's attendance at such a paradigmatically public spectacle. As a result, the familial circle is positioned as a last-ditch refuge from the social masquerade, rather than as an expansive social structure able to invade and domesticate it by the force of authoritative feminized language.[21]

BOOTH AND DR. HARRISON AS CHOICE-MAKERS

As determined as Richardson to test his readers' sociability, Fielding uses the dichotomized universe of his novel to invite the audience-as-judge to acquit or convict his heroine on the basis of her qualities as domestic exemplar. Beginning with Miss Mathews's cynical comments, the possible responses to Amelia range from accusations of prudery, to lust, to near-reverence of her as an angel. In the judgment of the authoritative Dr. Harrison, "she is one of the best Creatures I ever knew. She hath a Sweetness of Temper, a Generosity of Spirit, an Openness of Heart—in a Word, she hath a true Christian Disposition. I may call her [citing John 1:47] *an* Israelite *indeed, in whom there is no Guile*" (387). Although this invocation of a Christian, ungendered, and not specifically domestic standard of sociability appears at first to transcend the circumscribed sphere within which Amelia bounds herself, I believe it insists rather upon an equation between the values of the domestic circle and social virtues in general.

As representative choice-maker in the novel, Booth moves from an attempt to function in both public and private worlds, through the complete frustration of that attempt, to the choice of confinement within Amelia's circle as an expression of his freedom to choose. Like Charlotte Grandison, Booth feels the attraction of wandering, telling his wife that "large Companies give us a greater Relish for our own Society when we return to it" (362). But, again like Charlotte, he is ultimately forced to acknowledge the dangers that lie beyond the bounds of the domestic. Charlotte's fault, however, is part of her feminine essence, while Booth's inability to reconcile public and private indicates above all the irreversible corruption of the public world. Although married love is a paradise because of its stabilizing influence on individual desire, this is a world which prefers the masquerade as "a sweet, charming, elegant, delicious Place" to which "Paradise itself can hardly be equal" (248). Other social ideals besides that of marriage are equally perverted. The military code of honor, which once legitimately required Booth's participation in the Gibraltar campaign, has become a glorification of conflict and the defense of one's vices through dueling. Achievement and its rewards have been replaced by a system of bribery and arbitrary preferment. In an orderly public world, Booth's qualities of good nature, good breeding, and honor might allow him to live with a clear conscience in his public and private lives simultaneously, but given the moral polarization of the two, such a balance has become impossible.

As a consequence of his susceptibility to the corrupt values of English society, the Booth of most of the novel's action is living with a burdened conscience and is therefore incapable of choosing well between public evil and private good. Because he feels guilt over his adultery, he can be happy neither with Miss Mathews in Newgate nor with Amelia upon his release. The taint he thereby brings into the domestic circle obstructs the conversational process which is the ideal response to externally originating conflict. The attacks of the noble lord, James, and the bailiff alone cannot threaten the Booths united; when Booth is hiding the prison affair, a gaming debt, or an assignation with Miss Mathews, on the other hand, the resulting division of purpose renders the couple vulnerable. With actions such as Booth's selection of James as his confidante rather than Amelia, his manipulation of Amelia into a false quarrel, which therefore cannot be genuinely reconciled, and his abandonment of her in response to the call of the gaming table or the threats of Miss Mathews, the consensus of this intimate circle is much more seriously threatened than it could be by any outside enemy alone. Critics have often noted that Booth's early use of the doctrine of the ruling passion to excuse his unfaithfulness to Amelia indicates his refusal to acknowledge his own responsibility as choicemaker, either when the moment of choice presents itself or in its consequences. The novel's illustration of "the several small and almost imperceptible Links in every Chain of Events by which all the great Actions of the World are produced" (496) emphasizes the contextual nature of all such choices. Freedom, in this view, is the freedom to choose one's alignment; it is only Booth's "firm and constant Affection" for Amelia (415) which finally allows him to break out of the orbit of Miss Mathews. Because Colonel James's own marriage, by contrast, provides no such counter-pull to the charms of antisocial love, the colonel is last seen doting on a bloated and tyrannical Mathews in an illustration of the effects of the all-consuming vortex of self-love on individual freedom.

In contrast to Booth, Dr. Harrison is the individual who successfully bridges the gulf between the novel's domestic and public worlds. As I have noted earlier, he acts generally as a representative of domestic values outside of Amelia's home, and particularly as her voice at the masquerade.[22] Dr. Harrison's value for, and skill in, domestic conversation is revealed in the fact that he "is not only able to advise [Booth], but . . . knows the Manner of advising" (148). On occasion, Amelia is able to confide in the doctor when the interference of Booth's dependence on James and the potential effects of jealousy make it impossible for her to converse openly with her husband. Dr. Harrison's application of Christian ethical standards to public issues such as preferment and the support of literature is congruent with his concern for Amelia's right action in the family matters of attendance at the masquerade and prosecution of her sister. While he finally recommends that Booth flee the town because of his incapacity to function successfully in it, his own active pursuit of legal justice with respect to Murphy in the novel's dénouement illustrates his own "Maxim . . . that no Man [can] descend below himself in doing any Act which may contribute to protect an innocent Person, or to bring a Rogue to the Gallows" (523). He condemns the perverted code of honor through his use of conversational mediation as an alternative, shaming Colonel James, for example, into withdrawing and keeping secret his challenge to Booth.

In keeping with Fielding's insistence upon the interrelation of private and public virtues, the selfish Justice Thrasher, who originally consigns Booth to the social vortex of Newgate then sits down to the spoils in the local alehouse, is finally replaced by the good justice, who abandons his dinner table to collaborate with Dr. Harrison in bringing larger social structures into alignment with the Booths's domestic circle. When at the novel's resolution the good magistrate invites Harrison and Booth to share his dinner, his admirable public action in regaining Amelia's estate is rewarded by Amelia's arrival in her "clean white Gown" to grace the table. It is the doctor's role to pronounce authoritatively the meaning of this final alignment; he tells Booth, "Providence hath done you the Justice at last, which it will one Day or other render to all Men" (522).

SELF-NARRATION AND CONVERSATION

Although Dr. Harrison's judgments are ultimately given authority by the outcome of the novel, the larger social world, unlike Amelia and the repentant Booth, responds to his statements with mockery and abuse. Having rejected the voice of traditional authority and its interpretations of experience, the public world of *Amelia* is discursively cacophonic, a collection of individualistic voices each telling its own story and providing its own self-indulgent interpretation of that story. As a result, the individual is unable to learn from his or her own experience. The distorting influence of Miss Mathews's self-absorption is illustrated in her awkward syntax when she focuses on her self-justifications and mentions only as an afterthought the fact that her father's death was a result of her own actions: "When any tender Idea intruded into my Bosom, I immediately raised this Fantom of an Injury in my Imagination, and it considerably lessened the Fury of that Sorrow which I should have otherwise felt for the Loss of so good a Father; who died within a few Months of my Departure from him" (57-58). Booth's prison story, in turn, escapes the worst pitfalls of rationalization in its focus on Amelia rather than upon himself, but its romantic content nevertheless seduces him into an emotional state, which makes him only too ready to conclude with a grateful address of "great Tenderness" to Miss Mathews and a revival of the "much Affection" for her that he had presumably forgotten, if it ever existed, before the narrative began (150). Finally, Mrs. Bennet's story begins with details about her early life that suggest to the narrator that "she was desirous of inculcating a good Opinion of herself . . . before she came to the more dangerous and suspicious Part of her Character" (268). Fielding's narrator clearly views the potential of narration for portraying the self objectively as dubious; "we are . . . liable," he comments, "to much Error from Partiality to ourselves; viewing our Virtues and Vices as through a Perspective, in which we turn the Glass always to our own Advantage, so as to diminish the one, and as greatly to magnify the other" (31).

This sense of the unreliability of self-narration is reinforced by the fact that Amelia does not act as teller of her own tale in any portrayed conversation. Most frequently cast in the role of sympathetic listener, she confides in the doctor as adviser and surrogate father only under great necessity or at Booth's direction. Her recorded comments in fact suggest a lack of verbal facility in moments of self-consciousness that seems designed to mark a transparency and feeling not found in the more artful disclaimers of Miss Mathews or Mrs. Bennet. Amelia's response of "Well, nay, . . . I don't know what I am doing—well—there—" (482) when Atkinson at last confesses his love and begs the favor of a kiss is anticlimactic, to say the least. Booth admits that he does Amelia "an Injury" when he represents only her words of response at his mock-confession of love for another woman: "La! Mr. *Booth.*—In this Town. I—I—I thought I could have guessed for once; but I have an ill Talent that way—I will never attempt to guess any thing again." Indeed, it is "Her Manner, Look, Voice" which are "inimitable" and yet characterized in detail (for their "Sweetness, Softness, Innocence, Modesty," 71), rather than the actual content of her speech. As inarticulate heroine, Amelia avoids the egotism and delusion which apparently contaminate all self-representation. For her to tell her own story would require in her the self-consciousness of Sarah Fielding's Cynthia or Richardson's Pamela, a self-consciousness which for Fielding compromises the domestic heroine, and which he must therefore deny her even if that denial threatens the didactic authority of narration itself. For Amelia's self-abnegation requires that she resign portrayals of herself to others, most obviously in the instance of Dr. Harrison's verbal and Mrs. Atkinson's corporeal representations of her at the masquerade, and thereby abdicate the role, fulfilled by Pamela, of discursively ordering the social circle around her exemplary center.

If Amelia resembles the ideal narrator of *Grandison* in her unwillingness to represent herself, she is even more like Harriet Byron in her ability to be devious in a sociable cause.[23] In this society, in which individuals are all too ready to express their passions in a self-indulgent and destructive manner, Amelia is admirable in her readiness to be thought "mean, vulgar, and selfish" by her husband on the occasion of another man's assault on her virtue (134), or peevish at the snobbery of Mrs. James when in fact avoiding the attentions of the husband, or foolishly superstitious about dreams in hopes of preventing a meeting of the two men after James's challenge. That such affectation is again less than ideal is unquestionable, but that it is made necessary by a social code of honor which is an even greater evil is evidenced by its approval by Dr. Harrison, the Atkinsons, and even Booth (when cognizant of it). It should be noted that while Amelia's deceptions are gendered insofar as she encourages misinterpretation of her actions as expressing feminine foibles—selfishness, caprice, and imaginative excess, in the above examples—she also resembles Sir Charles Grandison in her "heroic" ability to bear her own troubles in silence for the sake of her social group. Her secrecy about the letter from Miss Mathews which reveals the affair with her husband is an example of this.

Amelia's concealments are congruent with her ideal virtue, moreover, in that she has no secrets of her own to hide. Unlike Miss Mathews or even Mrs. Bennet, who as a woman with a past is attractive but also potentially dangerous and certainly morally compromised, Amelia's watchful innocence and her focus of all her desires upon her husband and children mean her private story can be told with no cause for apology or rationalization. Even the narrator's scrutiny of her response to Atkinson's confession of love shows that it passes "without any Injury to her Chastity," as but "a momentary Tenderness and Complacence" (482-83) which she effectively channels into a celebration for her family of her "unusual good Spirits" (488). Finally, when revelations do become necessary, Amelia enlists the help of Dr. Harrison, indicating that a judicious selection of one's confidantes is as important as a careful guarding of dangerous secrets.

In contrast to the heroine's verbal self-discipline, the choice between secrecy and revelation for both Miss Mathews and Booth is dictated by undisciplined desire. Miss Mathews's entire story represents a failure to maintain the kind of secrecy which in a lady signifies, if not virtue, at least shame. Thus she reveals her passion prematurely to her lover in a manner which assures him of her subsequent easy yielding of her chastity; in then agreeing to hide this love from her father, she is equally indiscreet and self-indulgent. By the time she meets Booth, she laments, "now I have no Secrets; the World knows all." Rather than learn from the consequences of this failure to guard her words and her virtue, however, she now concludes that "it is not worth [her] while to conceal any thing," using past failure as a justification for revealing to Booth what he did not know of and what will ensnare him: her former affection for him (47). At one point the doctor enjoins Booth to silence regarding his letter on adultery as "a wholesome Exercise to [his] Mind" (424-25), an exercise which Booth shamefully fails to perform, using the letter instead as a weapon to unjustly accuse Amelia of secrecy in order to hide his own gambling debt. More important to the novel itself, Booth's error in not confessing to Amelia "a Crime . . . which he fore[sees will] occasion him so many Difficulties and Terrors to endeavour to conceal" exposes him to all of the conflicts inherent in plots and plotting instead of allowing him the resolution offered by "immediate Forgiveness from that best of Women" (176). Colonel James, the man in whom Booth does confide, is of course the worst possible choice because of his infatuation with Miss Mathews. Thus the secrecy motif again places the domestic circle, as a safe environment for intimate self-revelation, between deception, which protects the individual but disrupts relationships, and self-expression, which relieves the individual at the cost of unnecessary pain to others.

Because Amelia cannot have any secrets, or worldly experience, of her own, and because of her necessary isolation from the world as a domestic woman, conversation becomes her means of safely acquiring knowledge of the world. In his "Essay on . . . the Characters of Men," Fielding suggests that in a society marked by a disjunction between private virtue and public corruption, learning vicariously through narrative is safest, "since that open Disposition, which is the surest Indication of an honest and upright Heart, chiefly renders us liable to be imposed on by Craft and Deceit, and principally disqualifies us for this Discovery."[24] Thus Mrs. Bennet's story of the noble lord's seduction is a means for Amelia to gain knowledge without incurring the consequences of direct experience; like Mrs. Bennet, she is susceptible to a fall because of her similar delusions about the noble lord's friendship for her children and her husband. Amelia shows herself more capable of adapting example and of profiting from it according to her own high moral standards, however. Thus she uses her knowledge of the noble lord as an incentive to avoid him at all costs and even to her own apparent detriment, while Mrs. Bennet, even after the lord's attempt to deceive Amelia, permits herself to be compromised by playing his false game. Amelia's ability to apply this knowledge is indicated by her subsequent wary resourcefulness in avoiding Colonel James as a new threat; despite her relative seclusion, her awareness of the corruptions of London is in a very real sense greater at the end of the novel than is Booth's.

In fact, although narration similarly provides several other characters in the story with opportunities for knowledge, none of them passes the test so well as Amelia. Booth initially indicates through his responses that he understands the motives of vanity and self-justification underlying Miss Mathews's distorted account of her life; nevertheless, he appears unable to resist her sins himself when she turns her arsenal of admiration and approval upon his own narrative. As for Miss Mathews herself, her comments throughout Booth's story of his life with Amelia reveal her inappropriate and voyeuristic enjoyment of his detailed descriptions. This propensity to errors of judgment is paralleled by authoritative characters as well; Dr. Harrison admits at the discovery of James's villainy that he is "shocked at seeing it so artfully disguised under the Appearance of so much Virtue" and that "[his] own Vanity is a little hurt in having been so grossly imposed upon" (374). Readers have noted that even the narrator of *Amelia* seems unable to interpret his own story, hinting at explanations for characters' actions that are later shown to be manifestly false, and moralizing upon the basis of judgments which prove as superficial and inadequate as those of his characters.[25]

Indeed, Amelia's initial insensitivity to James's dishonorable intentions suggests, as do the blindspots of Sarah Fielding's characters, the necessity of combined knowledge as a means of arming the individual for interpreting experience. If Dr. Harrison, the narrator, and Amelia can all be so thoroughly,

albeit temporarily, deceived with respect to a character's motives, one must conclude that the collaboration of heroine, male and female friends, and adviser is
necessary in order to detect and thwart evil. In this way the conversational
group can provide epistemological support to the individual as an alternative
to that attitude of cynical suspicion which the narrator denies Amelia, but
"without some Use of which nothing is more purblind than human Nature"
(362). Thus, in contrast to society as a whole, the intimate community in
Amelia uses conversation to supplement fallible individual judgment by joining interpretive skills. The intimate and virtuous social group can find out evil
such as that of Colonel James, evil which is never fully revealed to Booth and
to society's individualists in general.[26]

An accurate identification of evil intentions is necessary to the group's
well-being; however, the ultimate goal of domestic conversation in Fielding's
model, as in that of his sister, is not moral truth, but intimate sympathy. Existing within a hostile social context, the unanimity of husband and wife in
Amelia can be achieved only through the medium of often-painful conversations, such as the debate, raised by the penetration of the noble lord into the
Booth circle, about Amelia's attendance at the first masquerade. Such conversations often conclude markedly short of facts known to the reader; the
narrative structure thus repeatedly and deliberately emphasizes unity over such
truth, resolving conversation rather with reconciliation and an embrace. It is
no accident, indeed, that the Booths's most successful verbal exchanges culmi-
nate in sexual conversation,[27] while their greatest unhappiness arises from a
thwarting of the conversational process either by physical separation or by the
spiritual separation occasioned by Booth's dishonesty. Truly sympathetic conversation ending in mutual comprehension seems, on the other hand, an
impossibility outside of the domestic circle. Such exchanges include the superficial conversation between Amelia and Mrs. James, "in which the Weather and
the Diversions of the Town, [are] well canvassed" (180), or the abortive conversation in which Booth attempts to "[open] his Heart" to Colonel Bath,
whereupon "the Colonel [is] got into his Stilts; and it [is] impossible to take
him down, nay, it [is] as much as *Booth* [can] possibly do to part with him
without an actual Quarrel" (195-96). If marital consensus is not always able
to produce truth, it presents the only alternative to an alienating and even
dangerous perversion of speech.

FROM REPETITION TO EQUILIBRIUM

The notion of domestic conversation as unique and precarious in *Amelia* makes
evident a contrast between domestic temporality as it is portrayed in *Pamela*
Part II and in this novel. Congruent language, excluded conflict, images of
stasis, and circulating nursery tales create a sense of an achieved heaven on earth

in Richardson's sequel that Fielding's focus upon marriage under attack never conveys. In fact, it is Miss Mathews who denies temporality in her attempt to revive a former attraction and thereby cause Booth to forget his intervening commitment to Amelia; the prison, what J. Paul Hunter has called a "timeless world of the moment where past and future can be temporarily construed as meaningless," is therefore the ideal setting for her seduction.[28] In *Amelia* the temporal mode of domestic harmony is rather a cyclical sequence of physical separations or misunderstandings followed by reconciliations that reestablish community. The seemingly endless repetition of the Booths's troubles at the hands of deceptive friends, which more than one critic has found claustrophobic, is transformed within the intimate circle into endless opportunities for what the narrator calls "exquisite Moments" of reunion and mutual endearment, of which "a very few . . . do, in Reality, over-balance the longest Enjoyments which can ever fall to the Lot of the worst" (359).[29] Although the equation here appears superficially similar to Mr. B.'s claim that one hour of married bliss outweighs a lifetime of guilty tumults, Pamela's husband is speaking of any hour in an unbroken series of tranquil hours, while the narrator of *Amelia* is referring to climactic moments of reunion after estrangement. The terms of this exchange are made explicit by Booth in describing the éclaircissement after Bagillard's attempted seduction of Amelia: "To say the Truth, I afterwards thought myself almost obliged to him for a Meeting with *Amelia,* the most luxuriously delicate that can be imagined" (133).

Since it is Booth who inhabits the liminal realm between the domestic world and the public sphere of repetitious and seemingly arbitrary crises, he is the source of this cycle of separation and return, rendering the heroine all the more admirable by contrast for her constancy at the center of the domestic circle. Steadfastness does not result in a transcendence of change and decay, however; unlike Pamela, who appears physically invulnerable despite smallpox, repeated lyings-in, and the deaths of her parents, Amelia begins her narrated life with an accident that leaves her scarred and ends that life described in qualified terms as "still the finest Woman in *England* of her Age"; it is only in the eyes of Booth that she remains "as handsome as ever" (533). Amelia's steadfast loyalty to Booth in a world of change is ultimately rewarded by Providence as the force that creates a meaningful sequence out of the cycle of vicissitude. Thus, it is a miniature of Amelia which initiates in its original thief Atkinson and the perjurer Robinson a chain reaction of love and pity that restores Amelia's fortune. This recognition of Amelia's essential worth, however, takes place only in the private sphere. Thus, for the pawn-broker, Amelia is simply a customer, and he advances her only the value of the framing gold and diamonds, calculating "the prettiest Face in the World . . . as of no Value into the Bargain" (487); Robinson, on the other hand, is awakened to a sense of guilt through the sight of the familiar face in this context.[30]

In what sense, then, is stasis achieved in this novel emphasizing mutability as a condition of the individual life? Although its most visible indications
are the restoration of Amelia's fortune and the removal of the Booths from the
city, the concluding stability of this novel resembles that of *Pamela* Part II, if
not in a defeat of mutability itself, in a permanent physical and spiritual union
of the central couple. The Booths, we read, "have, ever since the above Period
of this History, enjoyed an uninterrupted Course of Health and Happiness";
after paying his city debts, Booth "hath never since been thirty Miles from
home" (532). Nevertheless, the force of the values which the Booths represent
has not succeeded in aligning the city with the domestic circle. As the fates of
the novel's predatory individualists indicate, the only character who appears to
have changed is Booth, who has chosen Amelia as his center and therefore necessarily turned his back on the city. The tight self-enclosure of this domestic
unit is reflected in the *Pamela*-like reflexivity of the narrator's final suggestion
to Amelia that Booth has "the best of Wives" and her response that he has
"made her the happiest of Women" (533). This conclusion, however, suggests
less the optimistic construct of the exemplary heroine imitated by concentric
circles of admirers than the deterministic polarization of Pamela's nursery tales.
The novel thus concludes in a stylized divorce between the domestic circle and
the social vortex because of the refusal of larger social structures, and of the
self-serving individuals who operate within them, to allow the orderly model
to expand into a broader philanthropic and patriotic sphere.

As self-effacing and unselfconscious center of the domestic social circle
that is the starting point of virtuous male action for Fielding, Amelia herself
can have no direct role in the ordering of the larger social world. Indeed, her
vulnerability to verbal misrepresentation and sexual attack immobilizes her as
exemplary center. The exemplary heroine's vulnerability sharpens Fielding's critique of public corruptions; the failures of the novel's predominantly female
self-narrators nevertheless imply as well that any female attempt at narrative
authority is suspect. The domestic ideal therefore remains dependent upon
the inherent authority of the individual male. That male may be a wise and
devoted Christian patriarch such as Dr. Harrison; then again, he may be a
well-meaning but weak and morally tainted Booth. In the latter eventuality,
the female domestic center can finally prove attractive enough to fix the male
and ensure a circumscribed happiness, but it can never effect an ideal expansion of the circle into virtuous public action.

Thus the private circle and the public vortex remain in inevitable opposition, with the latter as an ongoing threat to be watchfully resisted by the
former. The resignation of moral initiative to the domestically peripheral male,
whose irresponsible default leaves the family circle exposed to an aggressively
hostile public world, reduces the authoritative conversational circle, so hope-
fully proferred as a model in *David Simple* and *Pamela* Part II and so fully

realized in *Sir Charles Grandison,* to the status of a private choice, a circumscribed retreat. Sarah Scott's *Description of Millenium Hall* and Tobias
Smollett's *Expedition of Humphry Clinker* develop more fully the image of
the circumscribed domestic circle as alternative and as retreat of the socially
marginalized; Sarah Fielding's *David Simple, Volume the Last* allows the public
world to pursue and destroy the intimate group even in its retreat. It is to these
works that I now turn.

6

Authorizing the Marginalized Circle in Sarah Scott's *Millenium Hall*

Recent readers have been intrigued by Sarah Scott's 1762 novel, *A Description of Millenium Hall,* particularly by its embedding of a utopian community of women within the narrative of "A Gentleman on his Travels," in its turn the anonymous work of a female author. Feminist analyses of this narrative structure have variously labelled it subversive or conservative. George E. Haggerty represents the former view, arguing that this is a lesbian narrative, eroticizing the maternal in a challenge to conventional patriarchy, while Vincent Carretta sees the novel's embedded structure as reinforcing the necessity of hierarchical order and a masculine agent in realizing a social ideal. Susan Sneider Lanser concludes rather that the novel remains divided between its voyeuristic male narrator, "reassur[ing] readers that women without men need not threaten the patriarchal status quo," and the women's stories as resistance to that public narrative.[1] Examining *Millenium Hall* as one of a series of fictions that model the ideal social circle offers a new set of terms, which absorbs issues of gender into those of sociability. In this chapter I will argue that in this fullest realization of the ideal of a feminized and intimate conversational community that I have discovered in the novels of the mid-eighteenth century Scott paradoxically renders her community inimitable because it becomes dependent upon the complete expulsion of masculinized qualities, which have been defined as incompatible with true sociability.

In both story and form, in other words, *Millenium Hall* affirms and elaborates the "conservative socialist" ideal of the conversational circle as I have generalized it.[2] The members of the circle are exemplary women, humble, dutiful, desireless, self-effacing. Yet while men of sensibility who esteem them are significant figures in these women's pasts, and remain at least theoretically welcome in their circle, the reality of this social world is that men are not merely superfluous, but disruptive, to its order. They are therefore excluded from the community, just as are women who are not sufficient in themselves, whose own desire is only to meet the desires of men. The community as a whole is stable and regular, entirely harmonious in its common interests and temporally static both for its members, who have arrived and will never leave, and in its ordering mechanisms, which ensure its economic and social perpetuity. Its expansive ordering capacity, like that of each of the communities I have described except Amelia's domestic circle, is pointedly demonstrated.[3]

The text's formal devices for portraying consensus and stability also resemble those of the earlier novels in this group. The unstable individual pasts which have been resolved in the formation of the female community are presented as a series of embedded narratives contained within the "description" of the novel's title, a continuous, routine present. This description is itself rationalized in exchanges in which the members of the community join to convey its principles in polite and sensible conversation. As in Sarah Fielding's *David Simple,* a male audience is used to elicit and authorize the stories of women; their reluctance to tell their own stories upholds the feminine ideal established in *Amelia.* The dynamic of sexual attraction is used to draw the male narrator to the female community and keep him attached there, according to the narrative model of *Sir Charles Grandison,* while the structural function of the wandering and individualistic male is expanded from that of Booth in *Amelia.*

It is in this reversal of the gendered narrative model of *Grandison,* placing the attracted male who "could not restrain [his] pen within moderate bounds" at the periphery of the exemplary circle,[4] and the simultaneous association of individualistic and socially disruptive desire with the masculine, that the paradoxical completeness and inapplicability of the social model of *Millenium Hall* lie. While the male narrator indeed functions as the traditional authorizer of the text's public presentation and didactic claims,[5] his relegation to the narrative level alone, without any active function in the community, renders him superfluous to the social circle itself. With male authority figures in the women's stories, like the narrator's companion Lamont, almost invariably shown to be antisocial agents, the resulting vacuum of authority within the text is manifestly filled by these active and articulate women. The marginalized, in other words, is made the center,[6] and once this has occurred there is no longer any need for a structure of desire to maintain the exemplary circle. Exclusion of the masculine rather becomes the implicit basis of the circle's viability, and hence the barrier to its free expansion into the larger social sphere. In thus solving the problem of destabilizing desire manifest in the gendered narrative structure of *Sir Charles Grandison* and *Amelia, Millenium Hall* has achieved an ideally stable form in which to embody the circle of consensus, but has limited its solution to an exclusively discursive one. In this chapter I will elaborate on the ideological and formal features which *Millenium Hall* shares with the earlier texts in this study, and then examine the means by which its feminized circle is endorsed and ultimately made the only possibility for realizing the ideal of sociability.

THE NATURE OF THE IDEAL COMMUNITY

The women of this community are represented as the ideal eighteenth-century centers of the feminocentric domestic circle. Their superior beauty is complemented by an excellent, if sometimes delayed, education, not only in the traditional female accomplishments and in languages and literature, but above all in the social and religious principles which will enable them to fill their intended roles as domestic women. Thus, they are humble and self-effacing, they prefer a retired life of reflection to one of public dissipation, they are able to place duty and reputation before their own desires, and they excel as nurses, family mediators, educators of the young, and household managers. The description of the schoolgirl Louisa Mancel, one of the first characters presented to the reader, exemplifies the ideal in its superlatives and hierarchy of qualities: "Thus her understanding opened in a surprising degree, and while the beauty and graces of her person, and her great progress in genteel accomplishments, charmed every eye, the nice discernment, and uncommon strength of reason which appeared in her conversation, astonished every judicious observer; but her most admirable qualities were her humility and modesty; which, notwithstanding her great internal and external excellencies, rendered her diffident, mild, bashful, and tractable" (61). The final story told, that of Harriot Trentham, reiterates the same theme: she is "complying and observant" as well as "extremely handsome and engaging," and she is capable from the age of eight of reconciling pure sociability with absolute transparency of the self, so that "Any thought . . . that could hurt she suppressed as an indispensable duty, and to please by her actions, and not offend by her words, was an essential part of the religion in which she was educated: but in everything whereby no one could suffer, she was innocence and simplicity itself; and in her nature shone pure and uncorrupted, either by natural or acquired vices" (178-79). Not surprisingly, Harriot finds herself mediating between the female cousins who hate her and their suitors and husbands, offering to give up part of her fortune to increase that of a cousin, taking upon herself the breaking of her engagement with her male cousin when he falls in love with a flighty woman, nursing her elderly grandmother in the country when the other cousins are all married, and finally banishing herself from the family home when her unhappily married cousin belatedly falls passionately in love with her. Disfigured by the smallpox, caught in one of her mediating missions, she returns to a life of retirement and reflection after a brief period of dissipation, and finds there the "Reason and piety" that enable her to "[restrain] her affection [for her cousin] once more within its ancient bounds of friendship" (194).

Harriot Trentham's successful rival, Miss Melman, is her opposite in much the same way that Miss Mathews represents the attraction of antisocial femininity in *Amelia*. Although pretty and vivacious, "a wandering unfixed look indicate[s] a light and unsteady mind" and her conversation is characterized by "all the common *routine* of discourse, and a fashionable readiness to skim lightly over all subjects" (184). Predictably, she is hopelessly undomestic, "imprudently vivacious in mixed companies, lifeless when alone with . . . her husband, who of his whole sex seem[s] the only person of no consequence to her. As her view [is] to captivate in public, she cover[s] a very pretty complexion with pearl-powder and rougé, because they [make] her resplendent by candle-light, and in public places" (189). In the end, her husband raises his two sons in the country and Harriot educates the daughter at Millenium Hall, "while their mother spends almost the whole year in town, immersed in folly and dissipation" (194).

The man caught, like Booth, between these two women, significantly named Mr. Alworth, is clearly an admirable figure in his recognition of Harriot's superior qualities and in his protection of and friendship for her. It is important, then, that unlike Booth Alworth chooses wrongly, falling victim to the manipulation of his own desires even though rationally aware of Harriot's superior worth. Miss Melman wins him because she knows how to "[keep] up the spirit of pursuit," "[increase] his desire to be certain" of her favor, and keep him in a state of "constant anxiety" and "continual transition from pleasure to pain" (185). When he informs Harriot of his discovery that "esteem and passion [are] totally independant, since she entirely possesse[s] the one, while Miss Melman totally engrosse[s] the other," Harriot becomes convinced of a more general truth: that "passion [has] greater power over his sex than esteem, and that while his mind [is] under the tumultuous influence of love, she must expect very little satisfaction from his friendship" (186). When he later falls in love with Harriot, he becomes proof of "the perverseness of human nature," inflamed by the impossibility of possession (190), but Harriot, who now also falls in love, is able to conceal her feelings while his are portrayed as uncontrollable, desperate, and obvious to all but his utterly self-absorbed wife. The fact that one of the most worthy male characters in the novel is congenitally prone to irresistible and socially disruptive desire suggests that the so-called perverseness of human nature resides in the masculine, and therefore that even the admirable man introduces a threat of instability into the intimate circle of friendship.

Other members of the male sex encountered in the women's stories represent the same fundamental threat of disruptive individualism, manifested in a range of sins against sociability. Mr. Hintman, Louisa Mancel's apparently altruistic guardian, is revealed to have been abusing the paternal relationship as a means of grooming her for his private pleasure; Louisa's friend Mrs. Morgan's husband, like the miserly previous owner of a mansion in the neighborhood of Millenium Hall, uses the country as a place of withdrawal "within the narrow circle of himself" (118); the local squires, whose social responsibility the neighborhood would have been, "grew rich, because they had our work [i.e., that of the poor], and paid us not enough to keep life and soul together" (39), while the miser's heir squanders in a year the money his uncle had accumulated, eventually having to sell the miser's mansion to the ladies of the community. The miser and his nephew lead the narrator to a daring comparison which aligns the feminine with a "superior" sociability and the masculine with limiting self-centeredness:

> How directly were we led to admire the superior sense, as well as transcendent virtue of these ladies, when we compared the use they made of money, with that to which the two late possessors had appropriated it! While we were in doubts which most to blame, he who had heaped it up without comfort, in sordid inhumanity; or he who squandered it in the gratification of gayer vices. Equally strangers to beneficence, self-indulgence was their sole view; alike criminal, though not equally unfashionable, one endeavoured to starve, the other to corrupt mankind; while the new owners of this house had no other view, than to convenience, and to reform all who came within their influence, themselves enjoying in a supreme degree, the happiness they dispersed around them. [176-77]

In perhaps the ultimate unsociable act, Sir Edward Lambton, when he is apparently thwarted in his love for Louisa Mancel, virtually commits suicide in battle under the influence of "impatience," "froward petulance," and "impetuous passions" (116), thereby separating himself from her irretrievably at the very moment when their marriage becomes possible. Again, even this most virtuous and suitable of men appears flawed in his capacity for true sociability.

As this gendered dichotomy of duty, self-control, and happiness on the one hand, and desire, self-indulgence, and misery on the other suggests, the female community represented in the novel is one in which the self is most fully expressed through sociable behavior. I have just noted that the women "themselves [enjoy] in a supreme degree, the happiness they [disperse] around them." Since the public world is informed by masculine individualism and disruptive desire, true society is relocated in the private or retired, as in the other works in this study. When Lamont questions the claim of these "ladies, who seclude themselves from the world in this solitary though beautiful place" to speak about society, Louisa Mancel insists on a distinction between "a crowd," or "the world," and "society." While the former is a Hobbesian "state of war," characterized by "a constant desire to supplant and a continual fear of being supplanted," by "unremitted tumult and envy" of mind, and by irrational action, the latter is "a state of mutual confidence, reciprocal services, and correspondent affections" (79).

The highest expression of such society, again, is in conversation that is "a free communication of sentiments," not "restrained by suspicion, or contaminated by detraction." "Large assemblies," in contrast, "drown conversation in noise" and are obliged (through masquerades) "to conceal . . . persons, in order to obtain . . . liberty of speech or action" (79-80). This exchange economy of language is paralleled and made visible, as it was in *David Simple,* by a free exchange of property; as founders of the community, Mrs. Mancel and Mrs. Morgan (then Miss Melvyn) establish very early the principle that "where hearts are strictly united," there can be "no notion of any distinction in things of less importance, as the adventitious goods of fortune." In fact, shared property is a sign of the dissolution of boundaries between selves: "The boundaries and barriers raised by those two watchful and suspicious enemies, Meum and Tuum, . . . [are] broke down by true friendship; and all property laid in one undistinguished common" (62). Thus the first rule the community sets for its sister establishments is that they maintain equality by the pooling of fortunes.

As the latter observation suggests, this community has been stabilized not merely through the resolution of the stories of its individual members, but also through the institutionalization of its practice. It has existed in a state of harmony and increasing prosperity for twenty years; the generalization of its philosophy into regulations allows not only the formation of spinoff communities to broaden the influence of Millenium Hall in the present, but also its continuation into perpetuity. In addition, Mrs. Maynard explains that the educational activities of the group are forming a second generation, trained in its utopian principles, that will allow for continued spatial and temporal expansion:

> By this sort of education my friends hope to do extensive good, for they will not only serve these poor orphans, but confer a great benefit on all who shall be committed to their care, or have occasion for their service; and one can set no bounds to the advantages that may arise from persons of excellent principles, and enlarged understandings, in the situations wherein they are to be placed. In every thing their view is to be as beneficial to society as possible, and they are such oeconomists even in their charities, as to order them in a manner, that as large a part of mankind as possible should feel the happy influence of their bounty. [122-23]

Not since Pamela's educational and authorial efforts has a social circle extended its influence so broadly beyond the domestic or familial. All social classes in the neighborhood of Millenium Hall have been ordered and harmonized. Even in the park of the Hall, "Man never appears . . . as a merciless destroyer; but the preserver, instead of the tyrant, of the inferior part of creation"; as in the biblical image of the millenium, "a perfect equality in nature's bounty [seems] enjoyed by the whole creation" (42). And despite the portrayal of true masculine sociability as a contradiction in terms, the narrator himself becomes a humble ambassador for the society, hoping that his description "may tempt any one to go and do likewise," and intending to embark on "a scheme to imitate [this society] on a smaller scale" (200).

The Form of the Sociable Narrative

As I have already noted, the plots of these women's individual conflicts in a society which places them in the power of corrupt male authority figures are located safely in the past tense and embedded in the fully stabilized present of Millenium Hall. If these plots may be said to provide narrative interest in an otherwise static utopian treatise, that interest arises at least partly in the deliberate disappointment of readerly expectation. Because these conflicts are invariably generated by corrupt male desire or by the susceptibility of male desire to manipulation by the stepmother, the ambitious grandmother, or the coquette who uses the patriarchal system for her individualistic purposes, comic resolution is effected not when the exemplary heroine marries but when she achieves independence, both social and financial, generally through the death of a wealthy parent or benefactor. When permitted to choose an alternative social alignment with a female friend, she enters the narrative frame of the novel, where plot is replaced by "description." Millenium Hall is portrayed as having been a place of perfect consensus from the start; internal conflict at this narrative level is deflected to the secondary community of ladies, who have themselves experienced only one expulsion and one voluntary retirement, disagreeable members finding "the fear of being dismissed" enough of an incentive to reform (86). As subcommunities of poor cottagers and show-freaks learn the principles of consensus, pride and quarreling give way to mutual aid and hospitality. When Mrs. Morgan's wicked stepmother visits the community as a widow, she finds it so dull and confining that she excludes herself, as have so many other faulty characters in this group of novels.

Indeed, the courtship plot and marriage ending are circumvented in every case but that of Mrs. Morgan, when they are superceded by her founding of the community.[7] This subversion of the "typical" novelistic plot is reinforced by repeated descriptions of the married state as one of irresolution and unhappiness caused by the instability of a mutable world and often exacerbated by the dangers of a forcibly created intimate society. Miss Selvyn, for example, argues that "enjoying perfect content [with Lady Reynolds, her mother], she [has] no benefit to expect from change" (163); she informs her suitor that "were you endowed with all the virtues that ever man possessed, I would not change my present happy situation for the uncertainties of wedlock" (166). For Mrs. Morgan, "linked in society with a man I cannot love, the world can afford me no pleasure, indeed no comfort, for I am insensible to all joy but what arises from the social affections. The grave, I confess, appears to me far more eligible than this marriage, for I might there hope to be at peace" (94). Even marriage to an admirable and loved man is represented as a confinement and deviation from an ideal possession of space and time; thus, Louisa Mancel is retrospectively thankful for the death of her lover,

> for had she married Sir Edward Lambton, her sincere affection for him would have led her to conform implicitly to all his inclinations, her views would have been confined to this earth, and too strongly attached to human objects, to have properly obeyed the giver of the blessings she so much valued. . . . Her age, her fortune, and compliant temper, might have seduced her into dissipation, and have made her lose all the heart-felt joys she now daily experiences, both when she reflects on the past, contemplates, the present, or anticipates the future. [123]

A second plot pattern rejected by *Millenium Hall* is the sentimental plot of the passive female victim, seduced or self-destroyed as the ultimate proof of her innocence. Although Lady Mary Jones represents the badly educated woman who promises to elope with an already-married man in one case and is lured towards an assignation in another, she is allowed to recognize her errors through reflection and to seek out actively the guidance she has never been offered. Louisa Mancel and Miss Melvyn are able, despite their situation as young women limited to boarding-school experience, to establish the inappropriateness of Mr. Hintman's behavior to his ward and, again, to find an adviser who can seek out for them the necessary knowledge of their adversary. Miss Selvyn's defense of her friend Lady Mary to her would-be seducer can be read as a general rejection of the notion that "levity" is in itself a sign of moral culpability: "I am sure . . . your lordship's hopes must have been founded on Lady Mary's folly, not her real want of innocence; a folly which arose from the giddiness of youth, and the hurry of dissipation; for by nature Lady Mary's understanding is uncommonly good" (165).

Virtuous women, in other words, deserve an escape from the two plots which constrain them, and an accommodating Providence offers that escape in the form of a rejection of the plot of individualistic desire altogether. By choosing to exclude themselves from such plots, which either objectify them as the ends of male desire or marginalize them as "fallen" women excluded from the marriage market, the women of Millenium Hall transform the peripheral into the central, the circumscribed into the powerful.[8] Although Lamont's initial witticism that King Nebuchadnezzar's "expulsion from human society" would have been a blessing if it had taken him into a paradise like this is frowned upon as revealing "the light turn of [his] mind" (32), it in fact points to the reconstruction of the socially desirable that the two men are about to experience.[9]

The enclosures of the text's structure as a whole, and of the Millenium Hall it describes, further serve to center and elevate the ostensibly marginalized community in a refiguring of the meaning of confinement. Using the dynamic of the male voyeur whose curiosity and desire draw him to penetrate the community ever deeper, noted by Lanser,[10] Scott emphasizes the attractiveness of the Millenium Hall community while insisting again on its reluctance to display its own perfections. Thus the narrator, searching for healing and suspecting that he has "sacrificed the greater good in pursuit of the less" of material wealth (30), is first drawn by paradisical fragrances, sights, and sounds towards the house, repeatedly describing the "attraction" of the scene and his own "desirous" response in statements such as "Curiousity is one of those insatiable passions that grow by gratification; it still prompted us to proceed, not unsatisfied with what we had seen, but desirous to see still more of this earthly paradise" (33). What has begun as an interruption in a journey is transformed into an arrival ("I believe I should have forgot that our journey was not at an end, if a servant had not brought in word," 36) and an increasing inability to leave the community that recalls the paralysis of Harriet Byron in *Sir Charles Grandison*. The writer and his companion are the ideal narrative instruments of exemplary women; when Lamont praises them as the best qualified to reform because of their own reformed practice, Mrs. Mancel replies demurely, "We do not set up for reformers, . . . we wish to regulate ourselves by the laws laid down to us, and, as far as our influence can extend, endeavour to enforce them; beyond that small circle all is foreign to us; we have sufficient employment in improving ourselves; to mend the world requires much abler hands" (127). Narrative self-deprecation meets the requirement of the domestic woman's avoidance of the public sphere, while masculine desire allows for the detailed anatomization of exemplary private sociability.

The novel's use of an embedding technique to control the effects of conflict and ultimately convey a rejection of the plot of conflict is reinforced by the fact that the women's stories are all told by Mrs. Maynard, one of the six community members, from the perspective of their female survivors. None of the women tells her own story (Mrs. Maynard's story is condensed into one sentence, which she adds to the end of her friend Mrs. Trentham's), and their refusal to talk of themselves is again made the sign of self-effacing virtue that it is in *Amelia* (82, 87, 89). Nevertheless, the use of a female proxy who is a member of the intimate circle helps convey a sense of celebration, of refusal to be made contingent to male satisfaction or the victim of male aggression; the effect can be contrasted helpfully with William Booth's narrative of his marriage to Amelia, where the reader is left with the impression that Amelia has no story to tell other than that of her relationship with Booth. Thus Scott gains the authoritative effect of autodiegetic narrative, pointed out by Lanser, without its suggestions of self-aggrandisement or subjectivity.[11]

Endorsing the Feminized Circle

I have already shown that the novel's structure of embedded narratives and of male desire as the source of descriptive energy serves to center and elevate the experience and communal practice of these women to an authoritative position in the text. In the portrayal of the Millenium Hall community itself, the community's authority as a model is endorsed by its possession of four qualities which were particularly legible in mid-eighteenth-century English culture: conversational skill, associated with the social sensibilities so highly prized in discourse of the time; the power of action, generally seen as belonging to the public, masculine domain; rational control over the passions, associated with the classical cultural tradition, transmitted and upheld by male representatives; and moral purity, grounded in the Christian tradition. The very centrality of these legitimizing modes to existing patriarchal structures of power serves to explain why characterization, private narratives, and narrative structure all tend in this novel to deny, and deflect attention from, the radical nature of these claims to authority.

In the case of conversation, this study has already established the revised ideal of the time, in which the feminized skills of moderator and consensus-maker are prized over those of the aggressive debater or wit, while women themselves are encouraged to play the role of audience rather than speaker. In *Millenium Hall,* the women are drawn into the speaker position by the men whose curiosity and admiration lead them to insist upon knowing more about the community. At the same time, they show no reluctance or difficulty in conveying the principles upon which they have established their utopia, thus using the requisite female compliance and charm as means of commanding a hearing for sociable truths. After-dinner conversation at the Hall is, the men discover, "particularly animated, and [leaves them] still more charmed with the society into which chance [has] introduced [them]"; "sprightliness of . . . wit" is paralleled by "justness of . . . reflexions," and "dignity" with "vivacity" (37), suggesting that here the traditionally male conversational strengths are combined with the female in a mode which avoids the excesses to which both are ostensibly prone. This pattern of persuasion is a feature of the embedded narratives as well, where the women are remarkably articulate in convincing suitors, for example, of their views of right and wrong courses of action. When Mrs. Selvyn forces Lady Mary's former pursuer to admit that he took despicable advantage of Lady Mary's naiveté, in the incident from which I quoted earlier, she does so in the context of that man's genuine proposal of marriage to herself.

Nor are these women reluctant to act out their sociability beyond the bounds of the properly domestic. Although their activities include, conventionally enough, the education of girls in their own household, the establishment of sister communities, and the care of the local poor, they also enjoy Sir Charles Grandison's favorite charity of giving dowries to local girls, "receive their own rents and direct all the chief concerns of their estates" (130), and have established and oversee a local carpet manufacture upon the innovative principles of high wages and social security for the sick and disabled.[12]

When the narrator praises the "justness" of the women's "reflexions" in the evening conversation described above, he goes on to observe "with how much greater strength the mind can exert itself in a regular and rational way of life, than in a course of dissipation" (37). The ability of the inhabitants of Millenium Hall, both in their trials before arriving and in their communal existence, to regulate their passions and act upon the dictates of reason is emphasized repeatedly in the novel. On one level, these exercises in self-denial reveal an extreme of internalized repression; when Louisa Mancel is forcing herself to refuse the man she loves because of her obligations to his grandmother, for example, she concludes that "while honour, truth, and gratitude, pleaded against inclination, they must be in the right, though their remonstrances were hushed into a whisper by the loudest solicitations of passion. Convinced that she could not be to blame, while she acted in contradiction to her secret choice, since the sincerity of her intentions were thereby plainly, though painfully evinced, she persisted in refusing to become Sir Edward's wife" (106). If the fundamental principle of the inherently blamable nature of all desire is a questionable one to today's reader, the mental process detailed here makes it very clear that the self-denial of these women is not to be seen simply as a learned reflex which has been externally imposed. Rather, Scott presents the reader with repeated instances of women making difficult choices as evidence of a rational strength, a properly ordered internal hierarchy of reason and passion, that is inherent in the female self rather than imprinted upon her through patriarchal control. Indeed, feminine reason can be most fully exercised when it is unencumbered by male passion or inadequacy. Louisa Mancel, I have noted, is freest to "reflect on the past, contemplate the present, or anticipate the future" when her lover's death has released her from "conformity to his inclinations." Similarly, her friend's mother, the first Mrs. Melvyn, devoted her intelligence to "sup-ply[ing] the apparent deficiencies in her husband's understanding," so that it was only after her death that "her extraordinary merit," and the fact that she had been the force behind any appearance of intelligence and good judgment in him, became evident (54-55). That the usual gendering of reason and passion has been reversed here is made clear from the start, when the narrator upon first entering into the presence of the women, "[can] scarcely forbear believing [him]self in the Attick school" (33). Appropriating the classical traditions of Athens and "Arcadia" (178) for its own use, this community again challenges the very grounds of the ideology of gender to which its individual members conformed so admirably in their earlier lives.[13]

In a related but even more radical centralizing move, the community of Millenium Hall thoroughly reinterprets the Christian tradition that has been used to uphold the patriarchal structures which have restricted its members' movements in society at large. As the narrator and Lamont originally move toward the Hall, they are drawn by a desire to see "the Primum Mobile of all we had yet beheld"; within, they find among the others Mrs. Morgan "drawing a landscape out of her own imagination" (33-34). Immediately thereby associated with the sustaining and creating roles of God, she is given the culminating description of "extremely majestic," dignified, benign, and portraying every virtue in her face. This list of godlike features concludes with the statement that "one would almost think nature had formed her for a common parent, such universal and tender benevolence beams from every glance she casts around her" (35). The effect is of an immediate and explicit feminization of the Christian God; the Christianity which is subsequently portrayed in the text is not, as some readers have argued, a repressively patriarchal, but rather a communal one.[14] In Haggerty's words: "When, finally, the women invoke God as the justification of their enterprise, they are not resigning authority but redefining what constitutes (final) authority in patriarchal culture and restructuring the hierarchy of power. The women create the world, that is, in their own image."[15]

The relationship between human beings and the rest of creation in such a system, for example, is governed not by pleasure in "a triumph of human reason," which allows wild beasts to be "tamed and subjected by the superior art of man" (43), but rather by a reciprocity which allows only interactions that bring benefit to both parties. Human relationships are similarly to be characterized by mutual kindness and forgiveness, and by a "reciprocal communication of benefits" (80). In such a view, "our time, our money, and our understandings" are to be used to imitate the "universal, . . . unasked, and unmerited" bounty of God; "What bounds then ought we to set to our good offices, but the want of power to extend them farther?" (196-97). For Scott, even a communal Christianity is indeed imaginable only in hierarchical terms, and *Millenium Hall* repeatedly assumes distinctions of station to be essential to society. However, the thrust of the community's social philosophy is that wealth is to be applied directly to the comfort of the poor and to their empowerment as contributing members of a community, rather than to luxuries that would benefit the local economy in a tangential, Mandevillian manner.[16] That such a Christianity would not have been the one familiar to the text's early readers is indicated by Lamont's difficulty in comprehending a mutuality between the poor and the wealthy, and by his view of interdependence as slavery rather than friendship (80). At the conclusion of the novel he has recourse to the New Testament in order to find the source of the "true" religion of this community, in contrast to that of other Christians, whose "doctrines seemed to have so little influence on their actions, that he imagined there was no sufficient effect produced by Christianity, to warrant a belief, that it was established by a means so very extraordinary" (200).

UTOPIA LIMITED?[17]

The conclusion of *Millenium Hall* seems entirely optimistic, almost euphoric: not only have six women escaped the plots of marriage and seduction to form a feminized community of friends, thereby transforming one English neighborhood, but their story has been rendered authoritative by the male observers who have been converted by it, will attempt to implement it, and hope that the reader will "go and do likewise." The sociable individual, moreover, has been shown to be the most fully independent and free; the women of Millenium Hall and the neighborhood they have re-ordered demonstrate the physical, economic, emotional, and spiritual well-being that can be achieved through interdependence and a commitment to one's sociable duty. With the promise of such rewards for the imitator, the potential for expansion of the ideal of the conversational circle seems unlimited.

The relation of this text to Sarah Scott's life reinforces this optimistic reading. Although the construction of an ideal female community had undoubtedly been authorized in part by the advocacy of men such as Richardson and his hero, Sir Charles Grandison, before Scott's novel was written,[18] Scott's literary and epistolary links with Richardson are arguably superseded, as is the male narrator of the novel, by the authority of personal experience. In what we know of Scott, her dependency upon a self-serving and ungenerous father and her short-lived and unhappy marriage contrast sharply with her intense, if variously defined, relationship with her sister, Elizabeth Montagu, leader of the bluestocking circle of the day, and with the domestic life she shared almost continuously with Lady Barbara Montagu for about fifteen years, until Lady "Babs"'s death in 1765. At the time of the publication of *Millenium Hall,* the two women were involved in extensive charitable, and especially educational, work resembling that of the fictional Hall, albeit on a smaller scale.[19] Thus the imaginative empowering of the community of Millenium Hall is ultimately based on an experiential conviction both of the need for a re-establishment of the bases of intimate community and of the potential for women to imitate such a model.

Nevertheless, Scott published her novel anonymously, thereby obscuring the gender of the voice which mediates it and weakening the image's link with the authoritative living model. As I indicated at the beginning of this chapter, the problem of implementation remains. Although two culturally authoritative male figures express in the novel their desire to imitate this community, its exemplary distinctness rests in its successful exclusion of individualistic desire embodied in the masculine, desire that inevitably compromises or confines feminine sociability when the two are made proximate. The intimate domestic circle founded upon a sexual dynamic has not been transformed because none of the male observers has established such a relationship with any of the text's exemplary women. Even Mr. Alworth, whose marriage is to all intents and purposes over, is not allowed the death of his wife as a means of achieving an earthly union with Mrs. Trentham; their spiritual "marriage" consists of a regular exchange of letters and their mutual efforts at educating their "daughter." Although the feminized community is made central and authoritative in the text, it remains marginalized and inaccessible within its heterosexual cultural context.

Ultimately, then, *Millenium Hall* points in the direction of two means by which the experience of the conversational circle is proven unattainable for its readers. In Tobias Smollett's *Expedition of Humphry Clinker,* the circle becomes a strictly discursive one, representing a range of perspectives on social experience that can never coalesce except at the level of the reader's imaginative response, and therefore cannot be incarnated in action. It thus elaborates on the structure of Scott's novel, in which a true conversational exchange between the masculine and the feminine can only occur within the static descriptive frame; the narrative mode of action in time—of experience, in other words—involves inescapable constraint and inequality. In *Volume the Last* of Sarah Fielding's *David Simple,* the intimate community is destroyed in this life and deferred onto an afterlife because of its fatal vulnerability to a larger society, which recognizes only the plot of aggressive individualism.[20] The elaborate enclosures separating *Millenium Hall* from a predatory patriarchal world, together with the otherworldly emphasis of its language of the paradisical, can thereby be seen to raise questions which Fielding's grim sequel answers.

7

Mobilizing the Community,
Immobilizing the Ideal in Tobias
Smollett's *Humphry Clinker*

Like *Sir Charles Grandison* and *Amelia,* Tobias Smollett's *Expedition of Humphry Clinker* (1771) is a final novel, published just a few months before its author's death. Typical of such a career placement is the novel's shift in plot and structure away from the author's earlier fictions, in which the protagonist is a placeless wanderer, even a picaro, at odds with an unsympathetic and alien society. Indeed, Smollett's very successful first novel, *Roderick Random,* published virtually simultaneously with *Clarissa* and *Tom Jones,* has probably contributed with these novels to the generalization that the novel genre is fundamentally committed to portraying the relationship between the individual and society as an inevitable conflict between desirous and deserving youth and a corrupt society blind to individual merit.

In his last work of fiction, Smollett joins Richardson and Fielding in idealizing rather the sociable self, making a harmonious domestic circle the goal and, in a sense, the protagonist, of his narrative. In this case, the group consists of a biological family and its personal attendants on a tour of the nation. Indeed, the title character, Humphry Clinker, is not introduced into the action until the tour is well under way, and then does not join the group of narrators, who foreground their own experiences and perceptions of events. Far from creating the effect of desire for an absent center produced by the delayed appearance of Grandison in Richardson's novel, however, this disappointment of readerly expectations emphasizes the novel's re-imagining of the ideal individual. In Wolfgang Iser's terms, "Clinker becomes real to us only insofar as he is seen by the other characters in the novel. Thus he inevitably loses that superiority which the cunning picaro always kept in the face of all adversity." As a servant, Clinker is an ideally sociable man in his refusal to claim even the individualized subjectivity implied by narration; like the exemplary women of *Grandison, Amelia,* and *Millenium Hall,* he is transparent and desireless, entirely devoted to the service of others. And like them, he becomes "the center around which the family forms."[1] His role in the novel is thus paradoxically peripheral and central; he is taken for granted and remains invisible during lengthy sequences, and yet plays the role of spiritual and literal savior of the family.

Meanwhile, the Bramble family's tour is, as readers have long noted, a domestic circuit, firmly anchored at its beginning and ending points to the house and lands of Brambleton-Hall, Monmouthshire. This circular structure and attachment to the Bramble estate, with its natural rhythms of planting and harvest, are juxtaposed with the random or vortiginous motion of the tour's stopping points, most notably Bath and London. While internal disharmony, both physiological and relational, initially characterizes the group's members (in a mirror-image of the society around them), the journey's ultimate achievement is a harmony of body, mind, and social situation, so that the travelers can finally take their rightful place as part of a "family of love, where every sole is so kind and so courteous, that wan would think they are so many saints in haven."[2] For the larger public world, on the other hand, reform seems as impossible as it was in *Amelia;* only in isolated corners of the nation can social order be preserved, and there only because the past has not been obliterated by the present.

Despite the physical displacement of the Bramble family, early reviewers complained of the novel's plotlessness, its "want of events." Like the other novels examined here, *Humphry Clinker* discusses questions central to the problem of social structure in a kind of conversational or "miscellany" style by having a series of characters comment on and illustrate them. This topical approach clearly highlighted the work's didactic project for its first readers; one such reader writes of its being "calculated at once to amuse the imagination, and release the understanding from prejudice," while the *London Magazine's* writer notes, "the reader will see, that much of the dreadful dangers, the surprizing escapes, the deep distresses, and the romantic passions which characterize our modern novel-writers, is not to be expected in this performance; in fact, it is something greatly preferable to a novel; it is a pleasing, yet an important lesson on life."[3] If the lessons of *Humphry Clinker* were persuasive, however, it was because of its appealing characters; Smollett's contemporaries clearly responded to the collection of eccentrics out of which he builds his community. While Sarah Scott portrays rather the exemplary than the exotic, both writers therefore use a similar strategy of focusing readerly attention on the nature of sociability by centering the marginalized, constructing the ideal out of what has been excluded.

These similarities to the mid-century novels already discussed suggest that Smollett was influenced, if not by these novels themselves, then by the same social anxieties felt by their authors. Moreover, his position as a perpetual outsider because of his Scottish origin and connections, exacerbated by his recent journalistic endeavors in support of the unpopular ministry of the pro-Scottish Lord Bute,[4] provides an interesting point of comparison with both Sarah Scott and Sarah Fielding, faced with unyielding constraints in their social positions as writing women despite the authorizing force of experience and publication. Perhaps it is this position of permanent marginalization that leads these three writers to take on ambitious projects of constructing the intimate conversational community as a (re)newed model of sociability and, at the same time, to render those communities unviable because of the very conditions upon which their models are founded. Thus Smollett's domestic circle is successfully stabilized only by the exclusion of the feminine, in a mirror image to the community of Millenium Hall, and by its placement in the past, effectively excluding the present generation. The possibility of expanding the influence of the ideal into society at large is thereby abandoned, even more evidently than it was in *Millenium Hall;* indeed, the novel's narrative structure finally suggests that conversational consensus can be achieved successfully only in the synthesizing response of the reader. In this discussion of *Humphry Clinker,* I will illustrate how both the novel's story and its narrative structure at once portray a model of sociability that is domestic, conversational, and consensual, and qualify these characteristics in affirming a nostalgically hierarchical and patriarchal structure of social authority and an individualistic notion of interpretive authority.

THE GROUP AS ONE AND AS MANY

Confronting the reader with an array of distinct characters and narrating voices from the start, and delaying the introduction of the ostensible hero, *Humphry Clinker* immediately not only divides the reader's attention among members of the Bramble party but also highlights the dynamics between them as members of a forcibly created and apparently less-than-consensual intimate community. Matthew Bramble's first letters complain that "domestic vexations" and "family-plagues" (13), including "those children of my sister [who] are left me for a perpetual source of vexation" (7), are aggravating his physical distresses. His nephew Jery finds his new "family of originals" potentially amusing to the outside observer but unpromising as a social unit; his uncle, in particular, is "always on the fret, and so unpleasant in his manner, that rather than be obliged to keep him company, I'd resign all claim to the inheritance of his estate" (10). The dislike is mutual; in Matthew's view Jery is "a pert jackanapes, full of college-petulance and self-conceit" (13). In addition to its detrimental effect on Matthew Bramble's health, this disharmony is mirrored and enlarged by the disasters the family seems to attract to itself; its arrival at Bath, notably, is accompanied by a cacophony of noisy encounters caused in part by the social chaos of that city, but also in part by the self-absorbed and confrontational impulses of the family members.

As these individuals continue in a society of correspondence and conversation, however, discord soon modulates into increasing harmony; in another metaphor, the emotional constipation that manifests itself literally in Matthew and the dog Chowder is relieved both by the epistolary "discharge" of "overflowings," which by "retention" would grow "intolerably acrimonious" (34), and by "the pleasures of society," which prove "a more efficacious, and, certainly, a much more palatable remedy" than the waters of Bath (48). Jery, for example, writes that "Mr. Bramble's character . . . opens and improves upon me every day" (29), while Bramble's niece Lydia is no longer one of his "family-plagues," but "one of the best hearted creatures I ever knew," who "gains upon my affection every day" (52). Although Tabitha Bramble's "avarice" and "perverseness" make her essentially individualistic and antisocial, "one of those geniuses who find some diabolical enjoyment in being dreaded and detested by their fellow-creatures" (59), even she, when Humphry Clinker's entry into the family forces her to choose between her unsociable dog and her brother, chooses human companionship, proving Jery's hypothesis that "she has . . . a most virulent attachment to [Matthew's] person; though her love never shews itself but in the shape of discontent; and she persists in tormenting him out of sheer tenderness" (60). As a result, by the time the party has completed its London stay, several of the writers have attested to a remarkable change in Tabitha and to the improving influence of the newly acquired Humphry Clinker on the family. In addition, Matthew's internal economy is in better order; although he attributes this to exercise, the juxtaposition of the change in Tabitha and the change in his health is telling: "[Tabby] and her dog have been remarkably quiet and orderly, ever since this expostulation [on the journey from Bath]. How long this agreeable calm will last, Heaven above knows—I flatter myself, the exercise of travelling has been of service to my health; a circumstance, which encourages me to proceed in my projected expedition to the North" (89).

By the end of the novel, not only has the health of Bramble improved significantly, but the group has become a family in both a literal and an affective sense: the near-drowning of Bramble has revealed not only the identity of Clinker as his bastard son, but also the true affections of his fellow-travelers (Lydia greets him with the words "Are you indeed my uncle—My dear uncle!—My best friend! My father!" 302).[5] The family has thus become worthy of joining an ideal domestic circle, that of the Dennison family, a union sealed by the marriage of Lydia to George Dennison. Here relationships are as stable over the generations as is the rhythm of the seasons; as the senior Dennison tells it, "In the course of two and twenty years, there has not been one hour's interruption or abatement in the friendship subsisting between Wilson's family and mine; and, what is a rare instance of good fortune, that friendship is continued to our children" (313). Thus, in the "enchanting" society of the

Dennison household, experience again, as in the households of the B. family and of Millenium Hall, takes on the timeless, present-tense aspect of routine; after days spent hunting, "In the evening we dance and sing, or play at commerce, loo, and quadrille" (318). To Jery, the appropriate metaphor is that of a "country dance" (319); to the servant Winifred Jenkins, it is that of a "family of love," and of "so many saints in haven" (324).[6]

At the same time, the novel stresses the inevitable fragmentation of experience, even in the most intimate society. The individual is portrayed as essentially isolated, on the plot level in terms of an incompatibility between his or her desires and the good of the group, and on the narrative level in terms of an unsurmountable subjectivity of perspective. The former is exemplified by Lydia, whose love for George Dennison, known only as the strolling player Wilson, causes her continued unhappiness and ill health despite the fact that her growing maturity leads to more rightly placed affection within the group and to an alignment of her judgment with the social perspective of her uncle. In other words, while she learns to mistrust the kinds of desire represented by Tabitha and Win Jenkins, and to confide in the good will and guidance of her guardian as her "best friend" and "father," her instinctive confidence in Wilson/Dennison's merit and faithfulness to her cannot be reconciled with the family's categorization of such confidence as naive and a threat to the social unit. Thus, even near the end of the novel, when the brother and sister encounter Wilson again, Jery immediately "act[s] the part of an indefatigable spy upon [Lydia's] conduct," perhaps "owing to his regard for [her] honour," but more likely as "the effect of his own pride" (297). Even Lydia's uncle, though her "best friend," cannot be confided in because Lydia's personal anguish is likely to make him "uneasy," and she "would rather suffer a thousand deaths than live the cause of dissension in the family" (297). In Jery's own ruminations on the situation, the possibility of a "clandestine correspondence with such a fellow" leads to avowals of "discard[ing] all tenderness" for his sister, replaced by the reassuring thought that "her simplicity and inexperience" render her incapable of acting on her presumably deceitful impulses. Only in conclusion does he resist this thought in turn with the assertion, "No—I can't think the girl so base—so insensible to the honour of her family" (299-300). No matter how fully Lydia has learned to sacrifice her desires for the good of the family, it appears that at least some members of it are unable to accept as truly sociable anyone whose desires have ever differed with those of the group.

Jery's version of the resolution of this tension illustrates how little the desires and judgment of the sister whom he claims to "love with uncommon affection" have to do with the formation of his ideal domestic circle: "You may easily conceive what pleasure I must have felt on discovering that the honour of our family was in no danger from the conduct of a sister, whom I love with uncommon affection; that, instead of debasing her sentiments and views to a wretched stroller, she had really captivated the heart of a gentleman, her equal in rank and superior in fortune; and that, as his parents approved of his attachment, I was on the eve of acquiring a brother-in-law so worthy of my friendship and esteem" (317-18). In the light of this revealingly subjective view of the family's interests, Jery's statement, in the same paragraph, that he is "mortified to reflect what flagrant injustice we every day commit, and what absurd judgment we form, in viewing objects through the falsifying medium of prejudice and passion," ironically underlines not what he has learned from his experience of misjudging George Dennison, but what he has not learned about the sister who is part of his intimate community, despite the travels he credits with "dispelling those shameful clouds that darken the faculties of the mind" (318).[7] Indeed, the novel appears to distinguish between prejudices about the phenomena encountered in travel, like spa life and Scottish hospitality, that can be corrected through sensory experience, and judgments of others, that can be radically influenced by one's state of health and even more radically by one's passions. If Tabitha's tendency to love a place while it offers the prospect of a husband and hate it from the instant that prospect is gone is the comic version of this phenomenon, Mr. Baynard's blindness to the coldly selfish character of the wife he dotes on and Jery's inability to see the gentlemanly breeding of a strolling player illustrate the threat to the health of the social unit posed by such subjectivity. The fact that the novel nearly ends with a duel between Jery and Lydia's lover, in a repetition of its opening incident, does little to convince the reader that the increased harmony of the Bramble group is a function of a new ability to achieve consensus rather than a mere happy conjunction of circumstances.[8]

CONSENSUS AS ACQUIESCENCE

If conversation leading to consensus remains unrealized in this novel in the sense that it has been portrayed in *Pamela* Part II or *Amelia,* for example, individualistic interpretation of experience is nevertheless modified in three respects: in the adjustment of the writer to his or her partner in oral or written conversation, in the matured understandings of characters such as Lydia Melford and Humphry Clinker through their travels, and ultimately in the reader's role as interpreter of the conversation that is the novel. The effect, however, is even less one of mutual modification than is the case in the Richardson novels I have discussed; rather, a traditional hierarchy of interpretive authority is modeled, in keeping with the reaffirmation of a traditional social structure that I will discuss later in this chapter.

When the novel's characters are first presented, their extreme idiosyncrasies are in need of modification, not only so that their relationships with fellow group-members will become less conflictual, but also so that the reader will be able to see through the exaggerated colors of their rhetoric to the "real" social phenomena of Bath, London, and rural England, toward which the novel's satire is directed. Thus, Jery and Matthew state opposing views of the effect on manners of the mixing of social stations at Bath, with Jery recording the difference as an argument that is settled by observing the behavior of the ladies at a tea-drinking. While Bramble's view that mixing is "destructive of all order and urbanity" and "vulgarize[s] the deportment and sentiments of those who [move] in the upper spheres of life" (49) proves the most accurate, Jery's attitude toward such incidents, that "they are truly ridiculous in their own nature, and serve to heighten the humour in the farce of life" (48), softens Bramble's cynicism and presumably determines the reader's own response, since Jery is the narrator of the tea-drinking story. Furthermore, having denounced Bath social life in the splenetic tone of a misanthrope, Bramble's response to winning the argument is to "[hang] his head in manifest chagrin, and [to seem] to repine at the triumph of his judgment" (51). In his early exchanges with Dr. Lewis, he similarly modifies his denunciations, admitting his biases as an elderly valetudinarian either by imagining Lewis's response ("Methinks I hear you say . . . ," 34) or by acknowledging the difficulties of the medical profession ("I grant that physick is no mystery of your making . . . ," 44). It is presumably this sense of strongly marked, individualistic voices and their softening through the accumulation of divergent viewpoints and implied responses that led William Hazlitt to describe the novel as "the most pleasant gossiping novel that ever was written."[9]

As the tea-drinking example illustrates, however, once Bramble's eccentric irritability has been accounted for, it is clearly his interpretation of English social relations that becomes authoritative for his group. The growing affection that Jery feels for his uncle, for example, is accompanied by a recognition that his views of the mixing of ranks, of the behavior of authors, and of the dishonesty caused by the spirit of party factions are objectively verifiable. Similarly, although Bramble and Lydia's responses to Bath and London represent opposite points on a spectrum that may initially imply an ideal middle position (in the midst of her breathlessly naive admiration of Vauxhall, Lydia admits, "my uncle . . . did not seem to relish the place. People of experience and infirmity, my dear Letty, see with very different eyes from those that such as you and I make use of—," 92), Lydia's statements are themselves subverted to indicate that her boarding-school romanticism disables her from reading accurately the information provided by her senses. At Vauxhall, for example, she has "the happiness to hear the celebrated Mrs. ___, whose voice was so loud and so shrill, that it made my head ake through excess of pleasure" (92). Lydia's viewpoint is thus reduced to the status of an illustration of Bramble's earlier description of the crowds at Vauxhall as objects of his compassion for their "temerity," of his contempt for their "want of taste and decorum," and of his horror at their "possess[ion] by a spirit, more absurd and pernicious than any thing we meet with in the precincts of Bedlam" (88-89). Even the Methodist Humphry Clinker, who at first poses a challenge to Bramble's authority when he asks, "may not the new light of God's grace shine upon the poor and the ignorant in their humility, as well as upon the wealthy, and the philosopher in all his pride of human learning?" immediately acquiesces to Bramble's definition of him as "either an hypocritical knave, or a wrong-headed enthusiast; and, in either case, unfit for my service" (135). In fact, he resigns any claim to interpret his own experience: "It becometh not such a poor ignorant fellow as me, to hold dispute with gentlemen of rank and learning—As for the matter of knowledge, I am no more than a beast in comparison of your honour; therefore I submit; and, with God's grace, I will follow you to the world's end" (136). Clinker's Methodism, with its rough edges rubbed off by Bramble's reminder of his servant status, is thus quickly incapacitated as a challenge to Bramble's interpretive authority and serves merely to reinforce his loyalty and submission.

As my argument about how interpretive authority is established in the novel implies, information provided by the multiple narrators is processed by the reader, who must determine their relative authority.[10] It can be argued, therefore, that the only true conversation of the novel, the only egalitarian exchange of points of view that results in a consensus, is the one which is conducted in the mind of the reader, who constructs the story out of the various versions provided.[11] In the text itself, on the other hand, subjectivity and a resulting fragmentation of perspective are givens that render impossible a mutual modification of views; only direct experience brings points of view together, and even such convergence is limited to the characters who are able to interpret rightly the information provided by their senses. Tabitha, for example, is notoriously prone to misinterpret, insisting on one occasion that Matthew must be pursuing an affair rather than extending disinterested charity when he offers a widow twenty pounds; she adamantly refuses to be "arguef[ied] . . . out of [her] senses" (24). For those who can learn to read experience, an acknowledgment of the authority of Bramble's interpretations is ultimately the result, and those interpretations do not alter throughout the novel, even if his tone softens from angry to sorrowful.

A WIDE BUT EXCLUSIVE CIRCLE

Bramble's version of social reality is of a dichotomy between a stable idyll of retired country life and a larger social world which is increasingly chaotic and disorderly, its instability caused by the ceaseless striving of every individual to imitate his or her social betters.[12] When Lydia has come to share this vision after her exposure to the larger world, she contrasts "repose and solitude" and "that disinterested friendship which is not to be found among crouds" with "the hurry and tumult of fashionable society," "the commerce of life," where "there is such malice, treachery, and dissimulation, even among professed friends and intimate companions, as cannot fail to strike a virtuous mind with horror" (296). In this dichotomy of public individualism and private sociability the novel resembles *David Simple* and *Amelia;* its use of anti-circular imagery to describe London life also echoes the latter. Frenetic social jostling is made visible in the form of unceasing, yet directionless motion:

> In short, there is no distinction or subordination left—. . . . The hod-carrier, the low mechanic, the tapster, the publican, the shop-keeper, the pettifogger, the citizen, and courtier, *all tread upon the kibes of one another:* actuated by the demons of profligacy and li-centiousness, they are seen every where, rambling, riding, rolling, rushing, justling, mixing, bouncing, cracking, and crashing in one vile ferment of stupidity and corruption—All is tumult and hurry; one would imagine they were impelled by some disorder of the brain, that will not suffer them to be at rest. The foot-passengers run along as if they were pursued by bailiffs. The porters and chairmen trot with their burthens. People, who keep their own equipages, drive through the streets at full speed. . . . [87-88]

When such individuals come together for the "diversions of the times," their collective motion is that of a mindless circle: "One half of the company [at Ranelagh] are following one another's tails, in an eternal circle; like so many blind asses in an olive-mill, where they can neither discourse, distinguish, nor be distinguished" (88). Both Matthew and Lydia suffer from giddiness as they watch the motions of their fellows, and near the end of the novel we hear that when Baynard's wife at first refused his request to remove to the country, "they continued to be sucked deeper and deeper into the vortex of extravagance and dissipation, leading what is called a fashionable life in town" (277).

This destructive and even demonic motion of course stands in contrast to the purposeful circle tour of Britain that provides the novel's structural backbone. More explicitly, as the Baynard example illustrates, the chaos of urban action is juxtaposed with the regular, health-giving motion of country life, which is both natural in following the rhythm of the seasons and rational in its pursuit of the good life as defined by the philosophers. Thus, even the comic detail of Tabitha's enquiries after her laying hens and the coupling of cow and bull reinforces the significance of Bramble's awareness of the progress of the haying and hunting seasons and the preparations to be made for a Christmas feast. The rhythmic ebb and flow of exercise and rest, summer work and "conversation, by the fire-side in winter" appears to be the ideal context of "a vigorous circulation of the spirits, which is the very essence and criterion of good health" (324-25). Ideal travel, from this perspective, is a deliberate pursuit of personal balance and knowledge that expresses as well a sense of social responsibility. Bramble's decision to travel beyond Bath is made in part to please and inform his wards, in part "for the benefit of my health," and in part because "it is a reproach upon me, as a British freeholder, to have lived so long without making an excursion to the other side of the Tweed" (64). Tabitha, on the other hand, is driven by the same demon of insatiable desire as the inhabitants of London; since "nothing in the shape of man can come amiss" to her (61-62), each new location is a social paradise for as long as it remains a potential source of a husband, only to be transformed into an intolerable confinement when no man will conform to her wishes.

If the Bramble family's travels generally reflect an ideal of openness and inclusivity in the use of sensory experience to modify preconceived ideas and in a willingness to see Scotland with unprejudiced eyes, the social truths discovered in this exploration reaffirm an exclusive and authoritarian model of ideal sociability. Far from representing the new domestic tourists visiting great houses as a means, in Carole Fabricant's terms, of "render[ing] pieces of privately owned land accessible—and in a vicarious sense possessable—by their often middle class audience,"[13] Bramble and his companions are self-consciously searching for the traditional hospitality of the lord of the manor, whose house is thrown open to the members of an extensive, but elite, social network. Indeed, a number of the country houses visited belong to kinfolk of Bramble, while others are those of university friends or of gentlemen approached through letters of introduction from other gentlemen; when Bramble feels he is not entertained fittingly, he can pronounce no greater insult than to call the place an inn (167-68, 282). The Dennison family, on whose "friendly shore" the group finally comes to rest (307), is first introduced as that of a gentleman who will not allow such a distinguished party of travellers to stay at a public house, while the true Wilson appears on the stage as a stranger who responds to Jery's absurd challenge to a duel with an immediate invitation to him, as a fellow gentleman, to "take the diversion of hunting with him for a few weeks" (299). In a social landscape conceived as a network of gentlemanly acquaintances, it is not surprising that the deciding factor in the resolution of Lydia's love affair is that "the slighted Wilson is metamorphosed into George Dennison, only son and heir of a gentleman, whose character is second to none in England" (321)—and, incidentally, who was once Bramble's "fellow-rake at Oxford" (307).

In this discussion of *Humphry Clinker* I have suggested that consensus is in fact achieved, both on the narrative and on the plot levels, through an alignment of perspectives and allegiances with Matthew Bramble. It is of course no accident that Bramble, as its eldest male, is head of this family, and that Lydia's final outburst of affection for him involves acknowledging him as her best friend and father. As an interpreter, she initially allows herself to be guided by her aunt, who assures her that her dislike of the heat and odor of the Bath public rooms is "the effect of a vulgar constitution, reared among woods and mountains; and . . . will wear off" (41); as a girl in love, she chooses the maid Win Jenkins as her "confidant" (12). Her growth to maturity involves becoming "truly ashamed of my own sex" as represented by these two women in their hypocritical use of religion as a "decoy" to catch a mate (251). Lydia's criticism of Methodism as a cover for, or an expression of, individualistic desire echoes her uncle's rationalist dislike of enthusiasm; she concludes, "If I could put faith in all these supernatural visitations, I should think myself abandoned of grace; for I have neither seen, heard, nor felt anything of this nature, although I endeavour to discharge the duties of religion with all the sincerity, zeal, and devotion, that is in the power of . . . " (251). It is Lydia's eagerness to please her uncle that wins his affection, and her weaning away from the dangerous female communities of first the boarding school and then her aunt and Win appears to be part of her education as an ideal female member of the domestic circle headed by a father or husband. The socialization of Humphry Clinker's spiritual impulses, referred to above, similarly reinforces this domestic structure, as does the fact that his primary qualifications as a servant are his humility and absolute loyalty. If the line between consensus and appropriation has been a fine one in the cases of Pamela's transformation of B.'s family and of Harriet's feminine narrative style, it is crossed here as the egalitarian implications of Methodism are displaced from Clinker to the enthusiasm of a Tabitha Bramble, leaving only a pious humility that makes him the ideal retainer in a traditional social structure.

Tabitha, on the other hand, does not willingly submit herself to her brother's governance. In this case, family harmony is achieved not through a mutual process of consensus-building, but rather through Matthew's assertion of his authority in making her choose between remaining in his household and keeping her dog; this incident is explicitly referred to by both Matthew and Jery as the beginning of the former's domestic happiness. In contrast to several of the novels in this study, which use brother-sister or husband-wife relations as a relatively egalitarian alternative to the father-daughter relation as it was conceived in the eighteenth century, Matthew's exercise of his prerogative over his sister seems deliberately to extend the authority of the male where it might be at its most questionable, to a sister of mature years and independent means. The suggestion that Matthew has been remiss in not asserting himself earlier is reinforced when he in turn reproaches his friend Baynard for "his unmanly acquiescence under the absurd tyranny which [his wife] exert[s]" (281). The Baynard families of this world are clearly part of the insubordination that characterizes faulty sociability; Baynard is "doomed for life" to a "rotation of absurdity" even after he has left the city (279), and Bramble asserts that "nineteen out of twenty, who are ruined by extravagance, fall a sacrifice to the ridiculous pride and vanity of silly women, whose parts are held in contempt by the very men whom they pillage and enslave" (283). The inability of either Tabitha or Mrs. Baynard to maintain a proper distance from their servants, whether indulging in billingsgate or encouraging insolence towards their masters, shows that such women create a breach in the family circle, a point of entry for the "democratical" influence of the mob, "incompatible with excellence, and subversive of order" (112).

REORDERING THE GENDERED DOMESTIC ECONOMY

In this study of novels of the domestic circle, I have argued that mid-eighteenth-century ideology of gender has been used to construct a model of sociability in which individualistic desire is contained, by its focus on the exemplary female at the center of the circle in the case of male desire, and by its sublimation of the self in the other in the case of female desire. I have also noted an increasing emphasis on silence, passivity, and domestic enclosure in the virtuous female character. Like several of these novels, *Humphry Clinker* portrays feminine desire as dangerously individualistic, most extensively in the character of Tabitha Bramble, but also in Win Jenkins and Mrs. Baynard. However, the essentially feminine nature of such desire as it is portrayed in characters such as Charlotte Grandison and Miss Mathews coexists uneasily in *Sir Charles Grandison* and *Amelia* with the portrayal of exemplary women such as Harriet Byron and Amelia Booth, whose admirably placed desires are necessary for social cohesion and harm only themselves. In Smollett's domestic circle, feminine desire is separated from the culturally feminized qualities of loyalty, passivity, humility, and spirituality; these admirable characteristics become those of the male servant Humphry Clinker who, as a result, is the essentially sociable being, devoting himself to bringing harmony and stability to the Bramble family.

That women in *Humphry Clinker* are inherently prone to irrational excess has already been suggested in this chapter. Of the characters who are most fully developed, only Lydia appears able to escape the pull of self-indulgent desire, whether expressed in the romantic fancies of a young girl, in Methodist enthusiasm, in the pursuit of fashion, or in lasciviousness. She escapes, though somewhat tainted, by distancing herself from the influence of her aunt, by a suitable choice of her uncle as guide to her behavior, and above all by suppressing her desire for Wilson to the point of illness and melancholy, in the pattern of a Harriet Byron. Even so, as we have seen, she never achieves the status of a fully trustworthy member of the family. Win Jenkins and Tabitha Bramble, on the other hand, are portrayed as incapable of rational self-control. Win is temporarily lured away from Humphry Clinker, "an English pudding, composed of good wholesome flour and suet," by the attractions of the Frenchified valet Dutton, "a syllabub or iced froth, which, though agreeable to the taste, has nothing solid or substantial," showing that in her vanity she is "as frail as any female in the kingdom" and deserving of her humiliation at the hands of the Newcastle mob (202). In her marriage to Clinker Bramble expects she will be "as great an enthusiast in love as in religion" (329), suggesting that the two are interchangeable as outlets for female propensities. While Win's faults are treated indulgently because of their "natural" state in an uneducated servant, Tabitha's illustrate more seriously the inefficacy of education and experience to contain female desire. Her array of antisocial faults—avarice, perversity, quarrelsomeness, hypocrisy, opportunism—are displayed at their worst when she shows signs of flirtation with the newly widowed Baynard on the eve of her marriage to Lismahago. Bramble concludes that such dishonorable and illogical motions "must be the instinctive efforts of her constitution, rather than the effects of any deliberate design" (328), a conclusion all the more damning of female nature.

Humphry Clinker, on the other hand, is the constant positive pole in a series of moral and social contrasts. While Win and Dutton go to the play in their tarnished finery, he accompanies Tabitha to a Methodist meeting; his Methodism teaches him to submit to his master while Tabitha "[takes] offence at his humility" and urges him to insubordination "for conscience sake" (136). As an English pudding rather than a French froth, Clinker offers the same reaffirmation of the domestic and the familiar as does Harriet Byron in contrast to the exotic Clementina. His refusal to take up a sword in response to Dutton's challenge, because "it doth not become servants to use those weapons, or to claim the privilege of gentlemen to kill one another when they fall out" (203), like his condemnation of swearing among servants, illustrates a purifying effect on his master's household like that of Pamela in Mr. B.'s. Indeed, his initial zeal for the saving of souls is rendered symbolic through his harmonizing effect on the family, and literal when he repeatedly saves his master and his family from the threats of fire and water, at first only perceived dangers, but finally an actual one in Bramble's near-drowning. On the latter occasion, immediately preceding the novel's resolution, Clinker passes the final trial of choice between desire and duty when he initially rescues his beloved Win, only to drop her back into the water upon realizing that Bramble remains in the submerged coach. Thus, Clinker's absence as a narrator from the novel named after him proves doubly significant: on the one hand, it highlights his ideal reluctance to narrate himself, and on the other, it points to the fact that, like the silent Amelia, he in fact holds the family together by his self-sacrificing sociability.[14]

Once antisocial and sociable traits have been gendered as respectively male and female, exclusion of dangerous desire from the ideal community be-

comes a matter of excluding the female, in a mirror-image of the structure of
Millenium Hall. This occurs most dramatically in the case of Mrs. Baynard,
who suddenly dies after the portrayal of her disastrous influence on her husband. Bramble feels no qualms about "being exceedingly pleased" at her death,
and within "a few hours" has persuaded his friend "that Heaven could not have
interposed more effectually to rescue him from disgrace and ruin" (326). Only
slightly more subtle is the effective marginalization of Tabitha at the end of the
novel, when Bramble rejoices that, through her marriage to Lismahago, "I, and
my servants, will get rid of a very troublesome and tyrannic gouvernante"
(263), while her husband will become a member of a male community together with Dr. Lewis, Bramble, and Baynard.

In fact, the differing treatments of Tabitha and Lismahago, as a pair of
equally eccentric "originals," illustrate the novel's distinction between the social
implications of female and male individualism. While in its female form it is
portrayed as a social threat to be suppressed if not excluded from the intimate
circle, individualism in the male is a harmless eccentricity which may initially
appear to impede sociability but in fact is its very basis. Critics have variously
suggested that idiosyncracy in Smollett is a sign of authority and trustworthi-
ness, or a vestige of an earlier, more virtuous age, or, at worst (in the form of
hypochondria), a socially benign expression of individualistic energy.[15] Thus
Bramble's irascibility and complaints of illness at the beginning of the novel
are shown to be signs of an extreme sensibility, which makes him a benevolent
guardian, master, and landlord. While at his most quarrelsome, Lismahago is
tolerated for his political insight and for his stimulating conversation;[16] when
he mellows at the prospect of a secure provision as Tabitha's husband, he
becomes "a valuable acquisition to our little society, in the article of conversation, by the fire-side in winter" (324). Part of the process of acceptance into
the gentlemanly community appears to be a pragmatic, even cynical approach
to marriage; thus Baynard's escape from his hen-pecked state is celebrated, and
Lismahago wins Jery's approval for the "languishing leer upon his countenance" at his wedding and for his exaggerated rapture after his wedding night,
which Jery has "no doubt" are ironical (333-34). It is acceptable, even desirable, in other words, for Lismahago to show a cynicism about his marriage to
Tabitha, while her reciprocal pragmatism in arranging a settlement for herself
is treated throughout the novel as lascivious, mercenary, and hypocritical.

This exclusion of the female and rehabilitation of the male in the domestic economy leads eventually to the same unviability as that of the social
ideal of *Millenium Hall*. In fact, this unviability is made much clearer in the
didactically inconclusive conclusion of *Humphry Clinker*. Some change has
been effected—Lydia has been successfully married into an ideal family, Baynard has been rescued and his estate set to rights, Lismahago and Clinker/Loyd
have become integral members of the community, and Bramble is renewed in

health and in his relish for the conversational circle of his friends. Nevertheless, the group which completes its journey with a return to Brambleton-Hall is in fact a sterile group of elders—two confirmed bachelors, a widower, and a couple past the age of childbearing. The price of the exclusion of female desire appears to be a sterility as complete as that caused by its excesses in the case of Mrs. Baynard's landscaping efforts, which turn a garden "well stocked with the best fruit which England could produce" into "a naked circus of loose sand, with a dry bason and a leaden triton in the middle" (275).

Of course one young couple that is likely to be prolific does return to Brambleton-Hall. Humphry Clinker, now Matthew Loyd, nevertheless exists in the social limbo of the illegitimate son, testimony to "the sins of [Matthew Bramble's] youth" in begetting and then not taking responsibility for this "crab of [his] own planting" (305-6). While his future place and that of his bride remain awkwardly difficult to determine, the younger generation of their social superiors has set off on another series of travels, its immediate destination Bath, the epitome of all that Bramble despises and fears. It remains unclear whether these young people have learned enough about ideal sociability to forge a more effective link between their intimate circle and the larger social world than did their elders. In fact, the lingering questions about Jery's growth to an unprejudiced maturity raise the possibility that the pattern of folly, disillusionment, and belated health that Matthew Bramble sees in his own life will simply be retraced. Any hope for the expansion of an ideal social order appears to be located in Lydia and George Dennison, an apparently ideal, but still very young and dependent, couple.

It is perhaps for this reason that *Humphry Clinker*'s claims to offer a vision of rebirth and transformation rest largely at the level of personal wholeness and of imagery, rather than of action. Change in a descriptive rather than prescriptive mode can be effected only at the level of an individual reawakening to social responsibility—and perhaps in the reader, who will synthesize and apply the lesson of a renewed sociability. The ideal of the intimate community, it seems, remains somewhere on the country estate of a bygone rural England, still visible in vestigial form in Scotland and on the Dennison estate, but largely preserved only in the memories of a few elderly men marginalized as eccentrics by their contemporaries. In *Volume the Last* of Sarah Fielding's *David Simple* the social ideal is similarly pushed beyond the horizon, not into the past, but into a future life.

8

Disembodying the Social Circle in Sarah Fielding's *Volume the Last*

In 1744, Sarah Fielding concludes *The Adventures of David Simple* with the confident assertion that "as strong a Picture as this is of real Happiness, it is in the power of every Community to attain it, if every Member of it would perform the Part allotted him by *Nature,* or his *Station in Life,* with a sincere Regard to the Interest and Pleasure of the whole." Even more optimistically, she envisions a world in which "all Mankind [were] contented to exert their own Faculties for the common Good"; in such a world, "real Happiness would be attainable, . . . and the various Humours, and the different Understandings with which Human Nature is supplied, would, instead of *Discord,* produce such a *Harmony,* as would infallibly make the whole Species happy."[1] This vision of difference accorded into harmony, however, has at the end of the novel been achieved only by David Simple's family, in part by its turning inward into a tightly closed intimate circle which acts as a haven from the self-interest driving the larger society, a self-interest that has proved a threat to each member of the group in turn.

In the gap between this optimistic declaration and the appearance in 1753 of Sarah Fielding's *Volume the Last,* it is known that she suffered certain effects of straitened financial circumstances and dependency, and within the space of seven months in 1750-51, the deaths of her three sisters and her eight-year-old nephew.[2] In contrast to such lived experience, Richardson's *Sir Charles Grandison* in this same period presented an intimate domestic circle empowered by a socially authoritative and wealthy male center to expand its moral influence over a broad sphere, while in *Amelia* the Booth family was permitted to retreat to a country estate where financial security guaranteed the fixity of William Booth within the domestic circle and thereby his moral reform. In other words, the social ideal of *Grandison* and *Amelia* depends for its realization on an unacknowledged foundation of wealth, which can command the respect and secure the means of power necessary to, at best, align the larger social world with the small society's values or, at the least, provide a barrier to the hostile incursions of that world.[3]

It is therefore plausible that for Sarah Fielding, like Sarah Scott, the authority of lived, rather than fictional, experience, and especially the kind of fictional experience provided by these newly authoritative male authors, lies behind her return to the story of David Simple's community in *Volume the Last*. Unlike Scott, however, Fielding uses her experience not to affirm the possibility of an influential community of the socially marginalized, but to portray "all the Horrors of Friendship" (431) in the face of the inescapable interdependence of individuals and of their communities in early modern England. Thus she elaborates on one of the most striking themes of her first novel, the problem of poverty for the wellborn, tracing its economic, physical, psychological, and ethical effects on her ideal social circle, and commenting on those effects with a new voice of authority. In so doing, she not only denies the ideal's assumption of communal self-determination, but also reveals the self-destructive logic inherent in the conversational circle idealized by Richardson, Henry Fielding, and Sarah Scott, as well as by her own first work.

At the same time, Fielding continues to affirm as transcendent the ideal's central social principle of placing the group before the self. She does so by displacing its realization from this world into another, the Christian heaven. Although David Simple's community is defeated by the combined forces of treacherous, passionate, and rational individualisms, its founding principle proves the only sociable option; full, permanent realization has simply been transferred to another plane of existence. *David Simple, Volume the Last* resembles Smollett's *Humphry Clinker,* therefore, in that the communal ideal does not succeed in transforming the rapaciously egotistical social climate. Rather, the potential for consensus has been transferred to an extra-textual and extra-social dimension: that of reader response, in both novels, and that of the afterlife, in *Volume the Last*.[4]

THE EARNED AUTHORITY OF THE AUTHOR

As "the author of *David Simple,*" Sarah Fielding was admired for her didactic essays and tales, and more qualifiedly, for her learning. This earned literary authority appears to have emboldened her, not to reiterate the ideal which her first fiction had espoused in hopes that she might effect an application of the text to social life, but to re-examine that ideal with stringent honesty.[5] The timid and anonymous writer of *The Adventures of David Simple,* apologizing for "the Work of a Woman, and her first Essay,"[6] has found the success she hoped for from its entertaining capacities, and now faces an audience prepared to be pleased. The preface to *Volume the Last,* written by "a Female FRIEND of the AUTHOR" (probably Jane Collier), sets the tone with an intimate and confident glimpse of the author's intent and compositional process, creating an effect very different from that of Henry Fielding's *David Simple* preface, with its distanced and patronizing stance. First, the original novel is, with the emphasis of threefold repetition, described as a completed quest; David Simple has arrived at "his desired Port" of friendship just as surely as Matthew Bramble and his family were "wrecked upon a friendly shore." Nevertheless, there appear to be realities that such a structure cannot comprehend, "natural and common Distresses of this World," which must be portrayed to illustrate the response of "a Society united by well directed Affections, and a Similitude of Mind" (309) to such distresses. Fielding deliberately puts herself on moral and artistic trial, moreover, claiming to return to familiar characters as an expression of "the unaffected Simplicity she has a Desire to recommend" and as a test of the "skilful Hand" required in producing variety from the known (309-10).

The note of confidence established in the preface is carried over into the creation of a more authoritative and self-assured narrative persona in the text itself. She launches forth with a confident advertisement of her story ("I . . . doubt not, but those Persons who were then pleased with [David Simple's] Character, will be no less pleased with knowing the Remainder of so very uncommon a Life") and continues with a detached, generalized observation that nevertheless points ironically, through the word "seems," to her own superior insight, much in the manner of a Jane Austen narrator: "A Man, actuated by neither Avarice nor Ambition, his Mind moving on no other Axis but that of Love, having obtained a Wife his Judgment approves, and his Inclination delights in; seeing, at the same time, all his Friends chearful and pleased around him, *seems* to be in a State of Happiness, in comparison of which, every thing in this World is trifling" (313, my italics). This greater assurance is reflected throughout the narrative itself in the form of unapologetic and definitive statements, made in the narrator's own voice, about moral issues raised by the story; one such digression begins, "And here, if I might be permitted a little to depart from the Brevity I promised in this first part of our History, I would detain my Reader by some Observations on the capricious Judgments that are shewn in passing Sentence on the Words and Actions of a Man, who is actuated by no other Motives than the simple Dictates of an honest Heart" (324).

Such comments are clearly designed to guide interpretation and appeal to sympathy, but in an even broader sense, they challenge the reader to growth in social ethics. Like parallel formal devices in *Grandison* and *Amelia,* one of the functions of the narrator of *Volume the Last* is clearly to socialize the act of reading itself. Thus the new assurance that is reflected in Fielding's deliberate choice of the sequel as a particularly demanding form and in the use of a more confident and dominant narrative persona extends to a determined resistance to audience demand for a pleasing plot. The preface and conclusion refuse to entertain complaints about the sequel's outcome, suggesting that such complaints reflect selfish failures of sympathy. David's death is "a Scene of real Pleasure"; "if any of my readers chuse to drag *David Simple* from the Grave, to struggle again in this world, and to reflect, every Day, on the Vanity of its utmost Enjoyments," the narrator will have no part of it, but will "chuse to think he is escaped from the Possibility of falling into any future Afflictions, and that neither the Malice of his pretended Friends, nor the Sufferings of his real ones, can ever again rend and torment his honest Heart" (432).[7]

Similarly, judgments passed on David Simple by characters in the text are paralleled with the kind of judgments made in the world at large, which are in turn made a test of reader response. When after repeated retrenchments David's family has settled into a yet-humbler cottage, for example, their contentment is juxtaposed with the misery of their neighbour Mrs. Orgueil, in despite of "an ample Fortune, without any real Misfortunes to afflict her, enjoying Plenty, Health, and every Blessing that can be thought on, in this World" (331); this neighbor holds the family in contempt as "a Set of lazy extravagant People" (328). The narrator then addresses in turn "those People (if any such there are) who cannot believe that Happiness can subsist without Riches," and finally those ideally sympathetic readers "who can have any Idea of the Happiness that still subsisted amongst our Society, and can conceive, that, exclusive of worldly Prosperity, they enjoyed the most perfect Harmony" (333-34). In other words, the narrator as naive alter-ego of the wandering hero in *David Simple* has been replaced by the narrator as authoritative social commentator in *Volume the Last;* increased authorial responsibility is reflected, in a variation on Carol Kay's model, in the increased social authority not of the protagonist but of the narrator.[8] As confidence in the practicability of the social ideal is undermined, the reader is invited to transfer that confidence to the narrator who exhibits so much control over the process of its demise and so much insight into its meaning.[9]

DEATH BY INTERDEPENDENCE

In chapter 2, I argued that the resolution of *David Simple* raises problems by insisting upon a reintegration of the egalitarian circle into the hierarchical social framework that it has rejected, by hinting that ideal friendship can incur the hostility of desirous individuals in the larger world, and by assuming that sympathy guarantees perfect happiness within the intimate circle. In the sequel, what Malcolm Kelsall has called "the potentialities of these ironies," whether or not the author was conscious of them in 1744, "come to maturity."[10] The community is rendered economically dependent upon a larger society structured according to principles inimical to its own, it is subject to continual misinterpretation and aggression on the part of the individuals whose egotism determines that social structure, and, in the face of the forced encounter with the outside, its own principles of consensus and selflessness prove mutually incompatible. Retrospectively, *David Simple*'s exotic story of Isabelle, in which David and Valentine share "great Admiration of the Marquis *de Stainville* and the Chevalier *Dumont*'s sincere and faithful Friendship" as an image of their own relationship (219), invites a reading of the tragic ending as foreshadowing the parallel losses that will fragment the community and leave David, like Isabelle, resolved upon "retiring from a World, in which it [is] impossible for [him] to meet with any thing worth [his] Regard, after what [he has] lost" (250).

Volume the Last reverses the amnesiac tendency of the original's teleological structure by placing a corrupt and unregenerate larger society in direct conflict with the little society of David Simple. In particular, the use of the Orgueil family as a continual point of contrast to, and source of attacks upon, David's family effectively transforms the optimistic progression from the sentimental picaresque journey to the conversational circle into a schematized tableau of social reality as a predetermined and recurrent triumph of selfishness over sympathy.[11] Supporting the chief aggressors, Mr. and Mrs. Orgueil, is Mr. Ratcliff as the London enemy, bringing the law and the political realm into play against the group. Even the experience of Cynthia and Valentine in Jamaica serves not as an escape to a newer, more sociable world, as it first appears, nor as a safely distanced threat, as did the story of Isabelle, but rather as proof that social evil is everywhere the same, and that attempted escape can lead only to repetition.[12] As Cynthia writes from Jamaica at one point, "I could almost have imagined I heard Mrs. *Orgueil* speaking; but such kind of Women are the Growth of every Climate; and I believe it is my Fate eternally to meet with them" (393)—referring, presumably, also to her experience as the tyrant lady's toadeater in *David Simple*. As a result of this inescapable recurrence, "Heaven in *David Simple,* captured, [David] had thought, on earth in the secluded community of Part I, is seen to be entirely distinct from it."[13]

At the start, however, for as long as the little society is granted a certain measure of economic independence, it thrives in its own rarefied element of sensible conversation, its "Chearfulness and Good Humour" free from the "*bon-mots, insulting* Raillery, malicious Ridicule, and murtherous Slander" so often mistaken "for the *Attic* Salt of Society" (315), while its "Family Affairs" are managed with perfect "Peace, Calmness, Concord, and Harmony" (316). The introduction of a few financial losses and the undesirable acquaintance of the Ratcliffs and the Orgueils appears to effect no significant changes while the group remains economically viable; at this point, dual modes of friendship— as a state of intimate sympathy between members of the group, and as civility without inclination between the group and its outside acquaintance—can be maintained at little cost other than inconvenience. In this portion of the text the word "still" takes on the nature of a refrain emphasizing the survival of the community's integrity and equilibrium through every stage of retrenchment: "they were still possessed of enough to gratify every innocent Desire, and no extravagant Wishes did they ever entertain" (316); "still might our Society be styled *the happy Family*" (327); and again, "Thus settled in their humble Cottage, still might our Society retain the Name of THE HAPPY FAMILY" (333).

When more desperate necessity follows, however, and preoccupation shifts to simply providing for the present and the future, the lines of economic dependency have already been knotted, and the cords begin to dig into the flesh. The losses, for one thing, have been incurred through the dishonesty of abusers of the law and through the bad advice of Ratcliff and Orgueil, while David and Camilla's eldest son has been, "by a strange Adoption, in a Manner excluded from his Birth-right" by being given his godfather Ratcliff's name of Peter (326), long before Ratcliff's whim dictates that he must be sent away from the family circle for an inferior schooling. Ratcliff as benign sponsor, the attorney as legal expert, the Orgueils as tolerated neighbors, all become tormentors with the capacity to influence group decisions through empty promises of favor and more real threats of displeasure. Since every decision must be weighed in financial rather than purely affective terms, the group is forced apart physically. After Peter's departure, the opportunity for Valentine and Cynthia to go to Jamaica forces them to place "any Prospect of Success in worldly Affairs" ahead of the previously primary value of a common life (336), and even the absolute separations caused by the deaths of Camilla's father and several of the children become the occasions of thankfulness that they are released from the community's increasing sufferings.[14]

In reducing her conversational circle to a state of poverty through such initially harmless and loose attachments, Fielding exposes the impracticability, in an increasingly interdependent economic structure, of a disinterested felicity as it is portrayed in Richardson and Henry Fielding and in her own first novel. In her detailed analysis of David's "Timidity" as a direct effect of the experience of "being, with a large dependent Family, in a Situation in Life, that you know not how to go out of, and yet are not able to support," possessed of a sociable nature whose "warm Affections . . . make you look with Dread and Horror on every Step you take, lest the Consequence of it should be any ways prejudicial to the chief Object of your Love" (351-52), Fielding confronts the ideal of the conversational circle with the implications of the fact that social man is not only sympathetically and epistemologically interdependent, but also economically so. This is of course not a new observation in the era of Mandeville, but its application to the model of the self-enclosed domestic circle arguably signals the end of the model's usefulness as a seriously posited alternative to, rather than a microcosm of, the larger structures which surround it.

At the start of this study, I noted the interchangeability of early eighteenth-century metaphors for commerce and conversation. In *Volume the Last,* the language of David Simple's property-sharing community is repeatedly portrayed as distinctive and incomprehensible to outsiders, as is the language of outsiders to David; this inability to communicate is particularly marked in the case of the most selfish and greedy characters of the novel. Conversations between Orgueil and David "always [leave] *David* in the highest Perplexity; for he [finds] all *Orgueil's* Discourse [leads] to something of which he [has] no Image" (364)—in other words, to self-admiration and the maintenance of the hearer's dependency—while David's own ability to flatter Orgueil is restricted by vivid visions of the needs of his wife and children. Similarly, Orgueil's definition of the word "friend" is so different from David's that it misleads his hearer in spite of himself into a state of greater enslavement. As for Orgueil's steward, the rapacious money-lender Nichols, David concludes, "You don't talk our Language, Sir" (369) after an abortive attempt to make him understand the sharing of property and sense of mutual obligation that characterizes his friendship with Valentine. Indeed, between members of David's family everything is "writ in the plural Number, 'if WE succeed,' and 'WE shall be happy,'" to express the assumed commonality of "one united Family" (362).

When Mr. Nichols visits David's household for the purpose of assessing his monetary value, the different worlds of meaning within which purely economic and purely sociable man exist are made particularly clear. Mr. Nichols, with his "Pair of Compasses, by which he [can] take as true a Measure of every Man's Disposition concerning Monies, as of his Lands" is, we are told, generally accurate in summing up the character of economic man—as long as he "[does] not meet with such Men as *David*" (371). A description of the industrious activity of David's household follows immediately upon Nichols' one-dimensional measure of the hero's value; in this description the fruits of orderly domestic labor, a flourishing garden, and a growing family are described in terms of "Plenty and Variety," "joyful Thanks," "the Height of Rapture," and "a Pleasure that the Great, at their luxurious Tables, might reflect on with Envy, and which all the Kingdoms of the Earth could not give to Minds unqualified for it" (373-74). However, the balance of labor and reward, production and consumption, which "our little united Family daily enjoy[s]" (374), proves founded on an illusion of the domestic circle as a closed and self-sufficient unit.

INDIVIDUALISM

Fielding repeatedly characterizes the larger society with which David's family is intertwined as driven by greed, pride, and envy, all manifestations of individualistic desire. Mr. Ratcliff, Mr. Orgueil, and Mrs. Orgueil respectively represent these antisocial impulses, which ironically combine and work through the hierarchical structures upheld by a traditional society to produce an effect of continual siege against the intimate community and what it represents. Mr. Ratcliff, for example, looks after David's legal interests in an "authoritative manner" (320), informally adopts his son, writing "what are called friendly Letters (though interspersed with that imperious advice which generally flows from superiority in point of Fortune)" (325), and solicits a pensioned place in government for David from "a very great Man" (336). It is only later that the reader is apprised of the fact that Mr. Ratcliff's ruling motives are the demands of his own "luxurious" nature and his passion for his vain and quarrelsome wife. When promises to David and his son become impediments to Mrs. Ratcliff's "great Necessity of a larger Fortune" in order to adorn herself in competition with a friend, the responsibility that attends authority is found entirely wanting, and desire easily defeats reason as Mr. Ratcliff convinces himself that to discard David and take the place for himself is but obeying the dictates of "Duty and Justice" (389).

Mr. Orgueil's need to preserve a rigid rationality in all of his actions, upon which he prides himself enormously, leads him to deflect true charity into meaninglessly theoretical advice about buying wholesale or heartless reproaches about expenses incurred in attempting to save his niece's life because "she was not his own Child; and it was a Shame for a Man, in *David*'s Circumstances, to spend his Substance on Strangers" (358). At the same time, he appears unaware that his supposed rationality is in fact a delight in keeping David in a state of abject dependence on him; we read that "Mr. *Orgueil*'s Wishes [are] all centered in keeping up to his Rule of Rectitude, in giving such Advice as might preserve and increase his Admiration of his own Wisdom, and still retain the Man he called his Friend in Slavery and Dependance" (364). Mrs. Orgueil's energies, on the other hand, are divided entirely between hatred of Cynthia as a rival wit and protection of the financial interests of herself and her daughter. Thus, as we have seen, she "[makes] herself a most miserable Woman, and perplex[es] and torment[s] her own Mind about nothing" (331), consumed with the possibility that her own social and financial power will be defeated by Cynthia's intellectual superiority, and that her beloved Miss Cassy "should . . . , during her whole Life, have one Jewel less for Mr. *Orgueil*'s Generosity" (361). Even her love for her daughter, we are told, reflects merely a preference for "something she [can] call her own," something that is "forced to yield the Preeminence," in its turn, "to a yet dearer Friend, namely, herself" (346).

Mr. and Mrs. Orgueil's complete self-enclosure as separate individuals paradoxically makes them together an example of egotistical domesticity. Conversation between Mr. and Mrs. Orgueil is a matter of aloof inattention to a weak woman's chatter on the part of the husband, who prefers "deep Debate with himself" (408), and of manipulation by flattery on the part of the wife. Unlike *Amelia,* with its implication that domestic loyalties are by definition virtuous, *Volume the Last* thus pointedly contrasts individualistic and sociable forms of domesticity. We are early informed that in David Simple's family, Cynthia and Camilla manage their household in those spare moments "when they [can] not have the Pleasure of conversing with their Husbands," conversation which "*David, Valentine,* and the old Gentleman" delight in as "amiable" (316); with Camilla, David "enjoy[s] the highest Pleasure that even his Imagination could ever have formed from the Union of two Hearts, capable of receiving, and disposed to give, reciprocal Delight" (322). Mrs. Orgueil is also pointedly contrasted to Cynthia in that her similar intellectual gifts are turned towards false rather than true social behavior. Thus she flatters Camilla as part of a plot to supplant Cynthia in her sister-in-law's favor, but her efforts are "fruitless" because these women's "extraordinary" friendship allows them to "[talk] over the Difference of their Capacities and Dispositions with the same Freedom as if they had been mentioning the Difference of their Height or Size" (330).

However, the Orgueils's conversational failings are not matched by a similar lack of influence over the physical well-being of the conversational circle which is so much their moral superior. Mr. Orgueil's refusal to give David more than useless advice contributes directly to the latter's ultimate recourse to Mr. Nichols, whose henchman, symbolically, destroys David's last house by fire; Mrs. Orgueil's cruelty and insensitivity to the children is directly responsible for several of their deaths. Even after the loss of all but the young Camilla has freed David from the greater part of his timidity, he is forced to seek a polite excuse for refusing Mrs. Orgueil's offer of educating his daughter because of the destructive potential of her hatred and anger if unleashed against the girl.

THE SELF-DESTRUCTION OF A COMMUNITY

In a dynamic similar to that established by Henry Fielding in *Amelia,* then, it appears that in Sarah Fielding's social vision the larger world in its corruption will inevitably resent and attack the little society which represents the ideal from which it has fallen; the group is in turn vulnerable because of its very virtues of conversational transparency, generous acceptance, and mutual affection. In *Amelia,* however, as well as in *Sir Charles Grandison* and *Humphry Clinker,* the domestic circle's vulnerability is located specifically in a desirous character who diverts or obstructs the ideal sociability of other members of the group through attempting to serve private ends. In the cases of William Booth, Charlotte Grandison, and Tabitha Bramble, some form of conversion to the domestic ideal finally establishes the stability of the little society. *Volume the Last's* circle, on the other hand, is invaded in its very retirement and is found vulnerable because of the perfect application of its ideals. For example, the economic power of Mr. Orgeuil and Mr. Ratcliff over the group is granted them in part because to be "guilty of even the Appearance of Rudeness or Ill-Manners, [is] repugnant to the Nature of any of this Society" (320), in part because the help offered them is what they would themselves have given without self-interested motives, but above all because David is "entangled in the Snare of his Love for others," whom he is afraid to see suffer (352). The reader is repeatedly told of the resulting "timidity" which leads the protagonist to act against the dictates of his own prudence and the advice of Cynthia; it is "by the Help of this Timidity [that] both Mr. *Ratcliff* and Mr. *Orgueil* [get] an

Ascendancy over the Mind of *David Simple,* that no Creature on Earth could ever have obtained, had SELF alone been his Consideration" (352). Because of his "Terror arising from Compassion" (354), David allows his "Inclination" to believe in his false friends to "[blind] his Judgment" (352).

Pursuing the implications of the communal ideal even further, Fielding makes the community's own expansion contribute to its vulnerability and inevitable destruction. In the relatively egalitarian spirit of *David Simple,* David's family becomes "exceedingly fond" of Farmer Dunster and his wife, tenant farmers of Mr. Orgueil, for their "Simplicity of . . . Manners," which prevents them from "affect[ing] to live *above their Station*"; nevertheless, through the farmer's dependency this relationship exposes them to the interference of Mrs. Orgueil. When they welcome to themselves the Dunster's daughter, teaching her to read and write and in turn learning from her knitting and spinning, Mrs. Orgueil pries her away from them "by taking her into [her] own Family" to learn "proper Employment for a Farmer's Daughter" (328), that is, to serve the whims of the Orgueils's spoiled daughter.

More extensively, *Volume the Last* emphasizes the circle's perpetuation of itself through its children and their education in the manner of *Pamela* Part II; we are informed that "the chief Study and Employment of our Society, was to improve the Understandings, and meliorate the Dispositions of their Children" (325-26). Unable to alter social structures as they are—the implication seems to be—the group will focus on the next generation as the basis of its hopes for expansion. However, the group is especially open to attack by virtue of this very self-perpetuation. Trusting, uncomplaining, and desirous of giving pleasure to others, the children of the circle are, especially when separated from their parents, easily victimized by the cruelty and negligence of Mrs. Orgueil. Her treatment of them is, as I have noted, a major factor in the deaths of three, and her final attempt to gain control over young Camilla is consciously motivated as an attack on the group: "although the long Friendship which had subsisted between *Cynthia* and *Camilla* had always baffled her Designs, yet . . . the young Mind of *David*'s Daughter would certainly bend under her Artifices, and yield to whatever Impressions she chose to give it" (416). More generally, David's concern for his children's financial provision leads him to submit them to the destructive "friendships" of the Ratcliffs and the Orgueils; in the case of "poor little *Peter,*" his death by smallpox becomes his escape from the influence of Mr. Ratcliff, who has destined him, in the name of kindness, to be "stigmatized with an Accusation of the highest and blackest Ingratitude" (389).

REAFFIRMING AND DISPLACING THE IDEAL

If these indications of the ideal circle's self-destructive qualities are taken in isolation, Lady Mary Wortley Montagu is not so facetiously off the mark as she herself clearly thinks, in writing to her daughter that Fielding's *Volume the Last* "conveys a usefull moral (tho' she does not seem to have intended it); I mean, shews the ill consequences of not providing against Casual losses, which happen to almost every body."[15] Such a reading of the novel, however, assumes that it is a descriptive narrative which accepts as given a society which is economically interdependent, and whose structures and relationships are controlled by individualistic self-interest. From this perspective, the ideal of a society held together by a complete congruence between the desires of individuals and the mutual good, the ideal upon which David Simple's community founds itself and for which it risks its future, is as "simple" as David's name and the reactions of others to him suggest. However, Fielding's denunciations of the abuse of those who are financially dependent provide a continuous thread, marked by some of her strongest writing, through both the original novel and its sequel, indicating that her critique is pointed more at the abuses of economic power than at the imprudence of those who find themselves without it. "Casual losses" may indeed "happen to almost every body," but Fielding insists that they are the result of immoral actions on the part of those who abuse social structures such as the law, and that their painful effects are exacerbated by those who do not feel the losses of others as their own. The sequel does not deconstruct the social ideal of the original; it heroicizes, rather, the perfect sympathy of this group, which survives individual weaknesses, suffering, and even death.[16]

By making social behavior an ethical issue in this way, Fielding makes response to the novel itself a matter of moral choice. This challenge is made explicit throughout the novel by means of the figure of the reader as judge. In differentiating "the capricious Judgments that are shewn in passing Sentence on the Worlds and Actions of a Man, who is actuated by no other Motives than the simple Dictates of an honest Heart," judgments generally made by "those who are blessed with Prosperity and Affluence," from "the Judgment of others, who, with the like beneficent Hearts [as David's], have been in the like Circumstances" (324-25), Fielding divides the implied audience into the Orgueils of this world and those who are able to sympathize with the central community. The reader is thereby put in a position much more like that of the narrator and his friend in Scott's *Millenium Hall* than that of the synthesizer of descriptions in Smollett's *Humphry Clinker*—she or he must decide whether or not to "go and do likewise."

Clearly, the reader is encouraged to align her- or himself with the imitators of David Simple, thereby becoming part of a community with the author and her characters. This community is bonded together by a sympathetic imagination; in the case of one "peculiar kind of tender Sensation" felt by David and Camilla, for example, the author "cannot pretend to give [her] Readers any Idea of [it], unless they will again assist [her], by the Help of their own Imaginations" (326). Such an implied community is portrayed in the preface as already created, broadening the base of the experiential authority claimed by the narrator: she has experienced what David has experienced, and is confident of the corroboration of readers who have shared in those experiences, if not in actual fact, through their reading of David Simple's story. Thus she presents the characters to her readers as "their old Friends, with whom if they were once pleased by them, they will undoubtedly not be displeased to renew their former Acquaintance" (309-10).

At the same time, Fielding implies that any community of sympathy consists of individuals who are ultimately alone. Conversation, for example, evolves from the pleasures of intense participation in one another's responses and of making one another happy in *David Simple* to an increasingly stoic silence on the part of each member of the group about their mutual sufferings, together with an acceptance of one another's commitment to the group that makes words unnecessary, in *Volume the Last*. This refinement of the conversational ideal is clearly intended as a contrast to the selfish affectation of Mrs. Orgueil, who parades her feelings in order to prove her sensibility, and to the hypocritical professions of friendship that roll so easily from the tongues of Mr. Orgueil and Mr. Ratcliff. Valentine's letter upon the death of his child and the prospect of his own financial success, for example, neither dwells on the "melancholy Subject" nor contains "Professions of Friendship" and "Promises of *lending* or *giving*" (362). In the same way, Cynthia's letter after the loss of Valentine leaves her own grief unspoken in consideration of the effect upon the letter's recipients and in confidence that their sympathetic imaginations will supply the rest. By Mrs. Orgueil, of course, Cynthia's reticence is misinterpreted as unworthy even the death of a pet monkey, while Mr. Orgueil is deaf to David's requests for help because they do not elaborate enough on his misery and desperate need of friendship to allow for grand professions of condescending kindness in return. At the conclusion of the novel, the conversation of David and Cynthia, the original and sole surviving friends, has been so purged of the unnecessary that the narrator can summarize it with the words "It is sufficient to say, that they spoke the Words dictated by the Hearts of *Cynthia* and *David Simple*" (427). Self-narration, which was accepted as an indicator of a sociable and transparently virtuous self for Cynthia and Camilla in *David Simple,* is now ideally absent as an indication of the self-control of individuals in consideration of the feelings of the group. This altered treatment of conversation indicates a new ideal of unselfconscious behavior; as in *Amelia,* the less articulate a character is, the less self-absorbed and, therefore, the more transparent and trustworthy.[17]

A corollary of this shift, however, one which becomes very visible in the novel's focus on David's state of mind, is the resultant isolation of the suffering individual even in the midst of the ideal community. As legal owner of the group's property, as husband and father, as a naturally naive idealist, David is the community's most vulnerable member. Because of this intense focus, un-interrupted by inset narratives and heightened by the sense of inevitability created by stating the story's outcome from the beginning, the group's gradual dismantling around him is felt primarily as his increasing loneliness in a hos-tile world. Exacerbating the effects of physical separation and death are the repeated points when, as we have seen, he feels forced to act against the better judgment of other members of the group, and when he is denied the help of the so-called friends who are his social cohorts as heads of families. Thus *Volume the Last* redefines the self in a shift opposite to that of the first part of *David Simple:* the well-being built upon the social foundation of a "Union of Hearts" is relocated in the individual "Christian Mind, whose Reliance on a future State is its only Foundation for Happiness" (333) and whose task is therefore an essentially solitary one.

It is upon the final inner state of David Simple rather than upon the future of the community he established that the novel's conclusion rests, and it is here that Fielding makes her last statement about the paradox of commu-nity which renders it unviable in this world. Motivated entirely by his desire to protect his wife and family, David has nonetheless seen all but his sister-in-law Cynthia and his daughter Camilla die. When he is reduced to virtual solitude by Camilla's death, David ironically regains a self-sufficiency which makes him immune to the assaults of this world; we read that "as Mr. *Orgueil* had not, with his whole Fortune, the Power of giving him equal Pleasure [as when Ca-milla was alive], so neither had he the Power of tormenting him, as when he cruelly refused to relieve his beloved *Camilla*. She was out of the Reach of feeling the Effects of Hardness of Heart, and consequently *David* could never again feel the same Strokes. His own Pains, indeed, might force from him a Groan; but it must be the Sufferings of another that could quite dissolve and overcome all his Resolutions" (414). Since social ties are inseparably linked to a state of economic connectedness, David can now transcend financial con-straints, "imagin[ing] himself possessed of great Riches, in Comparison of what he had been from the Time he dreaded his *Camilla*'s Distress" (414).

In a second twist of the ironic knife, however, even this regained im-penetrability comes too late, because the inevitable result of a perfect state of community, of a complete identification of the self with the being of another, is a fatal injury to that self's integrity, described by the narrator as "a Rent in [David's] Heart, which he vainly endeavoured to heal" (415). In striking con-trast to the physical motion which in the original novel allowed a solitary David to detach himself from disappointment and continue on in pursuit of his desire, the reader is told that "he attempt[s] not, by flying from Place to Place, to hide from his own Mind the Death of *Camilla*" because "he [knows], unless he [can] fly from himself, the picture [can] not be rooted from his Heart" (415). In the face of this paradox, David's only hope of resolution is in death.[18]

In this rewriting of the conversational community, then, Sarah Fielding neither modifies the terms of the model nor wavers in her insistence that it offers the means to the highest possible social happiness in this life. However, by tracing the progress of the ideal through a test situation, as it were, a situation of interrelated external and internal pressures,[19] she makes explicit the implicit assumptions which have enabled her contemporaries to construct an exclusive and static social circle in their fictions and then claim its applicability to the social world outside of the novel. Fielding thereby displaces the ideal community of shared conversational and material wealth back into the heavenly city of Bunyan's *Pilgrim's Progress,* proving that "although no Scheme for Happiness could be built on a better Foundation than [David Simple's]; although the Union of Hearts, which subsisted in that happy Family, was sufficient to compensate every common outward Evil; yet there may be such a Concurrence of Events, such heart-rending Scenes, arising from this very friendly Connection, as must undeniably prove the Truth of that Observation, . . . 'That solid and lasting Happiness is not to be attained in this World'" (313-14).

Although the prominence of death in Fielding's *Volume the Last* may at first seem a mawkish or melodramatic appeal to the reader's sensibilities, its overwhelming presence in fact lends force to an egalitarian vision by providing the only inescapable check to the egotism of characters such as the Orgueils.[20] That death which, according to David Simple's Christian schema, validates and will realize his own social ideal, is the same death which all of Mrs. Orgueil's schemes are designed to disguise; indeed, her sole "Grain of what is commonly called Compassion," unmoved by "any of the Vicissitudes or Chances of this mortal Life," is aroused by the occasional intrusion of "the Image, that both herself and her Miss *Cassy* must, one time or another, share the common Fate, and fall a Sacrifice to Death" (361). The mutability that has displaced the social ideal out of this life for David and his little society thus becomes the impetus to its replacement by a symbolic community of all humankind before this inexorably egalitarian end. The inability of such a community to penetrate the determined self-absorption of Mr. and Mrs. Orgueil in the former's supposed last illness emphasizes just how intangible it is as a basis for social relations. Nevertheless, given the prevalence of greed, pride, and envy in the fictional world of Sarah Fielding, the only hope for deflecting the individual from pursuit of his or her own private desires into a concern for the common good ultimately lies not in a social ideal which may motivate an exceptional few, but in a recognition of the common solitude of death. The task of the novelist thus becomes one of a portrayal of the common condition of humanity as an essential solitude whose potential recognition by the reader is in itself the fundamental act of community.

Conclusion

A Failed Plot? The Fate of the Conversational Circle in English Fiction

Of all things, banish the egotism out of your conversation . . . ; conversation-stock being a joint and common property.
                    —Lord Chesterfield, letter to his son

The conversable world join to a sociable disposition, and a taste for pleasure, an inclination for the easier and more gentle exercises of the understanding, for obvious reflections on human affairs, and the duties of common life, and for observation of the blemishes or perfections of the particular objects that surround them. Such subjects of thought furnish not sufficient employment in solitude, but require the company and conversation of our fellow-creatures, to render them a proper exercise for the mind; and this brings mankind together in society, where every one displays his thoughts in observations in the best manner he is able, and mutually gives and receives information, as well as pleasure.
                    —David Hume, "Of Essay Writing"

I hardly ever met with more simplicity and good sense than they both have, and it is with some degree of pleasure that I sit in an evening with them, and hear the discourse and gossipings of the day: it makes me smile often, and sometimes rises to a downright laugh; and whatever promotes and causes this, with innocence and good humour, is as eligible (as far as I know, in the way of conversation) and as worthy to be ranked of the sort called delightful and pleasing, as in the routs and hurricanes of the great, or at court, or even in company with my Lord Chesterfield.
                    —Mary Collier, letter to Samuel Richardson

To live in a family where there is but one heart, and as many good strong heads as persons, and to have a place in that enlarged single

heart, is such a state of happiness as I cannot hear of without feeling the utmost pleasure. Methinks, in such a house, each word that is uttered must sink into the hearer's mind, as the kindly falling showers in April sink into the teeming earth, and enlarge and ripen every idea, as those friendly drops do the new-sown grain, or the water-wanting plant. There is nothing in all the works of nature or of art too trifling to give pleasure, where there is such a capacity to enjoy it, as must be found in such an union.
—Sarah Fielding, letter to Samuel Richardson

I began this study of mid-eighteenth-century fictions of the conversational circle with these and other statements suggesting a widespread contemporary interest in the conversational circle as a paradigm for a renewed sociability. A significant number of the period's writers clearly felt a moral responsibility to both describe and model such a circle, thus at once claiming it to be a natural social formation and revealing it to be the product of the writers' desire for consensus and stability in the face of perceived societal fragmentation. The attempt to realize in fiction a social ideal that would in fact circumscribe and limit the perceived excesses of individualistic desire gave rise to a number of creative formal solutions, solutions deserving of recognition as a conservative strain in early English fiction.

And yet, as I have shown, portrayals of the mid-eighteenth-century ideal of the conversational circle contained from the start the seeds of its dissolution. Despite the temporary prominence of the ideal in the general cultural discourse and in fiction, it was doomed to failure ideologically, rather than formally, because of its reluctance to confront the tension between its egalitarian and expansive implications and a traditionally hierarchical and patriarchal (and increasingly class-divided) social structure. Sarah Fielding, the author whose *Adventures of David Simple* very early presents an idealized portrait of an intimate conversational circle emerging out of a fragmented society, is later the one to elaborate the most rigorous contest between that model conversational community and its social context. Against such an adversary, with its hierarchical structure open to abuse by egotistical individuals, the conversational circle, Fielding appears to conclude, is inviable. The sober warning, in the Preface to Sarah Fielding's 1753 *David Simple, Volume the Last*, that this is a narrative intended "to illustrate that well known Observation, that 'The Attainment of our Wishes is but too often the Beginning of our Sorrows,'" seems a long way from David Hume's confident project for constructing a "conversable world" through literary discourse, though only a decade separates the two texts.

In the meantime, however, the rich fictional experimentation fueled by this project deserves better than the critical neglect, if not outright derision, it has often received. Sarah Fielding's first novel and Samuel Richardson's *Pamela*

Part II succeed in evolving, out of confrontations between virtuous, essentially sociable individuals and a corrupt society, finely balanced and stable domestic communities—in Fielding's case, that community is the relatively egalitarian circle of David Simple and his family, in Richardson's case, the more authoritarian and tightly enclosed, but nevertheless feminocentric, circle of Pamela as Mrs. B. Richardson's *Sir Charles Grandison,* following upon his brilliant analysis of dysfunctional social structures in *Clarissa,* is perhaps the most ambitious and optimistic of the fictions I have discussed: in this his final work he models a conversational circle at once perfectly balanced and expansive, ultimately including such figures as predatory rakes, Italian Catholics, and greedy stepmothers among the converts to the virtues of domestic harmony. In the process, moreover, he creates a theory of feminized narration, exploiting an idealized female desire as self-effacing and utterly socializable.

With Henry Fielding's *Amelia* the wheel begins to turn. Although perhaps more ambitious than Richardson in foregrounding the problem of culturally approved but socially unruly male desire, Fielding resolves this problem by portraying a perfectly stabilized circle around a passive female center. As a result he posits only a private solution, not an expansively transforming one, and his perfected circle can only retreat from the vortiginous chaos of public life. In Sarah Scott's *Millenium Hall* and Tobias Smollett's *Humphry Clinker,* stasis and conversational consensus are realized only by marginalizing the intimate community and by sidestepping altogether the dynamic of heterosexual desire upon which the domestic circle is predicated.

As the publication dates of *Millenium Hall* (1762) and *Humphry Clinker* (1771) show, the formal structure of the intimate conversational circle survived Sarah Fielding's *Volume the Last;* however, its ideological promise of consensus and the stabilization of desire proved as short-lived as its marginalization in the two later novels suggests. Indeed, Sarah Fielding and Jane Collier's *The Cry: A New Dramatic Fable,* published in the year after *Volume the Last,* is a lengthy exemplum of the conversational ideal's unworkability in a hostile social context. This highly experimental work is taken up with the heroine Portia's painstaking defense of her thoughts and words, supported by Una, who represents truth, and continually interrupted by the Cry who, as the followers of Error, represent general public opinion. The heroine speaks of delightful exchanges in the intimate circle she shares with her husband-to-be and his sister, and ultimately forms a "sweet retreat" together with them and her former female adversary, now penitent. However, such conversation is never achieved in this fiction, despite the fact that the narrative consists entirely of dialogue; the exchanges portrayed are part of a constant debate between an embattled Portia and a mob which delights only in attack, no matter how arbitrary and unpredictable the grounds for it. The suggestion of Fielding's conclusion to *David Simple* seems borne out here: the ideal of the conversational circle, while it is yet to be embodied in such isolated fictional havens as Millenium Hall and the Bramble fireside, is doomed to be left waiting in the wings of the real world while the preliminary task of the virtuous individual—to justify her conduct before the hostile scrutiny of society—occupies the stage in an endless prologue.

Another conversational survivor, Laurence Sterne's *Life and Opinions of Tristram Shandy, Gentleman* (1759-67) spins out in multi-volumed detail its portrayal of the paralysis of the intimate domestic circle as a means to social change. At the same time, the subjectivity of Tristram telling his story becomes in itself the story, pointing to the future direction of the mainstream English novel. Consensus, if it occurs, takes the form of the momentary sentimental encounters of Sterne's *A Sentimental Journey through France and Italy* (1768), without any communal framework or conversational foundation to bring subjectively limited individuals into a common affirmation of more than the most generalized social truths.[1]

Later authors indeed draw on the formal possibilities of the novel focusing upon an intimate circle rather than an isolated individual—but as a means of portraying the self living among other selves in a social, moral, and economic microcosm. Frances Burney's 1796 *Camilla, or A Picture of Youth* develops the motif of a circle of characters whose experiences are all in some sense parallel, but whose life trajectories differ widely (as for the *Grandison* women) according to the complex variations of character and circumstance that are their lots, and (as in Smollett's *Humphry Clinker*) according to their range of subjective responses to experience. For the circle of children that surrounds the little Camilla as "fairy mistress of the ceremonies" at the novel's opening, the protective bounds of the domestic circle are soon broken; Camilla herself eventually returns from her wilderness to the encircling arms of family and lover, but for others there is no return to the exclusive circle. Community, for Burney, is subject to the divisive force of "individual experience" as the source of "injustice, . . . narrowness, and . . . arrogance" simply because "What, at last, so diversified as man? what so little to be judged by his fellow?"[2]

This full intrusion of plurality and epistemological uncertainty into the intimate group signals the chief formal contribution of the conversational circle to the novel. Jane Austen's novels, for example, explore the dynamics of the restricted circle to the fullest, using conversation as well as the internal states of characters to develop the relationship of the individual to her group, as that group's product and as a contributor to its corporate nature in turn. In Burney and Austen, it is the authoritative narrator, like the narrator of *David Simple, Volume the Last,* who presides over the text as guide to its meaning; this persona's voice is transparent and generalized, as though speaking for the reader the interpretive conclusions she or he is inevitably drawing. Epistemological authority, in other words, has been displaced from the represented conversational circle to a virtual circle of like-minded readers, whose own judgment is not unjust, arrogant, or narrow because it is socialized by the very act of reading.

Treatments of the conversational ideal in *The Cry* and *Tristram Shandy* thus support Michael McKeon's observation that after the mid-eighteenth century, the history of the novel records the process by which "hypostatized over against the individual, 'society' slowly separates from 'self' . . . , a ponderous and alienated structure whose massive impingement on the individual paradoxically signifies the latter's autonomy, the very fact of the individual's 'rise,' as well as the subjection of self to this greater power."[3] From a retrospective view of "the rise of the novel," then, the most explicit fictions of the conversational circle, those which most fully elaborate its social model, are roads not taken because their claim to be descriptive, to describe a newly formed conversable world, was quickly felt to be prescriptive and sterile, untrue to the realities of individual and social experience. At the same time, they hold a significant place in literary history because their formal innovations offered new modes of narration, characterization, and plot to the coalescing category of the novel as genre. More to the point, in my view, to overlook these fictions of Richardson, the Fieldings, Scott, and Smollett, together with the self-conscious prescriptive project they represent, is to skew our critical understanding of the range of technical and ideological experiments carried out in novels of the mid-eighteenth century. And above all, as I hope this study has shown, we as dismissive readers suffer a loss because of the inherent interest of these texts: as components of their authors' comprehensive social visions, as participants in the discourse of sociability of the mid-eighteenth century, and simply as unique fictions.

Notes

INTRODUCTION

1. David Hume, "Of Essay Writing," *Essays Moral, Political and Literary* (London: Oxford Univ. Press, 1963), 568. Further citations are to this edition, and are indicated in the text in parentheses.

2. John Mullan, *Sentiment and Sociability: The Language of Feeling in the Eighteenth Century* (Oxford: Clarendon, 1988), 25. Leland E. Warren ("Turning Reality Round Together: Guides to Conversation in Eighteenth-Century England," *Eighteenth-Century Life* 8 [1983]: 65-87) and Ralph S. Pomeroy ("Hume's Proposed League of the Learned and Conversible Worlds," *Eighteenth-Century Studies* 19 [1986]: 373-94) have also drawn attention to this essay.

3. See Ian Watt's *Rise of the Novel: Studies in Defoe, Richardson and Fielding* (London: Chatto and Windus, 1957), and more recently, Mikhail M. Bakhtin, whose insistently binary system leads him to read as the universal plot of the novel the struggle "to liberate [oneself] from the authority of the other's discourse" (*The Dialogic Imagination: Four Essays,* ed. Michael Holquist, trans. Caryl Emerson and Michael Holquist [Austin: Univ. of Texas Press, 1981], 348). Terry Castle similarly reinforces the inherited paradigm in *Masquerade and Civilization: The Carnivalesque in Eighteenth-Century Culture and Fiction* (Stanford: Stanford Univ. Press, 1986) when she adopts Bakhtin's interpretation of the narrative impulse as inherently subversive or carnivalesque; for this reason she elevates into prominence the masquerades of *Pamela* Part II, as an "escape from the tedium of plotlessness and the burdens of [Richardson's] own intractable ideological project" (152), and of *Amelia,* as "a submerged will toward scandal and impertinence" (199), thereby fitting even these recalcitrant fictions into a Watt-cum-Bakhtin critical understanding of the novel. Castle, indeed, suggests the inapplicability of this emphasis on individualism and subversion to a significant number of eighteenth-century novels when she concludes that although "subversive desire" has been the "charismatic hidden theme in European fiction since the eighteenth century," the masquerade device is only necessary until "the fate of the individual, rather than the representation of a shared public landscape, becomes the overriding subject of realistic writing" (343-44).

4. John Bender, *Imagining the Penitentiary: Fiction and the Architecture of Mind in Eighteenth-Century England* (Chicago: Univ. of Chicago Press, 1987), 61; see also 213, 274 n.27.

5. Michael McKeon, *The Origins of the English Novel, 1600-1740* (Baltimore: Johns Hopkins Univ. Press, 1987), 90, 22. Similarly, Leopold Damrosch (*Fictions of Reality in the Age of Hume and Johnson* [Madison: Univ. of Wisconsin Press, 1989] and William Ray (*Story and History: Narrative Authority and Social Identity in the Eighteenth-Century French and English Novel* [Cambridge, Mass.: Blackwell, 1990] have viewed their writers as striving at once "to elicit and to create the consensus to which they appeal" (Damrosch, 5). Ray finds that "more developed versions of individualism in the middle third of the century address the relationship of personal experience and collective authority positively, aligning individualism with the conscious interrogation and renovation of institutions of authority,

and redefining authoritative discourse as consensus opinion modeled on exemplary personal narrative" (98). Ray's argument is, however, limited in that he deliberately builds it, with respect to English fiction, on the canonical core of novels: *Robinson Crusoe, Moll Flanders, Roxana, Pamela, Clarissa, Joseph Andrews,* and *Tom Jones,* as well as *Tristram Shandy.* While this approach does provide a corrective in its reinsertion of individualistic narrative into the period's understanding of discourse as inherently communal, it reinforces, as a result, the impression that the story of eighteenth-century fiction is one of an ever-intensifying bid for mastery of the "social grammar" on the part of the individualist (101). Even though this story's moral, according to Ray, is the inevitable defeat of the individual by a system increasingly posited as abstracted and impersonal, the fundamental plot of the individual opposed to society remains unchanged.

6. I am invoking here Hannah Arendt's interpretation of authority as incompatible with either "external means of coercion" or "persuasion, which presupposes equality and works through a process of argumentation"; the stability of an authoritative framework for social relations "rests neither on common reason nor on the power of the one who commands," depending rather on an acceptance of the framework's (or "hierarchy"'s) "rightness and legitimacy" ("What is Authority?" in her *Between Past and Future: Eight Exercises in Political Thought* [New York: Viking, 1968], 93).

7. These terms are Betty Rizzo's, in *Companions without Vows: Relationships among Eighteenth-Century British Women* (Athens: Univ. of Georgia Press, 1994), 307.

8. Nancy Armstrong, in *Desire and Domestic Fiction: A Political History of the Novel* (New York: Oxford Univ. Press, 1987), locates in Victorian fiction the first instance of "a shift in moral emphasis from the claims of the individual asserted through female desire to those of the community, which required such desire to submit to rational control" (56). My examination of mid-eighteenth-century portrayals of individual desire subordinated to the demands of community suggests that this concern finds recurrent expression in the history of the novel rather than appearing as a break of the Victorian novel with its past.

1. CONSENSUS, THE CONVERSATIONAL CIRCLE, AND MID-EIGHTEENTH-CENTURY FICTION

1. See J.G.A. Pocock, *The Machiavellian Moment: Florentine Political Thought and the Atlantic Republican Tradition* (Princeton: Princeton Univ. Press, 1975), chs. 12-14, and Carol Kay, *Political Constructions: Defoe, Richardson, and Sterne in Relation to Hobbes, Hume, and Burke* (Ithaca, N.Y.: Cornell Univ. Press, 1988), 8, 19-44.

2. J.C.D. Clark, *English Society 1688-1832: Ideology, Social Structure and Political Practice during the Ancien Regime* (Cambridge: Cambridge Univ. Press, 1985); E.P. Thompson, *Customs in Common* (London: Merlin, 1991), 87-90, 71, also 31-33; Tom Nairn, *The Break-Up of Britain: Crisis and Neo-Nationalism* (London: NLB, 1977), 21-22, 28-29.

3. Robert Markley, "Sentimentality as Performance: Shaftesbury, Sterne, and the Theatrics of Virtue," in *The New Eighteenth Century: Theory, Politics, English Literature,* ed. Felicity Nussbaum and Laura Brown (London: Methuen, 1987), 216. See also John Mullan, *Sentiment and Sociability: The Language of Feeling in the Eighteenth Century* (Oxford: Clarendon, 1988), 8-12, 18-39, for a detailed study of Hume's adaptation of the Shaftesburean blend of philosophical discourse and politeness into a conversational style of social philosophy directed to readers of a "middle station" (12).

4. William Law, *A Serious Call to a Devout and Holy Life, Adapted to the State and Condition of All Orders of Christians* (New York: Stanford, 1856), 250-51.

5. Mary Collyer, *Felicia to Charlotte* (London, 1744 and 1749; rpt. New York: Garland, 1974), 101-2, 35-36, 28-29.

6. Joseph Addison and Richard Steele, *The Spectator,* ed. Donald F. Bond, 5 vols. (Oxford: Clarendon, 1965), 1:210. Further citations of *The Spectator* are to this edition and will be indicated in the text by volume and page numbers in parentheses.

7. Jack Prostko's "'Natural Conversation Set in View': Shaftesbury and Moral Speech," *Eighteenth-Century Studies* 23 (1989): 42-61, discusses some of the tensions inherent in turn-of-the-century concepts of the social self. His identification of the principal conflict as existing between a humanistic, gentlemanly view of conversation as a reflection of moral character and a bourgeois notion of proper speech as merely a matter of effective social formulas, however, assigns moral values along class lines in a too-generalized fashion that ignores the kind of synthesis attempted by mid-century writers.

8. J. Paul Hunter has identified this social stratum in *Before Novels: The Cultural Context of Eighteenth-Century English Fiction* (New York: Norton, 1990), chs. 3-5, as the primary novel-reading audience of the period.

9. Daniel Defoe, *The Family Instructor,* 2 vols. (1841; rpt., New York: AMS, 1973), 1:128, 139, 355.

10. Indeed, the ostensibly politically and socially neutral figure of the domestic woman, Nancy Armstrong argues, enables the aristocratic social model to be replaced in eighteenth-century England by a private, contractual, gendered model of the household, with the figure of a wife, mother, and household manager at its focal point (*Desire and Domestic Fiction: A Political History of the Novel* [New York: Oxford Univ. Press, 1987], 59-95). See also Lawrence Stone, *The Family, Sex and Marriage in England 1500-1800* (New York: Harper and Row, 1974), Randolph Trumbach, *The Rise of the Egalitarian Family: Aristocratic Kinship and Domestic Relations in Eighteenth-Century England* (New York: Academic Press, 1978), and Jean H. Hagstrum, *Sex and Sensibility: Ideal and Erotic Love from Milton to Mozart* (Chicago: Univ. of Chicago Press, 1980) for views of marriage ideals in the period as increasingly affective and egalitarian while also lingeringly patriarchal. Subsequent work has tended to emphasize the appropriation of the rhetoric of affect and companionship to patriarchal ideology (see Ellen Pollak, *The Politics of Sexual Myth: Gender and Ideology in the Verse of Swift and Pope* [Chicago: Univ. of Chicago Press, 1985], ch. 1).

11. John Locke, *An Essay Concerning Human Understanding,* ed. Peter H. Nidditch (Oxford: Clarendon, 1979), 405.

12. Thomas Hobbes, *Leviathan, Or the Matter, Forme and Power of a Commonwealth Ecclesiasticall and Civil,* ed. Michael Oakeshott (Oxford: Blackwell, 1947), 22.

13. The intimate connection between commerce and conversation has an impact, Pocock points out, on concepts of the self: "Once property was seen to have a symbolic value, . . . the foundations of personality themselves appeared imaginary or at best consensual: the individual could exist, even in his own sight, only at the fluctuating value imposed upon him by his fellows" (*Machiavellian Moment,* 440, 455-57, 464).

14. M[ikhail] M. Bakhtin, *The Dialogic Imagination: Four Essays,* ed. Michael Holquist, trans. Caryl Emerson and Michael Holquist (Austin: Univ. of Texas Press, 1981), 369.

15. Hobbes, *Leviathan,* 22.

16. Samuel Johnson, *The Plan of a Dictionary of the English Language,* in *Dr. Johnson: Prose and Poetry,* selected by Mona Wilson (Cambridge, Mass.: Harvard Univ. Press, 1963), 138. See Carey McIntosh, *Common and Courtly Language: The Stylistics of Social Class in Eighteenth-Century English Literature* (Philadelphia: Univ. of Pennsylvania Press, 1986), 46-53, for a discussion of the development of the prescriptive grammar in the second half of the century; although McIntosh places this phenomenon late in the century, the social concerns it reflects seem to me to have been present in a generalized form earlier in the period.

John Barrell, in *English Literature in History, 1730-80: An Equal, Wide Survey* (London: Hutchinson, 1983) also notes an increasing focus on polite speech, defined as the language of the disinterested landed gentleman, as a means of social regulation and of reinforcing existing social stratification.

17. Henry Fielding, *The Covent-Garden Journal* 4 (January 14, 1752), in his *"The Covent-Garden Journal" and "A Plan of the Universal Register-Office,"* ed. Bertrand A. Goldgar (Oxford: Clarendon, 1988), 35-38.

18. See, for example, *Spectator* Nos. 24, 49, 155, 521. I am thus identifying a model of conversation that sets itself against the public, urban, and masculine one frequently discussed in studies of the coffeehouse culture of the period.

19. Philip, Fourth Earl of Chesterfield, *The Letters of the Earl of Chesterfield to His Son*, ed. Charles Strachey, 2 vols. (London: Methuen, 1901), 1:281.

20. Edward Young, *The Complaint: Or, Night Thoughts*, in *The Poetical Works of Edward Young* (London: Bell and Daldy; rpt. Westport, Conn.: Greenwood, 1970), 1:29.

21. See Chesterfield, 2:3, 218, 143; James Boswell, *Life of Johnson*, ed. R.W. Chapman, corrected J.D. Fleeman (London: Oxford Univ. Press, 1970), 122, 543.

22. Mary Collier, in *The Correspondence of Samuel Richardson*, ed. Anna Letitia Barbauld, 6 vols. (London, 1804; rpt. New York: AMS, 1966), 2:74-75.

23. Leland E. Warren, "Turning Reality Round Together: Guides to Conversation in Eighteenth-Century England," *Eighteenth-Century Life* 7 (1983): 76. Similarly, Lennard J. Davis's "Conversation and Dialogue," *The Age of Johnson* 1 (1987): 347-73, speculates that conversation in novels is an ideological device for creating an illusion of dialogism while ultimately serving monologic and authoritarian purposes.

24. Barbara R. Hanning, in "Conversation and Musical Style in the Late Eighteenth-Century Parisian Salon," *Eighteenth-Century Studies* 22 (1989): 512-28, draws a further parallel between "polite society's elevation of conversation as an art form" and the new popularity of the musical *style dialogué*, especially in the string quartet (512).

25. See Mario Praz, *Conversation Pieces: A Survey of the Informal Group Portrait in Europe and America* (University Park: Pennsylvania State Univ. Press, 1971), 15-23, 34, 68-71, 128.

26. J.H. Plumb, "Lordly Pleasures," *Horizon* 25 (1973): 77.

27. Ronald Paulson, *Emblem and Expression: Meaning in English Art of the Eighteenth Century* (London: Thames and Hudson, 1975), 115, 121-36, 44-47. See also Paulson's *Popular and Polite Art in the Age of Hogarth and Fielding* (Notre Dame: Univ. of Notre Dame Press, 1979), 44-46.

28. Michael G. Ketcham, *Transparent Designs: Reading, Performance, and Form in the "Spectator" Papers* (Athens: Univ. of Georgia Press, 1985), 5.

29. See J.G.A. Pocock, *Machiavellian Moment*, chs. 10-12, and Robert D. Moynihan, "'Dwarfs of Wit and Learning': Problems of Historical Time," *Probability, Time, and Space in Eighteenth-Century Literature*, ed. Paula R. Backscheider (New York: AMS, 1979), 172, 179.

30. Jonathan Swift, *The Battle of the Books, A Tale of a Tub, with Other Early Works 1696-1707*, ed. Herbert Davis (Oxford: Blackwell, 1965), 150.

31. Edmund Burke, *Reflections on the Revolution in France*, ed. J.G.A. Pocock (Indianapolis: Hackett, 1987), 29-30. Ronald Paulson, in *Emblem and Expression*, summarizes the "Burkean" notion of the self's ideal fixity: "Central is the sense of place which promotes the moral conditions necessary for a stable social order: a sense of continuity in the collective life of man, personal attachment to the past, and a sense of the firmness and gravity of land and society. The self only exists as a part of and in relationship to his society, its social forms, institutions, and past, and the imperatives its welfare makes upon the individual. Personal happiness comes through the fond memories and instinctual ties a society engenders" (155).

32. Alexander Pope, *An Essay on Man,* in his *Poetical Works,* ed. Herbert Davis (London: Oxford Univ. Press, 1966), 1:86-90; 4:358, 363-72.

33. Fielding, *Covent-Garden Journal,* 218-19. In Thompson's words, the gentry "withdrew increasingly from face-to-face relations with the people in village and town. The rage for deer parks and the threat of poachers led to the closure of rights of way across their parks and their encirclement with high palings or walls; landscape gardening, with ornamental waters and fish ponds, menageries and valuable statuary, accentuated their seclusion and the defenses of their grounds, which might be entered only through the high wrought-iron gates, watched over by the lodge" (45).

34. Samuel Johnson, *The Rambler,* ed. W.J. Bate and Albrecht B. Strauss (New Haven, Conn.: Yale Univ. Press, 1969), 3:19-22.

35. One might ask if the fictions we are looking at, with their topical, repetitive, non-conflictual characteristics, are finally distinguishable from non-fiction works such as *The Spectator,* with its unifying persona and dramatic sketches. Nelson Goodman ("Twisted Tales; or, Story, Study, and Symphony," in *On Narrative,* ed. W.J.T. Mitchell [Chicago: Univ. of Chicago Press, 1981]) suggests as a guideline that although narrative can survive many transformations of temporal order, it is nullified when its topical, expressive, and aesthetic alignments completely supersede its chronology (111-15). I would add to this the indicator that in narrative fiction this relatively coherent chronological dimension is fixed to a character, or characters, not necessarily consistent in modern psychological terms, but at least continuous in terms of name and other identifying markers.

36. These generalizations about the novels I am examining parallel a number of David Mickelson's in "Types of Spatial Structure in Narrative," in *Spatial Form in Narrative,* ed. J.R. Smitten and A. Daghistany (Ithaca, N.Y.: Cornell Univ. Press, 1981): 63-78. Mickelson describes the "spatial form novel" as "an alternative to the *Bildungsroman.* It offers a *Bild,* a picture; it portrays someone who has *already* developed, who is largely past change. . . . The progress of the narrative, then, involves uncovering a more or less static picture" (65).

37. Laurence Sterne, *The Life and Opinions of Tristram Shandy, Gentleman,* ed. Ian Campbell Ross (Oxford: Oxford Univ. Press, 1983), 87. In its elaboration of the conversational circle to the point of absurdity, Sterne's novel testifies at once to the general cultural interest in the model and to its ultimate loss of prescriptive credibility. See my conclusion for further comments on *Tristram Shandy* and on the fate of the conversational ideal.

2. CONSTRUCTING THE CIRCLE IN SARAH FIELDING'S *DAVID SIMPLE*

1. Sarah Fielding to Samuel Richardson, in *The Correspondence of Henry and Sarah Fielding,* ed. Martin C. Battestin and Clive T. Probyn (Oxford: Clarendon, 1993), 130. Further references to this text will be indicated by *Correspondence* and page numbers in parentheses. Betty Rizzo's recent work on the community of women centered in the Bath area during Fielding's later life suggests that Fielding eventually, at least to some extent, found such a community for herself (*Companions without Vows: Relationships among Eighteenth-Century British Women* [Athens: Univ. of Georgia Press, 1994], ch. 13). See also ch. 8, note 4, below.

2. Rizzo, 307.

3. Sarah Fielding, *The Adventures of David Simple,* ed. Malcolm Kelsall (Oxford: Oxford Univ. Press, 1969), 304. Further references to the novel are taken from this edition, which is based on the 1744 second edition, and are indicated by page numbers in parentheses.

4. The broadening of "experience" through conversation, together with the reduction of direct conflict discussed below, are described by Malcolm Kelsall as a "refusal to render

the substance of life dramatically" (Introduction to Oxford edition, *Adventures of David Simple,* xii). Kelsall's comparison of this method to that of Steele in *The Tatler* suggests again the affinity of the conversational novel with both the methods and the ideals of early eighteenth-century periodical literature.

5. See Ronald Paulson's *Satire and the Novel in Eighteenth-Century England* (New Haven, Conn.: Yale Univ. Press, 1967), 237-45, for a discussion of how *David Simple* modifies the picaresque journey to serve satiric ends while rejecting the satiric stance as incompatible with naive goodness.

6. Sarah Fielding appears much more confident of the interpretive and representational capacities of female speech than does Henry Fielding in *Amelia,* or than even she herself will be in creating the story-telling Mrs. Orgueil of *Volume the Last.*

7. Gerard A. Barker ("*David Simple:* The Novel of Sensibility in Embryo," *Modern Language Studies* 12.2 [1982]: 69-80), makes a similar distinction between Grandison as man of principle and as active, worldly Man of Feeling, and David Simple as man of mere compassion and naive reaction. Barker goes on to admit, however, that David is "more forceful and resolute" (70) than his sentimental successors. In fact, most treatments of *David Simple* as an early novel of sentiment ultimately distinguish between this work, with its insistent link of the moral with the sentimental, as well as its confrontation of the flaws in sentimental philosophy as a workable social model, and novels of the later, more full-blown Cult of Sensibility. See, for example, Janet Todd's discussion of the novel in *The Sign of Angellica: Women, Writing and Fiction, 1660-1800* (New York: Columbia Univ. Press, 1989), 161-75.

8. Ronald Paulson, "The Pilgrimage and the Family: Structures in the Novels of Fielding and Smollett," in *Tobias Smollett: Bicentennial Essays Presented to Lewis M. Knapp,* ed. G.S. Rousseau and P.-G. Boucé (New York: Oxford Univ. Press, 1971), 65.

9. At the same time, the range of possible sub-relationships offered by such a foursome promises a maximum of stability and fulfillment; as Terry Castle has pointed out in her discussion of *Amelia* in *Masquerade and Civilization: The Carnivalesque in Eighteenth-Century Culture and Fiction* (Stanford: Stanford Univ. Press, 1986), such a *partie quarrée* "suggests a certain ideal geometry of social relations" (209). The misinterpretation to which the brother-sister relationship of Valentine and Camilla has been subject contributes to the sense of superior stability of the foursome.

10. For Deborah Downs-Miers, Cynthia is the text's real, though hidden, protagonist; for this reason she must be removed to Jamaica in the sequel to allow for an undivided focus on David ("Springing the Trap: Subtexts and Subversions," in *Fetter'd or Free? British Women Novelists, 1670-1815,* ed. Mary Anne Schofield and Cecilia Macheski [Athens: Ohio Univ. Press, 1986], 311). While agreeing with Downs-Miers's emphasis on Cynthia's intellectual superiority, I think this rhetoric of rivalry for the title of hero is reductive of the author's attempt to place a community, rather than an outstanding individual, at the center of her novel.

11. April London, "Sarah Fielding," *Dictionary of Literary Biography,* vol. 39, part 1, ed. Martin C. Battestin (Detroit: Gale, 1985), 197.

12. The use of "Man" in the passage quoted above to describe the possessor of "a greater Share of *Wit* than is common" provides a case in point. The description clearly applies to Cynthia, the intelligent woman, more than to any other character of the novel. Downs-Miers's argument about disguised female protagonists and their relegation to subtext is perhaps most relevant at this point in the work. This movement towards orthodoxy occurs in Fielding's later fiction as well; see, for example, the circle of school girls which regulates its own submission to Jenny Peace as senior girl, to Mrs. Teachum as governess, and to the families to which its members belong, in Fielding's *The Governess or, Little Female Academy* (1749; rpt., London: Oxford Univ. Press, 1968), or the "natural" friendship of Ophelia and

Lord Dorchester which ends when she discovers its indecorum, in *The History of Ophelia* (1760; rpt. New York: Garland, 1974).

13. That this legitimization is more symbolic than practical is indicated by the father's lack of power. Reduced by his error to the position of supplicant for his children's forgiveness, he is also reduced financially to reliance upon David, whose fortune will essentially support the extended household.

14. Some criticism has regrettably perpetuated this tone of condescension towards Sarah Fielding. See, for example, Robert S. Hunting's expression of pleasure, after a comparison of the first and second editions of *David Simple,* in the sensation of seeming "to peer over Henry Fielding's large shoulder as affectionately, patiently, whimsically, ironically, this very busy man read[s] through the brave and bungling literary efforts of a loving, trusting sister" ("Fielding's Revisions of *David Simple,*" *Boston University Studies in English* 3 [1957]: 121). Dale Spender has made some observations about the general tenor of such critical representations of Sarah Fielding in her *Mothers of the Novel: 100 Good Women Writers before Jane Austen* (London: Pandora, 1986), 180-86; recent work on Fielding has done a great deal to correct this tendency to read the sister only as a means of gaining access to the brother.

15. Jane Spencer, *The Rise of the Woman Novelist: From Aphra Behn to Jane Austen* (Oxford: Blackwell, 1986), 91-95; see also Aurélion Digeon's description of Sarah Fielding's position as "confidante and 'liaison officer'" between her brother and Richardson, in *The Novels of Henry Fielding* (1925; rpt. New York: Russell, 1962), 27.

16. Todd, *The Sign,* 162. Carolyn Woodward makes a similar point in "'Feminine Virtue, ladylike disguise, women of community': Sarah Fielding and the female I am at mid-century," *Transactions of the Samuel Johnson Society of the Northwest* 15 (1984): 58.

17. In fact, Woodward has seen David's feminized character as Fielding's strategy for exploring her ideal of female community (62-64).

18. Sarah Fielding, "Advertisement" to *The Adventures of David Simple,* 1st ed., quoted in Wilbur L. Cross, *The History of Henry Fielding,* 3 vols. (New Haven, Conn.: Yale Univ. Press, 1918; rpt. New York: Russell, 1963), 2:6-7.

3. Social Authority and the Domestic Circle in Samuel Richardson's *Pamela* Part II

1. T.C. Duncan Eaves and Ben D. Kimpel, *Samuel Richardson: A Biography* (Oxford: Clarendon, 1971), 149; Margaret Anne Doody, *A Natural Passion: A Study of the Novels of Samuel Richardson* (London: Oxford Univ. Press, 1974), 71. See also *Natural Passion,* 76-77, for criticism of the sequel's lack of plot.

2. Terry Castle, *Masquerade and Civilization: The Carnivalesque in Eighteenth-Century English Culture and Fiction* (Stanford: Stanford Univ. Press, 1986), 131, 135.

3. Castle, 132, 134, viii-ix.

4. Revisions of Ian Watt's reading of *Pamela* Part I have increasingly emphasized the novel's socially conservative implications. Robert Allan Donovan's treatment of Part I in *The Shaping Vision: Imagination in the English Novel from Defoe to Dickens* (Ithaca, N.Y.: Cornell Univ. Press, 1966), for example, emphasizes "the tightness and clarity of its social structure," a structure that is both "rigidly hierarchical and completely hermetic," and therefore sharply contrasted to Pamela's own ambiguous status before her marriage (54, 58, 55). Doody warns against an isolated focus upon subversive aspects of Part I that ignores "the emphasis upon the strength of family ties at the beginning and end of the novel" (*Natural Passion,* 67). William Ray, in *Story and History: Narrative Authority and Social Identity in the Eighteenth-Century French and English Novel* (Chicago: Univ. of Chicago Press, 1990),

describes Pamela as "gradually relinquish[ing] her claim to absolute individuality in favor of a program of mutual reality construal that defuses the potential antagonism between her and her erstwhile adversary"—in other words, "the husband, and collectively, . . . the roles dictated by society" (137).

5. Carol Kay, *Political Constructions: Defoe, Richardson, and Sterne in Relation to Hobbes, Hume, and Burke* (Ithaca, N.Y.: Cornell Univ. Press, 1988), 127, 129, 136, 8. Whereas Kay focuses on *Clarissa* as Richardson's response to *Pamela's* popular success, Part II of *Pamela* in fact more expressly formalizes an exemplary model of social authority as an alternative to the fictional structure patterned upon opposition between the individual and the group. Alan Dugald McKillop's early study, *Samuel Richardson: Printer and Novelist* (Chapel Hill: Univ. of North Carolina Press, 1936; rpt. Hamden, Conn.: Shoe String, 1960) notes the effects of heightened authorial status in the sequel, linking Richardson's newly "oppressive sense of responsibility" with a shift in his conception of Pamela from "shrewd, demure little serving-girl" to "the exemplar of the age" (57).

6. The spokesmen for these two parties here are Alexander Pope, quoted in Henry Fielding, *An Apology for the Life of Mrs. Shamela Andrews,* ed. Martin C. Battestin (Boston: Houghton Mifflin, 1961), 367n to p. 303, and Fielding, *Shamela,* 338-39.

7. Terry Eagleton, *The Rape of Clarissa: Writing, Sexuality and Class Struggle in Samuel Richardson* (Oxford: Blackwell, 1982), 36.

8. A number of readers have drawn on the figure of the circle in describing the marriage portions of *Pamela.* Nancy Armstrong's discussion of *Pamela* Part I in *Desire and Domestic Fiction: A Political History of the Novel* (New York: Oxford Univ. Press, 1987) notes that the married Pamela's voice "flattens into that of pure ideology," transforming a radical work into "a static paradigm" in which "the spirit of reform ripples outward in circles radiating from her center" (125, 131). Patricia Meyer Spacks, in *Desire and Truth: Functions of Plot in Eighteenth-Century English Novels* (Chicago: Univ. of Chicago Press, 1990), describes Pamela as "the representation of virtuous stability," who "will supply moral ballast for her more erratic husband" in Richardson's model of "balanced marriage" (95). Spacks's discussion of the defeat of "plot" by "story" (90-93) in Part I is also of interest to my discussion of the sequel.

9. Samuel Richardson, *Pamela,* ed. Mark Kinkead-Weekes, 2 vols. (London: Dent, 1962), 2:319. References to Part II are to this edition throughout and will be indicated simply by page number; occasional quotations from the first part are taken from the same edition and will be indicated by volume and page numbers. Although this edition is the most readily available source of both parts, its lack of editorial apparatus points to the need for a new edition of Part II.

10. Richardson, in *Selected Letters of Samuel Richardson,* ed. John Carroll (Oxford: Clarendon, 1964), 54. Further references to this edition will be indicated in the text using the abbreviation *Letters.*

11. The theme of boundaries is ubiquitous in the third portion of Part II, in which, I will argue, the movement of story and time is stilled by the abstractions of didacticism. Wit, according to the sequel, gives its male wielders the capacity to "throw down . . . those sacred fences which may lay the fair inclosure open to the invasions of every clumsier and viler beast of prey" (417). Female passion as well, swelled by "the *torrents* of *sensual love,*" can flood "the *banks* of *discretion*" unless the breach be stopped by a rare degree of "resolution and self-conquest" (447-48). Carol Houlihan Flynn has described Richardson's ideology of the female: "The sentimental woman, the artificial product of sublimation and repression, had to be guarded by her family and husband, matronized by her children, bound in by hoops and rules, to keep social morality properly fixed" (*Samuel Richardson: A Man of Letters* [Princeton: Princeton Univ. Press, 1982], 52). The successful ploy of the sequel, and of

all of Richardson's fiction, of course, is to convert the passive female into the active agent of her own circumscription.

12. Eagleton, 29.

13. Preface, *The History of Sir Charles Grandison,* ed. Jocelyn Harris, 3 vols. (Oxford: Oxford Univ. Press, 1972), 1:3.

14. Kay, 151-52; Castle, 139-46; Elizabeth Deeds Ermarth, *Realism and Consensus in the English Novel* (Princeton: Princeton Univ. Press, 1983), 128-30, 135-37. Ermarth uses the notion of instantaneous transformation acceptable in spiritual autobiography as a model for Pamela's changed behavior in her changed role. See also Patricia Meyer Spacks's *Imagining a Self: Autobiography and Novel in Eighteenth-Century England* (Cambridge: Harvard Univ. Press, 1976), for a detailed treatment of Pamela's theatricality as revealing her "well-developed and well-founded sense of the power of external judgment" and, indeed, her "authenticity" (209, 218).

15. A similar view is suggested by Kerry Larson's discussion of Part I ("'Naming the Writer': Exposure, Authority, and Desire in Pamela," Criticism 23 [1981]: 126-40) in terms of Richardson's control of his anxiety over unregulated desire through "an ideal of desublimated desire" (140).

16. M[ikhail] M. Bakhtin, *The Dialogic Imagination: Four Essays,* ed. Michael Holquist, trans. Caryl Emerson and Michael Holquist (Austin: Univ. of Texas Press, 1981), 335.

17. Aaron Hill, in *The Correspondence of Samuel Richardson,* ed. Anna Letitia Barbauld, 6 vols. (London, 1804; rpt. New York: 1966), 1:100.

18. Thus Pamela's past is not erased from public memory, as Castle suggests, but is more precisely remembered as prescribed by Richardson, by frequent reiterations of the original text's emphases upon Pamela's virtue and unique accomplishments. Far from intending that his reader forget the apparent contradiction between experience and precept, Pamela emphasizes it in statements such as "I don't mean that they [gentlemen] should all take raw, uncouth, unbred, lowly girls, *as I was,* from the cottage, and, destroying all distinction, make such their wives" (414, italics mine). The concern is apparently to emphasize the unique moral uniformity extending through Pamela's lowly past to her exalted present. This uniformity contributes greatly to Pamela's authority and is by contrast sadly lacking in the case of the fallen Sally Godfrey, who must now live in disguise as Mrs. Wrightson.

19. Mark Kinkead-Weekes, *Samuel Richardson, Dramatic Novelist* (London: Methuen, 1973), 74-75.

20. Kay, 140.

21. See Dolores Peters, "The Pregnant Pamela: Characterization and Popular Medical Attitudes in the Eighteenth Century," *Eighteenth-Century Studies* 14 (1981): 432-51.

22. Castle, 154, 131.

23. Richardson has prepared the issue of relative duties as the arena of conflict by having B. raise "the sleeping dragon . . . , *Prerogative* by name" (214) in the argument over the nursing of Pamela's child. Although Pamela acquiesces in this issue, reluctantly agreeing that breast-feeding may not be a mother's absolute duty, the debate makes it clear that should a case of moral imperative arise, even a husband's power would be superseded by the divine.

24. Castle, *Masquerade,* 167-68.

25. The issue of an authoritative point of view in this episode has proved a vexed one for critics. For Kinkead-Weekes, B.'s later account of the affair proves that "Richardson has learnt the lesson of the need for direct access to B.'s point of view" (82); Pamela's is a "fallible narrative" (84) because of her tendency to imaginative exaggeration, and her later defense of her own action is therefore for the author an aesthetically unfortunate fall "back into prudential calculation" (87). Eagleton rightly dismisses the realist biases of such a reading as irrelevant to Richardson's didactic project; however, he overlooks the fact that the

dissolution of conflict here, and in the text as a whole, does not simply make Pamela "the collusive victim of patriarchy" (36), but more precisely illustrates her clever strategy for moralizing, even feminizing, that hierarchy. The most helpful understanding of the issue of perspective, in my view, is suggested by Ermarth's description of the non-realist idea of self for Robinson Crusoe and Pamela as a concept which "does not involve a consensus among partial perspectives but rather a militant standpoint of the soul apart from time and space altogether. The presence of other viewpoints is not helpful, not mutually informative" (143). The rightness of Pamela's perspective, in other words, is premised upon her fixed position within an ideally congruent moral and social framework, and not upon the degree of overlap between her story and those of B. and the countess.

26. Lois A. Chaber, in "From Moral Man to Godly Man: 'Mr. Locke' and Mr. B in Part 2 of *Pamela,*" *Studies in Eighteenth-Century Culture* 18 (1988): 213-61, has examined the conversion of B. as the "actual overarching concern" of the sequel. This reading is one of the most effective I have seen in reclaiming all aspects of the work, including the lengthy discussion of Locke's *Some Thoughts Concerning Education,* and is, I believe, consistent with my emphasis on the authorizing of Pamela's moral authority as the primary impulse of the text.

27. Ian Donaldson, who bases his argument, in "Fielding, Richardson, and the Ends of the Novel," *Essays in Criticism* 32 (1982): 34, upon such representations of repetitive quotidian life at the end of the sequel, suggests that Part II represents a kind of realism not found in the reassuring formal completion of *Tom Jones,* for example.

28. The style of B.'s earlier response to the social threat of Pamela's rise illustrates the effect of a simultaneous invitation to virtue and denial of identity with Pamela: "If, I say, such a girl can be found, thus beautifully attractive . . . ; and after that . . . , thus piously principled; thus genteely educated and accomplished; thus brilliantly witty; thus prudent, modest, generous, undesigning; and having been thus tempted, thus tried, by the man she hated not, pursued . . . , be thus inflexibly virtuous, and proof against temptation: let her reform her libertine, and let him marry her; and were he of princely extraction, I dare answer for it, that no *two* princes in *one age,* take the world through, would be in danger" (171).

29. I do not believe that the language of these tropes justifies either Castle's qualification of them as "horrific" or her anachronistically negative coloring of the word "mechanism" and its synonyms (*Masquerade,* 148-49). The motion evoked is indeed "an endless turning in place" (149), but in the sense of a mutually satisfying harmonization of numerous individual functions (nature) into a living social structure (art). Ian Donaldson, in "The Clockwork Novel: Three Notes on an Eighteenth-Century Analogy," *Review of English Studies* n.s. 21 (1970): 14-15, points out that eighteenth-century analogies drawn from human craftsmanship are related to notions of the intricacy of human action and its motives.

4. SOCIALIZING DESIRE AND RADIATING THE EXEMPLARY IN SAMUEL RICHARDSON'S *SIR CHARLES GRANDISON*

1. Samuel Richardson, *The History of Sir Charles Grandison,* ed. Jocelyn Harris, 3 vols. (Oxford: Oxford Univ. Press, 1972), 1:3. Subsequent references are indicated in parentheses in the text. Commentators on Richardson have noted the similarity between *Grandison* and *Pamela* in their emphases upon manners rather than moral conflict. See, for example, Margaret Anne Doody, *A Natural Passion: A Study of the Novels of Samuel Richardson* (Oxford: Clarendon, 1974), 67, 98, and Mark Kinkead-Weekes, *Samuel Richardson: Dramatic Novelist* (London: Methuen, 1973), 59, 72, 76.

2. Sending an early printing of volumes one and two of *Clarissa* to Aaron Hill, for example, he requests return of the copy, complete with "loose Papers paged, put in, with your

Corrections" (Samuel Richardson, *Selected Letters of Samuel Richardson,* ed. John Carroll [Oxford: Clarendon, 1964], 63). Further references are indicated by the abbreviation *Letters* in the text.

3. Of interest here is Tom Keymer's sustained argument for Richardson's conscious, subtle, and developing theory of reading as integral to his didactic project (*Richardson's "Clarissa" and the Eighteenth-Century Reader* [Cambridge: Cambridge Univ. Press, 1992], see esp. 56-84). Describing the epistolary effect in *Clarissa,* Keymer writes, "Typically, each letter . . . challenges the reader's opinions, puts questions, and above all sends him back to re-examine the text. It is geared not to explanation but to interrogation, and rather than correcting readers it invites them to correct themselves" (65). Unfortunately, Keymer says little about *Grandison* beyond asserting that Richardson's "last novel . . . gives the method its freest rein" (72).

4. Richardson complains repeatedly of women's favorable responses to the villainous Lovelace and the immoral Tom Jones; see *Letters,* 92, 102-3, 126-27, 141, 143-44. Florian Stuber's introduction to *Clarissa* (New York: AMS, 1990) suggests that Richardson's insertion of new letters from Anna Howe's relatively colorless lover Hickman into the third edition moves in the direction of this attempt to simultaneously accommodate and redirect female desire (35-38).

5. One is reminded here of Nancy K. Miller's conclusion, in *The Heroine's Text: Readings in the French and English Novel, 1722-1782* (New York: Columbia Univ. Press, 1980), that the "plot to undo feminine virtue," exemplified by *Clarissa,* embodies "an unsaid ambivalence on the part of male writers toward the very existence of female desire, and an unsayable anxiety about its power" (134).

6. John Mullan, *Sentiment and Sociability: The Language of Feeling in the Eighteenth Century* (Oxford: Clarendon, 1988), 83. Mullan identifies many of the features of the text that I will discuss here, including Sir Charles's creation through repetitious female praise, the lack of conflict in the novel, and its conversational and familial emphases (82-93). At the same time, he underplays the dynamic role of female narrative energy itself in providing interest and material for discussion.

Reading *Grandison*'s hero as the creation of readerly desire suggests an interesting complementarity of the novel to the *Clarissa* of William Beatty Warner's *Reading Clarissa: The Struggles of Interpretation* (New Haven, Conn.: Yale Univ. Press, 1979), with the important distinction that the desiring male reader of Richardson's heroine implicitly becomes her violater, while the passivity characteristic of female desire limits it to either the relatively positive mode of speculation, discussed below, or the self-destructive mode of lovesickness. Mary V. Yates associates *Grandison*'s metaphor of seduction with eighteenth-century pedagogical methods in which "the philosopher is polished, given accomplishments, dubbed a gentleman, and brought into the drawing room," and thereby "subtly eroticized" ("The Christian Rake in *Sir Charles Grandison," Studies in English Literature 1500-1900* 24 [1984]: 559).

7. To understand this socialization of narrative as it is embodied in *Grandison* is to glimpse something of Richardson's participation in the feminization of novelistic discourse and the social control of desire in fictions of the late eighteenth century. *Grandison* provides us not only with an early manifestation of what Nancy Armstrong has called the "rise of female authority" in "domestic fiction" (*Desire and Domestic Fiction: A Political History of the Novel* [Oxford: Oxford Univ. Press, 1987], 28-58), but also with a narrative strategy for circumscribing this authority within the bounds of a traditional social structure. Armstrong's insistence that through the gendering of discourse "legitimate monogamy—and thus the subordination of female to male—would ultimately be affirmed" (29) undergirds my argument in this chapter. My intent, however, is to point out that Richardson

self-consciously, formally, and within one text enacts a process that Armstrong extends over a half century.

8. The phrase is Jean H. Hagstrum's, in *Sex and Sensibility: Ideal and Erotic Love from Milton to Mozart* (Chicago: Univ. of Chicago Press, 1980), 214.

9. In fact, the novel is less about this plot than about waiting for the saving arrival of Sir Charles, fearing for his virtue and his safety in his absence, debating the nuances of drawing-room behavior, resisting men's attempts to elicit declarations of love, fantasizing about multiple possibilities for plot closure, and above all, rehearsing and elaborating upon the perfections of Sir Charles. John Sitter has similarly provided two summaries of the novel's plot, an active and a topical one, in *Literary Loneliness in Mid-Eighteenth-Century England* (Ithaca, N.Y.: Cornell Univ. Press, 1982), 202-3, 209-11.

10. Sitter, 211, 213; see also Lois A. Chaber, "'Sufficient to the Day': Anxiety in *Sir Charles Grandison*," *Eighteenth-Century Fiction* 1 (1989): 293-94.

11. Gerard A. Barker, *Grandison's Heirs: The Paragon's Progress in the Late Eighteenth-Century English Novel* (Newark: Univ. of Delaware Press, 1985), 17-18.

12. Anonymous, *Critical Remarks on Sir Charles Grandison, Clarissa and Pamela. Enquiring, Whether they have a Tendency to corrupt or improve the Public Taste and Morals. In a Letter to the Author. By a Lover of Virtue* (London: J. Dowse, 1754), in *Three Criticisms of Richardson's Fiction, 1749-1754* (New York: Garland, 1974), 58. Added to this absorption into Sir Charles's reported activities is the imaginative activity generated by his conspicuous absence from this novel bearing his name, not only during its first portion, but also during a considerable part of its remainder, when he is ostensibly wooing Harriet and presiding over his estate. These lengthy absences are for the women in the family circle, led by Harriet, the source of endless lament and speculation about duels of honor and love entanglements. Harriet's obsessive fears about Sir Charles's activities at the inn where he is staying during their courtship, for example, encompass everything from his murder to his being a secret carouser, and her sleep is haunted by dreams of tragic and pathetic endings to her own romance. These "imbecillities" supply much of the narrative interest in an unimpeded courtship.

13. Sir Charles has been described by Sitter (208) and Doody (*Natural Passion*, 337) as a static hero because of Richardson's emphasis on virtue as restraint of the passions; while such terminology is helpful in pointing to the absence of portrayed internal struggles on the part of the hero, it can be misleading if taken to mean a physical fixity similar to that of Pamela as wife and mother, or of Harriet as domestic woman, for example.

14. The circular metaphor of expansion outward from a center is more accurate to the text, I believe, than is Kinkead-Weekes's image of excess (315-21) which, in its apparent contradiction of the ideals of balance and uniformity, confuses what is in fact a coherent cluster of images associated with Sir Charles in the novel.

15. Cynthia Griffin Wolff (*Samuel Richardson and the Eighteenth-Century Puritan Character* (Hamden, Conn.: Shoe String, 1972) has suggested that the emphasis on Sir Charles's pecuniary generosity is one feature of the externalization of inner life in the novel (187-90).

16. Thus Hagstrum describes *Grandison* as "represent-[ing] a climax in the domestication of heroism" (214). Doody has argued in "Richardson's Politics," *Eighteenth-Century Fiction* 2 (1990), that Sir Charles is Richardson's ideal, "unbigoted Church of England" alternative to Charles Stuart, and that the novel "embodies a dream of restoration, reconciliation, and wholeness to an England badly divided and given to division" (125, 126).

17. Wolff has commented on the convenient death of the immoral and selfish father, Sir Thomas Grandison, as a necessary prerequisite to the operation of Sir Charles's brotherly benevolence (193-94). Although by no means non-patriarchal in nature, as Marijke Rudnik-Smalbraak has pointed out, in *Samuel Richardson: Minute Particulars within the*

Large Design (Leiden, Neth.: Leiden Univ. Press, 1983), 160, playing indulgent brother, selecting a wise and discreet father-figure in Dr. Bartlett, and managing his uncle at the latter's invitation are nevertheless acts which allow Sir Charles and his author to counteract the association of hierarchy with abuse of power and with inevitable conflict. In its emphasis upon brother-sister relationships, the *Grandison* family model in fact attempts a blend of the best features of the family, the marriage, and the friendship; Jocelyn Harris's discussion of the marriages based upon such a relationship in "'As if they had been living friends': *Sir Charles Grandison* to *Mansfield Park,*" *Bulletin of Research in the Humanities* 83 (1980): 383, elaborates on this point.

18. See Doody, *Natural Passion,* 279.

19. See 2:76, for example; also Sylvia Kasey Marks, "Sir Charles Grandison": The Compleat Conduct Book (Lewisburg, Penn.: Bucknell Univ. Press, 1986), 63, and Sitter, 215-16.

20. Doody points out further that when suspense is allowed to build, in such cases as the threatened duel of Sir Charles and Sir Hargrave, these "small knots of complexity are unravelled over several successive scenes" rather than contributing to a sustained intensity like that of *Clarissa* (*Natural Passion,* 301). See Kinkead-Weekes, 305-12, for a detailed analysis of the effects of the averted duel scene. Only when the reader is intended to feel with Harriet or Sir Charles the suspense of his Italian entanglement is the dramatic potential of conversation exploited in any extensive way. Indeed, the Italian subplot of the novel functions much like the parallel plot of Isabelle in *David Simple* or the countess affair in *Pamela* Part II, deflecting conflicts between passion and duty out of the central circle of characters and even onto foreign soil. Like the failure of David's group to avert the final isolation of Isabelle, Richardson's inability to resolve Clementina's story seems again to hint at the limit of the intimate group's capacity for achieving authoritative consensus in the face of an absolute disjunction between an individual's desires and the will of the group.

21. Sir Walter Scott, *Sir Walter Scott on Novelists and Fiction,* ed. Ioan Williams (London: Routledge and Kegan Paul, 1968), 43-44.

22. Doody's detailed discussion of music and dancing images in *Grandison* (*Natural Passion,* 352-64) provides a helpful elaboration of the importance of gesture in the novel.

23. Marks has pointed out the dearth of concrete acts of charity performed by women in the novel (112).

24. Terry Eagleton, *The Rape of Clarissa: Writing, Sexuality and Class Struggle in Samuel Richardson* (Oxford: Blackwell, 1982), 95. Wolff has pointed out that the wish of the exemplary Richardsonian heroine is for a "male-dominated society which is stable and continuing" and within which she is "permitted . . . to assume her rightful place" (191).

25. Jocelyn Harris, *Samuel Richardson* (Cambridge: Cambridge Univ. Press, 1987), 144.

26. An intriguing precursor to Sir Charles's use of withdrawal is that of the father in Daniel Defoe's *Family Instructor,* 2 vols. (1841; rpt., New York: AMS, 1973), 1:129. See also p. 11 above. Carol Houlihan Flynn has drawn a more extensive parallel between the two works, showing how both reveal "eighteenth-century society's contradictory desires for mutual subordination and voluntary compliance. Both Defoe and Richardson, creating the newly reconciled 'self' for their domestic fictions, endorse compliant behaviour that strains against the belief in the individual that their culture was inventing" ("The Pains of Compliance in *Sir Charles Grandison,*" in *Samuel Richardson: Tercentenary Essays,* ed. Margaret Anne Doody and Peter Sabor [Cambridge: Cambridge Univ. Press, 1989], 134).

27. George E. Haggerty has argued, in "*Sir Charles Grandison* and the Language of Nature," *Eighteenth-Century Fiction* 2 (1990), that Charlotte's secret promise to a lover is "a perversion of the public role of language" (136); he does not deal with the issues of necessary secrecy and the gendering of frankness that complicate this generalization. Doody, on the other hand, observes that the male desire to penetrate female reserve in *Grandison*

suggests the "sexually attractive" nature of that reserve ("Identity and Character in *Sir Charles Grandison,*" in Doody and Sabor, 125).

28. Sir Charles's latent resemblance to the intriguing Lovelace has been noted frequently by commentators on Richardson. See Yates, especially, for a detailed study of the function of these parallels in characterizing the exemplary hero through the safe method of mere allusion to the rake's faults. The parallel between Sir Charles and a rake is repeatedly drawn by the female narrators, by exclamations such as "it is well he is a good man!" (3:127), in an application of their discursive imaginations that provides some of the spice of plot while relegating its dangers to the realm of impossibility.

29. The comparison to Adam is found on 2:609. For discussion of this passage, see, for example, Doody, *Natural Passion,* 271-72.

30. When necessary, Harriet also self-consciously assumes male discursive prerogatives, writing, for example, of Sir Charles's "philanthropy" because "Why should women, in compliance with the petulance of narrow-minded men, forbear to use words that some seem to think above them, when no other single word will equally express their sense?" (1:389).

31. It is worth noting here that in a reversal of these roles, Sir Charles is asked to resolve for Clementina her conflict between religion and love; unlike the hero, however, she is the target of thinly veiled accusations of bigotry and a lack of generosity in her treatment of Sir Charles.

32. Charlotte's use of martial imagery, as well as of that of a trial and of captured prey, is reminiscent of the prominent hunt, trial, and conquest metaphors embodying the intensely conflictual structure of *Clarissa*'s plot. Such metaphors in *Grandison* are consistently marginalized through their association with Charlotte, or distanced through the perspective of the female narrator looking out from her safe enclosure at a wilderness full of hyenas, or rendered benign through their reapplication to the game of courtship (from which they were originally drawn in *Clarissa*). Thus, exclusion on the level of imagery strengthens the sense of domestic enclosure associated with feminized narrative in the novel. As Doody has pointed out for the parallel case of Charlotte with her baby, the use of animal imagery to give sexual relations the much more loving and orderly connotations of protection and petting rather than hunting and preying conveys the notions that "nature is tractable, and civilization is the apotheosis of nature, not a mask concealing the horror beneath" (*Natural Passion,* 344).

33. In Paul R. Crabtree's words, "the presence of people" is in *Grandison,* as in the later novel of manners, "the great subject or problem; . . . a familiar, enveloping quality without which life could hardly be imagined—and yet at the same time, on a level too deep for conscious awareness, . . . something *wrong,* not the felt evidence of community but a continuously alien pressure" ("Propriety, *Grandison,* and the Novel of Manners," *Modern Language Quarterly* 41 [1980]: 159). This portrayal of the relation between public and private selves as a superimposition due to virtue rather than an ideal congruence is also noted by Wolff, 199-200.

34. A number of writers have heard this undertone in *Grandison.* Doody has commented specifically on the imprisonment of Charlotte (*Natural Passion,* 293). John Allen Stevenson, in "A Geometry of His Own: Richardson and the Marriage Ending," *Studies in English Literature 1500-1900* 26 (1986): 469-83, argues that Grandison is in fact "the anticourtship hero *par excellence,* a glittering image of the endlessly unattainable" as a reflection of Richardson's fear of the sexual release of marriage as closure (474). See also Chaber ("'Sufficient'"), who writes of the anxiety underlying the novel's plot despite its ostensible manifestation of providential order.

35. Richardson's newly expansive idealism about the potential influence of *Grandison* as material for debate is attributed by Kinkead-Weekes to the development of the author's circle of admirers into an intimate community of feeling and moral casuistry (280-84). Pa-

tricia Howell Michaelson's thesis that a novel such as *Grandison* was likely to be received into a domestic reading circle led by a male family member or friend, rather than being perused by a solitary female reader in her closet ("Women in the Reading Circle," *Eighteenth-Century Life* 13 [1989]: 59-69), suggests that the social dynamics of Richardson's novel and the model of interpretation established in the correspondence together reflect contemporary strategies for circumscribing the female imagination.

36. See, for example, *Letters,* 215-16, 253, 270, 277-78.

37. Richardson does appear to point the way to the narrative centered around the silent, exemplary heroine in one portion of *Grandison,* when Sir Charles becomes the representative narrator-reader of Clementina's story.

5. SILENCING THE CENTER IN HENRY FIELDING'S *AMELIA*

1. Henry Fielding, "Essay on the Knowledge of the Characters of Men," in *Miscellanies by Henry Fielding, Esq,* 2 vols., ed. Henry Knight Miller (Middletown, Conn.: Wesleyan Univ. Press, 1972), 1:176-77.

2. See Fielding's use of the Stoic image of the self-sufficient soul as a smooth ball in "Of the Remedy of Affliction For the Loss of our Friends" (*Miscellanies,* 213), and *The History of Tom Jones, a Foundling,* ed. Fredson Bowers, intro. and commentary Martin C. Battestin (Middletown, Conn.: Wesleyan Univ. Press, 1975), 471-72, 760-61. *Amelia,* with its urban setting, has been seen as the author's most fully developed portrayal of social interdependence by James E. Evans, in "The Social Design of Fielding's Novels," *College Literature* 7 (1980): 92, 99-101.

3. Thus *Amelia* provides an early version of a fictional structure that Nancy Armstrong describes in *Desire and Domestic Fiction: A Political History of the Novel* (New York: Oxford Univ. Press, 1987) as contrasting "the marketplace driven by male labor . . . imagined as a centrifugal force that broke up the vertical chains organizing an earlier notion of society" with "the nuclear family, a social organization with a mother rather than a father at its center," conceived as a "centripetal" force holding isolated social units together (95).

4. Peter Sabor has argued that in their final novels Richardson and Fielding move towards a similarly psychological-social model of characterization ("*Amelia* and *Sir Charles Grandison:* The Convergence of Fielding and Richardson," *Wascana Review* 17.2 [1982]: 3-18).

5. See, for example, Henry Fielding, *"The Jacobite's Journal" and Related Writings,* ed. W.B. Coley (Middletown, Conn.: Wesleyan Univ. Press, 1975), 127-29, and *"The Covent-Garden Journal" and "A Plan of the Universal Register-Office,"* ed. Bertrand A. Goldgar (Oxford: Clarendon, 1988), 40.

6. *Covent-Garden Journal* No. 7 (Sat., Jan. 25, 1752), *"Covent-Garden Journal,"* 57-66.

7. This structural dichotomy is reflected in criticism of the novel for a failure to resolve tensions between private and public, ideal and real, good and evil, instruction and delight, freedom and necessity, satire and sentiment; see, for example, Robert Alter, *Fielding and the Nature of the Novel* (Cambridge, Mass.: Harvard Univ. Press, 1968), 141-48 and C.J. Rawson, *Henry Fielding and the Augustan Ideal under Stress: "Nature's Dance of Death" and Other Studies* (London: Routledge and Kegan Paul, 1972), 68-70, 96.

8. John Cleland, *The Monthly Review,* 5:510-15, qtd. in Ronald Paulson and Thomas Lockwood, eds., *Henry Fielding: The Critical Heritage* (London: Routledge and Kegan Paul, 1969), 304. Bonnell Thornton in turn parodies *Amelia's* narration of domestic routine in a description of the heroine's "little family . . . squatted upon the hearth close by her knees, and gnawing each of them an huge luncheon of bread and butter," crying "'Mammy!—

where's Pappy?—Mammy!—where's Pappy?—Mammy!—where's Pappy?'" (*Have at You All: or The Drury-Lane Journal,* qtd. in Paulson and Lockwood, 322).

9. Cleland, 308-9. See also A.R. Towers, "*Amelia* and the State of Matrimony," *Review of English Studies* n.s. 5 (1954): 144-57, for a general discussion of the significance of the novel's focus on marriage.

10. Henry Fielding, *Amelia,* ed. Martin C. Battestin (Middletown, Conn.: Wesleyan Univ. Press, 1983), 15. Further references are to this edition.

11. Terry Castle, in *Masquerade and Civilization: The Carnivalesque in Eighteenth-Century English Culture and Fiction* (Stanford: Stanford Univ. Press, 1986), 190-204, notes the lack of forward momentum and the sense of fragmentation created by Booth's suspension, in the first half of the novel, "between two worlds: that of Miss Mathews, the embodiment of lassitude and corruption; and that of Amelia, representative of moral purity and the domestic virtues" (203). I disagree with Castle's view that this dichotomy is subverted later in the novel, as my discussion will make clear.

12. As Kim Ian Michasiw has put it: "At the heart of Fielding's city yawns a vacancy; there exists no centre of moral authority" ("The Plot of Sensibility: Emotion and Narrative Form in English Fiction, 1750-1800" [Ph.D. diss., Univ. of Toronto, 1984], 93).

13. In comparing the novel's dénouement to a lottery (246), Castle deflects Fielding's metaphor into a reading that is consistent with her own view of the novel's events as arbitrary, but is inconsistent with the narrative's actual revelation of the order in the apparent disorder which proceeds from the masquerade. In general, Castle's insistence upon reading the text as amoral allows for valid observations, yet must remain limited in its refusal to deal with the fact that contrasts are so explicitly moralized in the work.

14. John E. Loftis has pointed out, with reference to the anonymity of the masquerade's mocking rakes, that "Christian, natural, legal, and human values all are virtually non-existent in contemporary London; they have been replaced by the oaths, cant phrases, and self-centered actions of virtually anonymous men" ("Imitation in the Novel: Fielding's *Amelia,*" *Rocky Mountain Review of Language and Literature* 31 [1977]: 223). Alter has similarly interpreted the anonymity of the noble lord as signifying "the ubiquitous spirit of corruption of a degenerate aristocracy" (152).

15. As the subsequent discussion of Amelia's role in the novel will indicate, I use the word "active" advisedly here to describe the heroine's hardworking, but reactive and spatially circumscribed, efforts to maintain her virtue and her family's equilibrium.

16. Booth also describes his country life with Amelia as a paradise. This repeated metaphor suggests Fielding's use of the country-city distinction as a tonal backdrop to his primary contrast of idealized marriage and other social institutions, as Loftis has pointed out. Loftis has also noted the souring of the Booths's original country sojourn as evidence that Fielding is not, however, idealizing rural life (227). The failure of Booth's farming venture provides an interesting point of departure for a study of Sarah Fielding's *Volume the Last,* in which economic pressures felt in a country setting, rather than sexual ones associated with the city, become the means of attack upon the social circle.

17. The novel's reconciliations and éclaircissements are almost all located around tables, first around the breakfast table, with Mrs. Atkinson, Booth, and Amelia, and then at the dinner table of the Jameses, presided over by Dr. Harrison. Finally, the Booths and Atkinsons travel to Amelia's country house, where the final table scene occurs.

18. The egalitarian nature of Amelia's circle marks an important shift from *Tom Jones;* John Richetti, in "The Old Order and the New Novel of the Mid-Eighteenth Century: Narrative Authority in Fielding and Smollett," *Eighteenth-Century Fiction* 2 (1990), finds in the earlier novel a concentration of authority in the narrator similar to that of "the Hanoverian-Whig oligarchy" (190) and that makes no place in its hierarchy for the miser-

ies experienced by a character such as Partridge (191-93). Although both Morris Golden, in "Fielding's Politics," in *Henry Fielding: Justice Observed*, ed. K.G. Simpson (London: Vision, 1985), 34-55, and Rawson (3-29) argue for democratic tendencies in *Amelia*, the strong gender dichotomy on which the Booths's marriage, and therefore the novel, is structured, supports Armstrong's claim that "the gendering of discourse" ultimately reinforces marital hierarchy (28-29; see also chapter 4 above).

19. Alter views the masquerade as this corrupt world's "central rite," allowing "hungry sexual egos" to forget "the limitations and obligations imposed by family and society in ordinary maskless life" (155).

20. Amelia's reaction to the ostensible deathbed confession of Sergeant Atkinson's love is not intended to falsify this claim, but rather, to indicate its volitional nature.

21. Castle insightfully observes the parallel between the scene of Amelia's unmasking to Booth after her accident and the masquerade itself (178-80, 198); however, her view that this undermines the moral significance of the masquerade in the novel overlooks the consistency in Amelia's selection of an appropriate moment for, and witness to, her intimate self-revelation, a self-revelation which notably does not reveal any hidden fault. Castle also identifies this second masquerade as the "hub" and "kernel" of the plot (232-33), but her argument that it is morally compromising to Amelia seems somewhat specious to me because Amelia's use of "deceit" is carefully rationalized and distinguished from that of other characters (as will be seen below), and because the good which apparently arises out of the masquerade can as well be attributed to forces such as Amelia's refusal to compromise and Atkinson's love for her as to a subversion of all of the novel's moral indicators.

22. Hugh Amory's "Magistrate or Censor? The Problem of Authority in Fielding's Later Writings," *Studies in English Literature 1500-1900* 12 (1972): 503-18, opposes the fundamental and intuitive religious authority of Harrison to the utilitarian magisterial and rational authority of the justice of the peace and the writer of "histories," suggesting that there is no common ground for effective action between the two. In having Dr. Harrison "incarnate" his religious authority as humble citizen aiding the justice in implementing the novel's resolution, however, Fielding does, I believe, bridge that gap while modeling the action of the Christian hero who is in, but not of, the world.

23. For a fuller study of this issue see Donald Fraser's "Lying and Concealment in *Amelia*," in Simpson, 174-98.

24. Fielding, *Miscellanies*, 156.

25. For an example of the first case, see the narrator's original suggestion that Mrs. Bennet's dislike of the noble lord is a manifestation of her jealousy at his admiration of Amelia (204). The latter inadequacy is illustrated in the narrator's early lament, inspired by James's generosity, "that so few are to be found of this benign Disposition; that while Wantonness, Vanity, Avarice and Ambition are every Day rioting and triumphing in the Follies and Weakness, the Ruin and Desolation of Mankind, scarce one Man in a thousand is capable of tasting the Happiness of others" (170); James is of course later revealed to illustrate exactly this incapacity of sympathy for Booth.

26. I am indebted to Eric Rothstein here for his treatment of the "epistemological empathy" created by the novel's narrative method (*Systems of Order and Inquiry in Later Eighteenth-Century Fiction* [Berkeley and Los Angeles: Univ. of California Press, 1975], 154-57).

27. Thus, for the sake of contrast between the marriage of cold convenience and ideal wedded conversation, the narrator at one point follows Mrs. James throughout an evening of "talk[ing] again and again over the Diversions and News of the Town" and finally to her solitary bed, and then describes the Booths, who, after a humble meal and pleasant conversation, retire "happy in each other" or, according to the first edition, "with mutual Desires,

and equal Warmth, [fly] into each other's Arms" (180 and App. VI, 569). The implicit link between verbal and sexual conversation becomes a dangerous one in Newgate, where the long exchange of stories between Booth and Miss Mathews ends in a week of "criminal Conversation" between the two prisoners (154).

28. J. Paul Hunter, *Occasional Form: Fielding and the Chains of Circumstance* (Baltimore: Johns Hopkins Univ. Press, 1975), 194.

29. Hunter, for example, has written of "a certain claustrophobic, smothering sense of frustration, panic, and doom" created by "Booth's seemingly endless petitions to great men, his furtive routine calculated to avoid the eternal pursuit of creditors, the pointless circularity of the masquerade, the silliness and failure of the wine-basket device to gain Booth access to Amelia." Hunter sees only the dark aspects of this repetition as a portrayal of "the absurdity of trying to cope in a world where evil is relentless and goodness has few allies" (194-95); while this may be the case at moments during the text, I believe the rapturous unions, the Sunday freedom of Booth and his family, and even the simple pleasure his company affords Amelia during his confinement are intended to indicate the possibility for transformation and transcendence of the prison house of repetition.

30. Rothstein explains the novel's resolution in favor of Amelia as an affirmation of what she symbolizes in contrast to the systems of the larger social world: "What Amelia is, and what she providentially brings to the Booths' marriage, also leads to preferment higher and more significant than anything Mrs. Atkinson could have won as a false Amelia from my lord, or that James, as a would-be Booth in Amelia's arms, can offer" (*Systems,* 200).

6. Authorizing the Marginalized Circle in Sarah Scott's *Millenium Hall*

1. George E. Haggerty, "'Romantic Friendship' and Patriarchal Narrative in Sarah Scott's *Millenium Hall*," *Genders* 13 (1992): 108-22; Vincent Carretta, "Utopia Limited: Sarah Scott's *Millenium Hall* and *The History of Sir George Ellison*," *The Age of Johnson* 5 (1992): 303-25; Susan Sneider Lanser, *Fictions of Authority: Women Writers and Narrative Voice* (Ithaca, N.Y.: Cornell Univ. Press, 1992), 224-31.

2. The phrase is used by Betty Rizzo in *Companions without Vows: Relationships among Eighteenth-Century British Women* (Athens: Univ. of Georgia Press, 1994), 307, as I indicated in my introduction.

3. In the novel's sequel, *The History of Sir George Ellison,* it becomes clear, however, that only a male, Grandison-like hero can carry the influence of this society outward to the broader sociopolitical sphere which, while it can be regulated, is not in fact transformed into a radically non-patriarchal structure. Rizzo points out that "Ellison can operate from the normal domestic sphere whereas the women of Millenium Hall must forgo marriage and live entirely outside the patriarchal system in order to put their ideas into practice" (317).

4. Sarah Scott, *A Description of Millenium Hall,* ed. Walter M. Crittenden (New York: Bookman, 1955), 200. Further references will be indicated in parentheses in the text.

5. This is the basis of Carretta's reading of the text as socially conservative. If nothing else, the doubling of the narrator by a male companion who is even more in need of conversion than the narrator weakens the argument that the masculine observer's position must be a straightforwardly authorizing one.

6. Nina Auerbach has described this as a common element in literary portrayals of communities of women as "simultaneously defective and transcendent," and therefore as "a rebuke to the conventional ideal of a solitary woman living for and through men, attaining

citizenship in the community of adulthood through masculine approval alone" (*Communities of Women: An Idea in Fiction* [Cambridge, Mass.: Harvard Univ. Press, 1978], 5).

7. For a helpful discussion of the rejection of the marriage ending and the creation of a female subject position in *Millenium Hall* see Haggerty, 108-11.

8. Caroline Gonda states, in "Sarah Scott and 'The Sweet Excess of Paternal Love,'" *Studies in English Literature 1500-1900* (1992): 511-35, that "the abiding impression of the novel is not one of limitation or conservatism, but of women empowered by experience and eventual good fortune to choose the direction of their own lives and to benefit those of others" (523-24).

9. In a related argument, Carretta has noted that the text returns repeatedly to the paradox of confinement that is in fact freedom (309-15). Carretta interprets this as an emphasis on happiness as achieved through placement within a traditional order and hierarchy; while I will argue that freedom for the individual is indeed attained through self-discipline and service to others in this novel, I feel that the transformation of what the larger, traditional social structure understands as exclusion into an alternative order is more socially radical, more egalitarian in its implications, than Carretta would have it. Thus, the Hall is first represented as the refuge of hay-makers, who run to it "as to an assured asylum against every evil" (33), and the women explain to Lamont that for the freaks hidden behind the pale in the wood, enclosure is not a "confinement" but an "asylum" (44).

10. Lanser, 226-28; see also the frontispiece reproduced in the Crittenden edition.

11. Lanser, 19 and 230. Thus, the women's refusal to act as self-narrators need not necessarily be read in Lanser's terms, as a tacit disapproval of the portrayal of their community to society at large (227-28).

12. Sarah Scott's earlier novel, *The History of Cornelia* (1750, rpt. New York: Garland, 1974), while its plot is that of a more traditional courtship story, also devotes considerable time to descriptions of Cornelia's various means of making herself useful to several employers while hiding from her evil guardian and separated from her lover. These activities include financial management and the operation of extensive charities.

13. In emphasizing the rational, dispassionate nature of this community I do not wish to skirt the issue of lesbian desire, which the novel raises at least for today's reader. I agree with Haggerty that the emotional intensity of the relationship between Louisa Mancel and Miss Melvyn, for example, contrasts strongly with their dispassionately dutiful behavior in courtship (see also Lanser, 230). However, it seems to me that much of the force of Scott's narrative comes from the portrayal of the female community's relationships as a rational and orderly retreat from the disorderly desires that mar male-female interaction, and I suspect that for her original readers female friendship would have easily been assumed to be asexual in the case of exemplary women. Certainly the original responses to the novel (see Carretta, 304) suggest this assumption; it is supported as well by Lillian Faderman's discussion of "The 'Fashion' of Romantic Friendship in the Eighteenth Century," in *Surpassing the Love of Men: Romantic Friendship and Love between Women from the Renaissance to the Present* (New York: Morrow, 1981), 74-84.

14. See Lanser, 226-28; while Carretta agrees that the heads of Millenium Hall are portrayed as "earthly surrogates for God the Father," he sees this portrayal as limited only to this case, in which "the intervening males are lacking" (312).

15. Haggerty, 118-19; see also Rizzo, 307.

16. See, for example, 39-41, describing the encouragement of the local poor to mutual dependence, and 197-98 regarding the use of wealth, as well as my earlier description of the carpet manufacture established by the women.

17. I am applying Carretta's title in a different sense here; see note 1 above.

18. Carretta has suggested a process by which male authority figures "authorized [feminist] ideas that earlier women had authored" (305).

19. The best source of information on Sarah Robinson Scott's life, and on her involvement in the "Bath community" specifically, is Rizzo, chs. 2 and 13. Another useful biographical sketch is found in Jane Spencer's Introduction to the Virago edition of *Millenium Hall* (1986), v-xvi.

20. Like Sarah Fielding, Scott is clearly aware of the financial basis upon which her community's self-enclosure rests; Fielding, however, goes a step further in stripping her community of its economic independence and thereby portraying its destruction.

7. MOBILIZING THE COMMUNITY, IMMOBILIZING THE IDEAL IN TOBIAS SMOLLETT'S *HUMPHRY CLINKER*

1. Wolfgang Iser, "The Generic Control of Aesthetic Response: An Examination of Smollett's *Humphry Clinker,*" *Southern Humanities Review* 3 (1969); rpt. in Tobias Smollett, *Humphry Clinker,* ed. James L. Thorson (New York: Norton, 1983), 380; Robert Folkenflik, "Self and Society: Comic Union in *Humphry Clinker,*" *Philological Quarterly* 53 (1974): 198. Folkenflik's article is a useful discussion of the novel's portrayal of "comically limited" selfhood (195) modulated by "a recognition of the necessity of human relationships" (200).

2. Tobias Smollett, *The Expedition of Humphry Clinker,* intro. and notes Thomas R. Preston, ed. O.M. Brack Jr. (Athens: Univ. of Georgia Press, 1990), 324. Further references will be indicated in parentheses in the text.

3. *The Gentleman's Magazine* 41 (July 1771): 317; *The Critical Review* 32 (August 1771): 81-88; *The London Magazine* 40 (June 1771): 317; all qtd. in the Norton edition of the novel, 329, 328, 333.

4. See Robert Crawford, *Devolving English Literature* (Oxford: Clarendon, 1992), 55-75, for a discussion of *Humphry Clinker* as a Scot's response to the problem of Scotophobia specifically, and of prejudice in general.

5. B.L. Reid, in "Smollett's Healing Journey," *Virginia Quarterly Review* 41 (1965): 549-70, has discussed both the change in views of family on the part of the novel's characters (550-53) and the specific image of retention and discharge (550-51).

6. Edward Copeland, in *"Humphry Clinker:* A Comic Pastoral Poem in Prose?" *Texas Studies in Literature and Language* 16 (1974): 493-501, has noted the novel's use of such pastoral motifs to underline its resolution into stability.

7. Robert Spector's recent book, *Smollett's Women: A Study in an Eighteenth-Century Masculine Sensibility* (Westport, Conn.: Greenwood, 1994), concurs with many of these observations about Lydia's unreconciled position in the family (see 60-80), as well as with some of my later observations about the maturation of Lydia as involving the imposition of "masculine" self-discipline and reason upon her "feminine" propensities. In general, Spector argues convincingly for the marginal place of women in Smollett's social vision.

8. Indeed, K.G. Simpson claims, in "Tobias Smollett: The Scot as English Novelist," in *Smollett: Author of the First Distinction,* ed. Alan Bold (London: Vision, 1982), that the travelers of *Humphry Clinker* do not develop significantly in their understanding of one another and of society; the novel is rather an "in-depth investigation of individual limitation" (88).

9. William Hazlitt, *The English Comic Writers,* in his *Complete Works,* ed. P.P. Howe 21 vols. (London, 1931), 6:117.

10. See Iser, 382.

11. Indeed, not all readers have agreed that the novel strongly authorizes Matthew Bramble's social vision. Ronald Paulson, for example, argues that "None of these views is valid in itself, but a special circumstance of illness, callow youth, or young love, and must be sublimated, dehumored, or in some way corrected—as many are by the end of the novel" ("The Pictorial Circuit and Related Structures in Eighteenth-Century England," in *The Varied Pattern: Studies in the Eighteenth Century*, ed. Peter Hughes and David Williams [Toronto: A.M. Hakkert, 1971], 180). I concur, however, with Paulson's conclusion that the novel's interest in differing views of the same phenomenon reflects a "sweeping change from belief in the primacy of reason to belief in the primacy of experience" (168), a change that contributed to that anxiety about the basis of sociability which gave rise to the fictions of this study.

12. For a detailed examination of English luxury as the chief theme of *Humphry Clinker*, see Part III of John Sekora's *Luxury: The Concept in Western Thought, Eden to Smollett* (Baltimore: Johns Hopkins Univ. Press, 1977), 213-82.

13. Carole Fabricant, "The Literature of Domestic Tourism and the Public Consumption of Private Property," in *The New Eighteenth Century: Theory, Politics, English Literature*, ed. Felicity Nussbaum and Laura Brown (New York: Methuen, 1987), 259. See also Ian Ousby, *The Englishman's England: Taste, Travel and the Rise of Tourism* (Cambridge: Cambridge Univ. Press, 1990), ch. 2.

14. Thomas R. Preston, in his introduction to the Georgia edition of the novel, discusses the dichotomy between financial power, represented by Matthew Bramble, and "active" concern for others, represented by Clinker (xxix-xxxi). This reading offers an interesting parallel to mine in its placement of Clinker in the economically powerless, yet truly sociable role; unlike the female centers of the social circles I have examined, however, Clinker is able to play a physically active part.

15. See, respectively, Robert D. Spector, "Smollett's Traveler," in *Tobias Smollett: Bicentennial Essays*, ed. G.S. Rousseau and P.-G. Boucé (New York: Oxford Univ. Press, 1971), 242-45; Simpson, 75; Virgil Nemoianu, "The Semantics of Bramble's Hypochondria: A Connection between Illness and Style in the Eighteenth Century," *Clio* 9 (1979): 47-48.

16. Louis M. Martz, in *The Later Career of Tobias Smollett* (New Haven, Conn.: Yale Univ. Press, 1942; rpt. 1967), ch. 7, has illustrated at length how Lismahago represents the author's own views of Scotland and its relations with England.

8. Disembodying the Social Circle in Sarah Fielding's *Volume the Last*

1. Sarah Fielding, *The Adventures of David Simple*, ed. Malcolm Kelsall (Oxford: Oxford Univ. Press, 1969), 304-5. This edition contains both the 1744 novel and its 1753 sequel, referred to here as *Volume the Last*. Further references to both parts are taken from this edition and are indicated in parentheses in the text.

2. See April London's "Sarah Fielding" in the *Dictionary of Literary Biography*, vol. 39, Part 1, ed. Martin C. Battestin (Detroit: Gale Research, 1985), 195-204, and the general introduction to *The Correspondence of Henry and Sarah Fielding*, ed. Martin C. Battestin and Clive T. Probyn (Oxford: Clarendon, 1993), xviii-xliii, for biographical summaries.

3. Kelsall has suggested that although "*her* outlook is narrower," in her sequel Sarah Fielding takes a "*harder* look at some of the dilemmas of human kind" than does either Henry Fielding's comedy or Richardson's psychology (Introduction to Oxford edition, xvii).

4. Through the *David Simple* series alone Fielding earns the title of "theorist" of the Bath community of independent women, awarded by Betty Rizzo in *Companions without*

Vows: Relationships among Eighteenth-Century British Women (Athens: Univ. of Georgia Press, 1994), 307. Sarah Fielding appears never to have become actively involved in the communal and utopian projects of Scott and Montagu, however. Whether this indicates that she truly was more interested in theory than in application, or whether it suggests that she was less convinced than the others of the worldly viability of the conversational circle, as this chapter argues, must remain open to conjecture. In my reading, the correspondence by and about her after her retirement to the Bath area in approximately 1754 draws a portrait of a lonely, yet insistently solitary, individual who sees the impracticability of the ideal intimate community even as she longs intensely for it.

5. Gerard A. Barker, in *"David Simple:* The Novel of Sensibility in Embryo," *Modern Language Studies* 12.2 (1982): 69-80, has described Fielding in the sequel as "willing to test David's 'little Society' empirically in the stress and strain of everyday domestic life" (78).

6. These quotations are taken from Wilbur L. Cross, *The History of Henry Fielding,* 3 vols. (New Haven: Yale Univ. Press, 1918; rpt. New York: Russell and Russell, 1963), 2:6-7. Cross cites Sarah Fielding's first-edition "Advertisement" in full.

7. Because of statements like these, I disagree with Janet Todd's view that in *Volume the Last* "the sense of [the afterlife] is less able than in *Clarissa* to compensate for the generalised ills in this world" (*The Sign of Angellica: Women, Writing and Fiction, 1660-1800* [London: Virago, 1989], 165).

8. Carol Kay, *Political Constructions: Defoe, Richardson, and Sterne in Relation to Hobbes, Hume, and Burke* (Ithaca: Cornell Univ. Press, 1988), 8; see also my chapters 1 and 3.

9. In claiming that Fielding acquiesces to received definitions of the female sphere by not dramatizing herself within her own narrative, Jane Spencer overlooks this significant shift to a more authoritative narrative voice (*The Rise of the Woman Novelist: From Aphra Behn to Jane Austen* [Oxford: Blackwell, 1986], 95). Similarly, *Volume the Last* serves as an exception to Todd's rule that female writers of the mid-eighteenth century found it inadvisable to claim authoritative power within their narratives (*The Sign,* 125-27, 141-42). Susan Sneider Lanser's study of female narrative voices, *Fictions of Authority: Women Writers and Narrative Voice* (Ithaca, N.Y.: Cornell Univ. Press, 1992), while it does not refer to *David Simple* and its sequel, describes the claims to authority implied by such an "overt authoriality" as that of *Volume the Last* as extending "to 'nonfictional' referents" and "allow[ing] the writer to engage, from 'within' the fiction, in a culture's literary, social, and intellectual debates" (17). Lanser's observation that "women writers' adoption of overt authoriality has usually meant transgressing gendered rhetorical codes" (17-18) is useful here as well. John Butt, in *English Literature in the Mid-Eighteenth Century,* ed. and completed by Geoffrey Carnall (Oxford: Clarendon, 1979), has identified the narrator's "firmly analytical manner" as the device that "controls the paralysing hopelessness that constantly threatens to dominate the story" (452).

10. Kelsall, xiv. Because it resumes action immediately where the original left off and orients itself in relation to the original, *Volume the Last* is generally treated as the true sequel to *The Adventures of David Simple,* despite the intervening *Familiar Letters between the Principal Characters in David Simple* (1747).

11. The reappearance of Mr. Orgueil from the journey portion of *David Simple* heightens the gloomy effect of Fielding's rearrangement of structural elements, from the earlier pattern of progress from evil to good into the oppositional scheme of evil opposing good.

12. See Kelsall, xv. Even the starving man who is aided by David's family towards the end of *Volume the Last* reinforces the impression of a world entirely consumed by self-interest; he tells a tale of woe featuring a disinheriting father and a will-altering nephew that parallels the experiences of the central community (see 395-96).

13. Todd, *Sensibility: An Introduction* (London: Methuen, 1986), 102-3; see also Todd's

The Sign, 173, for a comment on the effect of contextualization upon the ideal of the benevolent community.

14. Both Todd (*Sensibility,* 97-99) and Robert Palfrey Utter and Gwendolyn Needham (*Pamela's Daughters* [New York: Russell, 1936; rpt. 1972], 114) have discussed the significance of the poverty motif in *Volume the Last* as a convention of the sentimental novel. They include in the motif, however, a disdain of work or of ameliorative action, an attitude which is explicitly disowned in narrative features such as Valentine's move to Jamaica, David's subsistence gardening, the group's pleasure in young Camilla's learning to spin and knit, and the text's evident approval of the wellborn beggar's having taught his children "to earn their Bread by Labour" (395).

15. Lady Mary Wortley Montagu, *The Complete Letters of Lady Mary Wortley Montagu,* ed. Robert Halsband, 3 vols. (Oxford: Clarendon, 1967), 3:67.

16. As Todd has put it, although sentimental beliefs cause suffering there is "no decent alternative" to them (*The Sign,* 166).

17. The quantity of recorded conversation is also greatly decreased in *Volume the Last* in favor of the authorial commentary and narration of mental and emotional states already noted. The exceptions to this rule are in themselves significant; Mrs. Orgueil's stupid and spiteful partiality, for example, is captured in her distorted and self-contradictory style when she compares the dying child Cynthia and her own spoiled daughter: "The little Hussey sets up for such Delicacy! she pretends she has got a Cold, and fancies she lay in a wet Room the first Night of our Arrival; but I know it is all Humour, because she was contradicted. Nothing would serve her, truly, but to lye with my Miss *Cassy,* though she knows the poor Child hates to lye with any one, but her own Maid, whom she is very fond of; for it is a gentle, loving, little thing; and I will not suffer her to be vexed, and spoil her Eyes with Crying, to please any humoursome Brat in *England*" (343). Similarly, the conversation between Mr. Nichols and David, "in which neither Party [can] well comprehend the other," is presented in full in order to illustrate the differences in language and values between the steward, who can talk only of security and interest, and David Simple, who says "I have no Bond, or Note, Sir; *Valentine* is my Brother, my Wife's Brother, and that's the same thing" (368).

18. If children prove the downfall of the conversational community at its point of greatest potential for expansion, the group's educational emphasis is nevertheless affirmed in that the sole survivors of the general destruction are the young Camilla and her aunt Cynthia, whose relationship has always been one of pupil and mentor. Cynthia's successful mission to gain a promise of protection for them both after David's imminent death means that this nucleus of a new community will not have to set out on a renewed journey in search of a friend. The modification in the sequel of the communal ideal from one of earthly possibility to one of a momentary, vulnerable, and partial foretaste of the heavenly city suggests, however, that the premises of the surviving community will be different from those expressed in the confident manifesto of its original founding. For Todd, this ending, with its promise of a "providentially supported female community," "moves towards the escapism of noneconomic, nonpolitical female bonding, characteristic of the novel of sensibility. Power through sentimental struggle in an evil world has been denied, but the extreme importance of women promises a quasi-magical power entirely outside the bourgeois economy in which the rest of the novel has functioned" (*The Sign,* 174). Although I agree that a commonality of interest and a priority of the group over individual desires will continue as the basis of the surviving community, Cynthia is to teach Camilla, says David, "to consider [my Death] as my Deliverance" (432), just as he has already taught her to prefer the loss of her mother to the sight of her "painful Passage through this World" (414).

19. Ann Marilyn Parrish's summary of the sequel's argument in mathematical terms accords well with the sense of an empirical experiment: "The nature of this world is such that

friendship with another only doubles one's potential disappointment and heartbreak. In a perfect community of eleven, the potential for disaster is a mathematic nightmare" ("Eight Experiments in Fiction: A Critical Analysis of the Works of Sarah Fielding" [Ph.D. dissertation, Boston University, 1973], 74).

20. In fact, the treatment of deathbed scenes is less problematic here than in most of Sarah Fielding's works, where almost the only, and certainly the most infallible, means of bringing a character to acknowledge truth and to desire change is through the experience of a real or imagined deathbed.

Conclusion

1. See John Mullan, *Sentiment and Sociability: The Language of Feeling in the Eighteenth Century* (Oxford: Clarendon, 1988), 114-46, for a discussion of the retreat of sentimental virtue into a narrowly domestic and aesthetic space. Ronald Paulson, in "The Pictorial Circuit and Related Structures in Eighteenth-Century England," in *The Varied Pattern: Studies in the Eighteenth Century,* ed. Peter Hughes and David Williams (Toronto: A.M. Hakkert, 1971), 165-87, also views changing uses of a circular structure in eighteenth-century English art, including the novel, as reflecting a shift in interest from a range of expressions focused on a central object to the disparity between perceptions themselves.

2. Fanny [Frances] Burney, *Camilla, or A Picture of Youth,* ed. Edward A. Bloom and Lillian D. Bloom (Oxford: Oxford Univ. Press, 1972), 18, 913.

3. Michael McKeon, *The Origins of the English Novel, 1600-1740* (Baltimore: Johns Hopkins Univ. Press, 1987), 419.

Index

Note: The central texts upon which this study is based have been indexed under the titles of the works. General references to these texts, however, are indexed under the author's name. Concepts fundamental to the study are indexed for the introductory and concluding portions of the book; the reader is also invited to consult individual text entries for further references to these concepts.

Addison, Joseph, 9. *See also* Spectator
Alter, Robert, 151 n 7, 152 n 14, 153 n 19
Amelia (Fielding, Henry): Amelia as domestic heroine in, 50, 72, 76, 78, 81, 86, 152 n 15; Booth as choice-maker in, 50, 70, 72, 75, 78-79, 85-86; circle image in, 74-75, 76-77, 85; conversation in marriage in, 153 n 77; Dr. Harrison as authoritative speaker in, 50, 70-71, 77, 78, 79-80, 81, 86, 153 n 22; epistemology in, 71, 83-84; expansiveness in, 70-71, 75, 86; exclusivity in, 76; feminine circle in, 50, 68, 69-70, 71-72, 74-75, 76-77, 82, 86-87, 133; ideology of gender in, 76-77, 81, 86; individualism in, 70, 72-74, 77, 78, 79, 80, 86; Miss Matthews as anti-heroine in, 70, 72-73, 75, 76, 78-79, 80, 82, 85, 154 n 27; narrator of, 83, 153 n 25; plot structure of, 70, 71, 72, 85-86, 152 n 11; reader's role in, 71, 78; self-narration in, 70, 77, 80-82, 86, 153 n 21; stabilization of plot in, 70, 84, 154 n 29; table image in, 75-76, 152 n 17; traditional structures of authority in, 152 n 18; vortex image in, 70, 71-74, 79. *See also* Fielding, Henry
Amory, Hugh, 153 n 22
Arendt, Hannah, 138 n 6
Armstrong, Nancy, 6, 138 n 8, 139 n 10, 144 n 8, 147 n 7, 151 n 3, 153 n 18
Auerbach, Nina, 154 n 6
Austen, Jane, 134
authority, 138 n 6; of conversational circle, 5; and individual experience, 5; and sociable self, 9-12; and traditional social structures of, 2, 8-9

Bakhtin, Mikhail, 2, 3, 13, 41, 137 n 3
Barker, Gerard A., 55-56, 142 n 7, 158 n 5
Barrell, John, 140 n 16
Battestin, Martin C., and Clive T. Probyn, 157 n 2
Bender, John, 3
bourgeoisie, 2-3, 7, 8-9, 10
Bunyan, John, 2, 17
Burke, Edmund, 18
Burney, Frances, 134, 160 n 2
Butt, John, 158 n 9

Carretta, Vincent, 88, 154 n 5, 155 nn 9, 13, 14, 17, 156 n 18
Castle, Terry, 36-37, 39, 44-45, 137 n 3, 142 n 9, 145 n 18, 146 n 29, 152 nn 11, 13, 153 n 21
Chaber, Lois A., 146 n 26, 148 n 10, 150 n 34
Chesterfield, fourth earl of, 14, 15, 131
circle image, 19, 160 n 1
circular structure, 5, 17-19
Clark, J.C.D., 8
Cleland, John, 71-72
Collier, Mary, 15, 131
Collyer, Mary, 9-10
commerce. *See* language
consensus: in conversational novel, 5, 20, 137 n 5; and ideology of conversation, 3, 14-15; and language, 5; as social ideal, 2, 4-5, 131
conversation, 13, 139 n 7; in domestic sphere, 15; ideology of, 2, 14-15, 132,